Movies, Rock & Roll, Freud

Movies, Rock & Roll, Freud:

Essays on Film and Music

by Ken Fuchsman

Published in 2021 by the
ORI Academic Press, New York, NY

Copyright © 2020 by Ken Fuchsman

All rights reserved.

For permissions to reproduce more than 500 words of this publication, email ORIPressEditor@Gmail.com or write to ORI Academic Press Editor @ 7515 187th St, Fresh Meadows, NY 11366.

Printed in the United States of America on acid free paper.

Library of Congress Control Number: 2021946657

Cataloging Data:

Fuchsman, Ken. Movies, Rock & Roll, Freud / Ken Fuchsman. Psychohistorical Dialogues Series.

1. Music and Cinema – Psychological aspects. 2. Psychohistory. 3. Psychoanalysis. 4. Analytical sociology. 5. Race relations. 6. Unconscious communications.

ISBN 978-1-942431-16-9 (soft cover)

Book design, editing, and book cover - by MindMendMedia, Inc. @ MindMendMedia.com

To

Liz and Jack

TABLE OF CONTENTS

ACKNOWLEDGEMENTS (xi)

CHAPTER 1. INTRODUCTION (1)

MOVIES

CHAPTER 2. LETTING LIGHT INTO DARKNESS: JOHN HUSTON'S 1962 BIO-PICTURE: *FREUD* (7)

CHAPTER 3. GREATNESS AND PARADOX: SIGMUND FREUD IN THE 1890S AND BEYOND (17)

CHAPTER 4. FREUD AND SARTRE: JEAN-PAUL SARTRE'S *THE FREUD SCENARIO* (37)

CHAPTER 5. A DANGEROUS METHOD: A FILM REVIEW (55)

CHAPTER 6. ROMAN POLANSKI'S *CHINATOWN* IN ITS TIME AND OURS (59)

CHAPTER 7. STEVEN SPIELBERG: THE QUEST TO BE A MORAL MALE (71)

CHAPTER 8. SPIELBERG'S *THE POST*: A REVIEW AND PSYCHO-HISTORICAL COMMENTARY (79)

CHAPTER 9. ARTHUR MILLER'S SELF-UNDER-STANDING IN *THE CRUCIBLE* (87)

MUSIC

CHAPTER 10. FOREVER YOUNG: 1960'S-1970'S COUNTER-CULTURE ROCK (93)

CHAPTER 11. THE AGE OF MIRACLES AND WONDERS: PAUL SIMON AND THE CHANGING AMERICAN DREAM (135)

CHAPTER 12. DELIVER ME FROM THE DAYS OF OLD: 1950'S ROCK & ROLL (151)

CHAPTER 13. WHERE HAVE ALL THE FLOWERS GONE: A MEMORIAL TO PETE SEEGER (163)

CHAPTER 14. JAZZ, RACE, AND POLITICS, 1955-1975 (169)

CHAPTER 15. ABOUT THE AUTHOR (193)

AKNOWLEDGEMENTS

I thank Paul Elovitz, editor of *Clio's Psyche,* first for his encouragement of my work over the years, and also for permission to publish the review of *A Dangerous Method,* the two articles on Steven Spielberg films, the comments on Arthur Miller's *The Crucible,* and the memorial tribute to Pete Seeger, all of which appeared in *Clio's Psyche.* The *Journal of Psychohistory* has kindly given me permission to reprint here my analysis of the film *Chinatown* and the article on Paul Simon's career that appeared in that publication.

CHAPTER 1

INTRODUCTION

This book is a collection of papers written for various occasions. They grow out of my love for music and movies, and my long immersion in Freud. Also informing these essays is Montaigne's finding that as humans we are double-sided creatures who do not believe what we believe and cannot rid ourselves of what we condemn. I too find contradictions, paradoxes, and divisions within individuals and movements.

The films and songs I write about are products of the consumer culture built on advanced technology and large corporations. Hardly any of that is dealt with in these papers. A good deal of what follows combines applied psychoanalysis with cultural-historical perspectives. Part of the dialectic of modern life since the 16th century Reformation is divisions about paternal authority and rebellion in the name of liberty, though there is often an unrecognized allegiance to that which is protested. This applies not only to what is prevalent in the lyrics of counterculture rock songs, but also divisions about paternal authority in Freud himself and the doctrines he develops.

My journey to these outlooks started long ago while reading Norman O. Brown's chapter "Liberty" in his Love's Body. He was a classics professor, a disillusioned leftist who turned to Freudian theory to see where Marxism failed. Brown analyzes John Locke's Two Treatises on Government. Instead of explicating the influential second treatise, he turns to the first essay, which is a critique of Robert Filmer's 1680 Patriarcha, a defense of kings. Brown uncovers how liberal ideology is a rebellion of sons against fathers, and is an example of how the Oedipus complex applies to political phenomenon. This was illuminating to me. Over time I could see how in early modern times, this dynamic applied to the Protestant reformation, the revolts against monarchs, science's challenging the hegemony of the Catholic church, entrepreneurs fighting against the guild's restrictions, and the father's power within the family. This notion of liberty as contradictory rebellion also was manifest later in a repeated pattern within American liberal and radical political movements.

MOVIES, ROCK & ROLL, FREUD: ESSAYS ON FILM AND MUSIC

My perspectives on the dialectics of modernity and the cycle of American left of center political movements developed while I was working on my doctoral thesis. My dissertation was on the American Progressive era cultural radical Randolph Bourne, who was a champion of youth and an anti-war critic. I found in his inner struggles and his public career a pattern that both his and later generations of reformers and radicals would reproduce.

Much of what influenced my thinking during my doctoral research were the writings of Erik Erikson and Sigmund Freud. It should not then have surprised me that a decade or so later I turned to Freud, and focused on the Oedipus complex. Three of the essays in this book are connected to how Freud is depicted in some screenplays and movies, and a fourth is an interpretation of Freud's inner struggles in the 1890s and how it impacted his doctrines. The first written is a review of the 2011 film *A Dangerous Method*, which is about Carl Jung, Sabina Spielrein, and Sigmund Freud. The film had a screenplay by Christopher Hampton, and is based on his play *The Talking Cure*. Hampton's drama on the subject was based on John Kerr's book *A Most Dangerous Method*. The film makers shortened the book's name when giving a title to their movie. The other three Freud connected articles were written especially for this volume: one on the 1962 movie *Freud,* the second is an essay on Freud's conflicts over fathers that covers much of the same time-frame as Huston's film. The third is about Sartre's original but unused draft for that movie. Esteemed film director John Huston in the late 1950s decided to do a film biography of Sigmund Freud. Huston contracted with this famous French playwright and philosopher to compose a screenplay.

The Frenchman's first version turned out to be way too long for a comercial release. Eventually Huston commissioned two other men to adapt and shorten Sartre's drafts, which they did. Sartre then requested his name not be used in the film's credits. The movie itself covers the period in the 1880s when Freud became interested in hysteria to the late 1890s when he developed central doctrines of psychoanalysis. I review the 1962 release of Huston's *Freud,* then in a separate essay fill in the gaps in Freud's divided psychology the movie does not sufficiently cover. I rely heavily on Sigmund's revealing letters to the German physician Wilhelm Fliess, Freud's own writings, biographies of Freud, and comments by other analysts to give a fuller portrait of Freud and his ideas than the movie

CHAPTER 1: INTRODUCTION

does. It is in discussing Freud's personal and intellectual journey in the late 1890s that I apply Montaigne's notion that we are double sided and Brown's ideas on the divisions about paternal authority to Freud's life and thought.

The next essay is on the first version of Sartre's script for Huston's proposed movie. I had known that Sartre had written such a screenplay and had also heard that it was published several years after he died. I read a good amount of early Sartre, and had written a paper on his ideas about bad faith in graduate school. Then I was more impressed with his capacity as a philosopher to develop a long and complex argument than with his ideas in themselves. My own thinking was more in tune with his one-time friends Maurice Merleau Ponty and Albert Camus than with Sartre. So I was surprisingly bowled over by the excellence of Sartre's Freud scenario. The Parisian made Freud's former intimate friend Wilhelm Fliess a catalyst in his account, while Fliess does not even make a cameo appearance in Huston's film. Sartre not only shows how Freud and Fliess stimulated each other's thinking and how they confided in each other, but how their relationship helped alter Sigmund's connection to his mentor Josef Breuer and to the dynamics of Sigmund's marriage to Martha. Through his fictional creations Sartre illuminates these personal dynamics in ways some biographers do not. He also has a greater gift for character than is present in Huston's movie. *The Freud Scenario* is not only better than other dramas with Freud as a character. it can also help us understand how Freud became Freud.

The next movie I discuss is 1974's *Chinatown*. The film is a descendant of the film noir genre which owes a great deal to the hard-boiled detective school writing of Dashiell Hammett, Raymond Chandler, and James Cain. Set in 1930s Los Angeles, *Chinatown* has a remarkable Freudian-tinged screenplay by Robert Towne, directed brilliantly by Roman Polanski, and with memorable performances by Jack Nicholson, Faye Dunaway, and director turned actor, John Huston. In its own way, it is about paternal authority and sexuality. The movie was released in May 1974 during the Watergate crisis. This time was filled with disillusionment, and corresponds to the last stages of a liberal and radical era. So, *Chinatown* then is an illustration of both issues surrounding authority and hope for change.

MOVIES, ROCK & ROLL, FREUD: ESSAYS ON FILM AND MUSIC

Director Steven Spielberg's films, which I discuss next, are generally removed from Freudian and film noir themes. But many are concerned with how to be a moral and heroic male. His first blockbuster movie, 1975's *Jaws* was made while Spielberg was in his twenties and contrasts the questionable actions of politicians when a killer shark terrifies a beach town to the more noble and professional pursuits of a sheriff and scientist. Later, Spielberg's hit Indiana Jones films present a Superman like character masquerading not as a mild-mannered journalist but an archeologist battling evil across the planet. These are fun adventures with a heroic male lead. They are akin to *Jaws* where a man defeats mortal threats.

From his mid-forties on, the director somewhat changes direction. He is still concerned with moral males in the midst of danger, but they are less centered on adventure and fantasy than on ethically complex and often evil settings. For this 2016 published paper, I cover *Schindler's List* and *Saving Private Ryan*, both set in World War II, *Munich* which starts during the 1972 Olympics, *Lincoln* at the end of the American Civil War, and *Bridge of Spies* set during the Cold War. These are all historic films with men facing tasks with much moral significance and frequently mortal danger. In another piece, I later review Spielberg's 2017 movie *The Post*, which is set in the Watergate era. It features not only a heroic male grappling with ethical concerns, but a female heroine making a moral decision of much significance for the United States.

I had viewed many Spielberg movies, but it was seeing *Saving Private Ryan* that got me interested in his career. When the movie came out, it received glowing reviews. My wife did not want to see it, but my 13-year-old son did, as did I. The two of us went to a Sunday matinee. As a Vietnam veteran myself, the quality of its war scenes and its psychology hit me deeply. I could not speak after the film concluded, which had only happened to me once before. Since *Saving Private Ryan,* I have seen all Spielberg's films, with *Munich* standing out to me as placing the male hero in the most morally complex situation of any of his films.

Next, I respond to psychoanalyst Jim Anderson's 2011 symposium paper on artistic creativity with reference to Arthur Miller's 1953 play *The Crucible*. The symposium appeared in the psychohistory journal, *Clio's Psyche*. Miller's drama was made into a movie in 1996, with a script by

CHAPTER 1: INTRODUCTION

the playwright. Jim had claimed that in *The Crucible*, Miller exhibited extensive self-knowledge. In my response included here, I questioned that conclusion.

Now to music. I think in song lyrics. In conversation or while teaching, a lyric relevant to the discussion will pop into my head, and I will quote it. Unlike some people, I read and write better when music is playing. My love of music unexpectedly turned into an opportunity for me. In the small city where I live, in the late 1990s, I helped a new non-commercial radio station get on the air, and then had two weekly radio shows. One was on the history of rock and roll. The other was entitled the jazz spectrum. I would often do theme shows, such as jazz versions of Joni Mitchell songs, a history of New Orleans rhythm and blues, the career of Carole King from her days of writing songs for others until the present. After five years, when the demands of my job increased, I no longer had the time to prepare, and so stopped being a disc jockey.

A few years after I gave up my radio programs, in 2005 Professor Paul Elovitz asked me to give a talk on music to the history club he ran for students at New Jersey's Ramapo College. I played songs and gave a paper on the cycle within counterculture rock of the 1960s and 1970s. As the cultural radicalism of this period largely echoed the pattern of Randolph Bourne's generation, with some modifications I applied my ideas on this recurring cycle to the 1960s generation. Recently, I ran across a hard copy of the paper, and liked what I had written. It was too long for the journals for which I usually write. I then conceived of collecting my writings on song and film into a book. And so here we are.

Dr. Elovitz in the next decade asked me to deliver a paper on music at the Psychohistory Forum in Manhattan. He has run this group since the early 1980s. I chose to write on the long recording career of Paul Simon. I focused on the changing nature of the American dream in his songs. Simon's compositions are also featured in the preceding counterculture rock paper. My 2015 Forum presentation got a good response and there was even a question on comparing Simon to Sinatra. The version reprinted here was originally published in the *Journal of Psychohistory*.

The earliest paper in this collection goes back to 1983. It is on themes of sex, relationships, dancing, and rock and roll in 1950s records. I delivered it at a popular culture association conference in Wichita, Kansas. It too features the divided sensibilities in the lyrics of that decade.

After Pete Seeger died, Paul Elovitz requested I publish a memorial on the famed folksinger in his journal, *Clio's Psyche*. Seeger's songs spanned many decades, and at least three of his compositions became Top 40 hits in the 1960s. Seeger was even mocked in a Phil Ochs song from 1966. Seeger himself kept his political faith throughout his life and was less subject to the fluctuations of many other 1930s and 1960s radicals.

The last paper in this book is on jazz, race and politics from 1955 to 1975. It has been recently revised, but was originally given as part of a panel on jazz with myself, historian Dave Beisel, and therapist Irene Javors at the 2015 psychohistory conference. This is its first publication. The politically related jazz records followed the divisions that occurred within the civil rights movement and its fracturing with the rise of black power. I try to present the various components and stages within the history of these jazz recordings as well as the music's richness and diversity. This paper is roughly derived from my ideas on the divisions within liberal and radical movements.

For me revisiting the older papers and writing the three new ones has been a rewarding experience. I hope it is for you as well.

CHAPTER 2:

LETTING LIGHT INTO DARKNESS: JOHN HUSTON'S 1962 BIO-PICTURE: *FREUD*

How often individuals are cited on Google Scholar is compiled by an arm of the Spanish Ministry of Education. A few years ago, Sigmund Freud was the most frequently referenced of everyone. As of November 7, 2019, he was ranked fifth. He is the only person of the top ten who was born in the nineteenth century and remains highly influential in the twenty-first (Consejo Superior de Investigaciones Cientificas, 2019). Unlike many prominent thinkers, Sigmund Freud did not make his major discoveries until midlife. He was 41, when in 1897, he clarified the role of unconscious fantasies and promulgated the Oedipus Complex.

The Movie

Many have discussed Freud's journey from being interested in hysteria in the 1880s to founding psychoanalysis in the 1890s. Include in the list the prominent film director, John Huston, whose 1962 *Freud* covers this formative period. In some releases of the movie, the subtitle is "The Secret Passion." To me, the whole movie might be titled "How Freud Became Freud" or "After Missteps, How an Obscure Viennese Physician Discovered the 'Science of the Unconscious.'"

By the time the film was made, crucial documents about this period of Freud's life were in circulation. The first volume of Ernest Jones magisterial biography of Freud up to 1900 was published in 1953, and an expurgated version of Freud's revealing letters to his intimate friend, the Berlin physician Wilhelm Fliess, came out in 1954. Freud was more open about himself in the correspondence with Fliess, a more rawly human writing on his struggles, discoveries, and self-analysis than in the remainder of his life. In 1896 and 1897, he tells Fliess about his being uprooted, neurotic, and a hysteric. Yet it is out of this inner turbulence that Freud discovers and develops psychoanalysis, addresses some of his complexes, and leaves others lingering. His life in this time frame is a fine subject for a film.

Huston's *Freud,* by and large, presents the founder of psychoanalysis in a heroic light, as do some of Freud's biographers. As well as admirers and devotees, there have also been the Freud Wars. From the beginning to the present day, psychoanalysis has been severely criticized. Huston's film shows the hostility towards Freud while asserting that his psychoanalysis opens up the key to understanding the human psyche.

The origins of psychoanalysis grow out of a mixture of evolving doctrine and Freud's own psychological turmoil. Huston's movie portrays a fictionalized account of the processes Freud went through to get to the core psychoanalytic principles. It sometimes does and sometimes does not capture the founder's internal struggles. This paper evaluates the film. The following chapter attempts to show how the personal and the intellectual mixed together as Freud by 1900 weaved his way towards greatness and paradox.

By the time Huston was making a movie about Freud's life, he had directed *The Maltese Falcon, The Treasure of Sierra Madre, The African Queen, The Red Badge of Courage,* and *Moby Dick.* All were based on exceptional novels. His film before the Freud project was *The Misfits,* written by the acclaimed playwright Arthur Miller. As Huston was drawn to literature and high accomplishment, making a movie about Freud fit into his interests.

The idea for the film came to Huston and Wolfgang Reinhard in 1940 while they were writing the script for *Dr. Ehrlich's Magic Bullet,* a film about a 19th century Nobel Prize winning German Jewish physician and scientist (Wollen, 1999, p. 156). Ehrlich was born two years before Freud. Though it took two decades for this idea to come to fruition, it was not a great leap from one contemporary Jewish European physician to another. To write the screenplay about Freud, Huston in 1958 hired Jean-Paul Sartre. In 1964, Sartre would be awarded the Nobel Prize in literature. Like his French contemporaries Albert Camus and Simone de Beauvoir, Sartre's writings were not confined to one area. Not only was he a renowned philosopher, but also wrote important short stories, plays, novels, biographies, screenplays, and psychological works. Sartre was a reincarnation of a Renaissance man.

CHAPTER 2: LETTING LIGHT INTO DARKNESS

In his 1943 philosophical treatise, *Being and Nothingness*, he expressed his doubts about the Freudian unconscious (Sartre, 1943/1953, pp. 93-96). The scenario he wrote in 1959 was brilliant, but would have been a 5-hour movie. Huston and Sartre met to discuss how to revise and shorten the script. The meeting did not go well, Huston thought Sartre talked endlessly and Sartre thought Huston could not concentrate for more than five minutes (Roudinesco, 2008, pp. 44-45). When Sartre then tried to revise his screenplay, it turned out to be longer than his first version. An exasperated Huston then turned to two other writers. Sartre did not like what they composed and had his name removed from the final product (Meyer, 2011, pp. 184-185).

Much of the final script was written by Wolfgang Reinhardt, who was mostly known as a producer, and who is so credited for this film. His last writing for film had been in 1939. Charles Kaufman was the other author; he wrote stories for *The New Yorker* and had been a screenwriter for a quarter century. What they composed borrowed a good deal from Sartre's scenario. Reinhardt and Kaufman's version received a nomination for the 1962 academy awards, but did not win.

Freud begins and ends with voice-over narratives by Huston. The director states that before Freud we believed we were ruled by our conscious will alone, but Freud revealed another part of our mind. "which functions in darkest secrecy and can even rule our lives." Huston says this movie is the story "of Freud's descent into a region almost as black as hell itself, man's unconscious and how he let in the light." Given this introduction, it is not surprising that the film treats Freud as a courageous hero.

A motif of the movie is that in his path to greatness Freud had to deal with the objections of the Vienna medical establishment. The film opens with Freud's advocacy of hysteria, which his mentor Dr. Meynert told Freud were patients who were faking their symptoms. There is also an early scene where Freud presents his views on hysteria in a hall to the doctors of Vienna. When Meynert critiques Freud's presentation, the audience breaks out in applause. Towards the end of the movie, there is a scene where doctors walk out of Freud's presentation in an auditorium. These scenes are reminiscent of Frank Capra's 1939 *Mr. Smith Goes to Washington*, where a beleaguered U. S. Senator played by Jimmy Stewart on the floor of the Senate chamber is derided by his colleagues. The noble hero with a righteous cause meets opposition. As with Senator Smith, so with Sigmund Freud. Both films follow a Hollywood biographical tradition where noble leaders encounter resistance. While Mr. Smith in Washington faced an organized campaign against him, Freud also confronted inner demons. His path to heroism led through a psychological and intellectual crisis.

At the end of the 19th century, Freud went from advocating the study of hysteria, which was stimulated by studying at the feet of Charcot in Paris, then later to collaboration with his friend and mentor in Vienna, Josef Breuer. In 1895, they co-authored *Studies on Hysteria*. In the book, it was clear that Freud was focusing on the centrality of sexuality in the etiology of hysteria. Breuer could only partially follow Freud down this path. Afterwards, on his own in 1896 Freud published articles promoting the thesis that adult perpetrators performed sexual acts with pre-pubescent victims. With the 1897 announcement of the Oedipus complex actual adult sexual abuse is no longer central, the origins become the child's psychological love for the mother and jealousy of the father. By the fall of 1897, Freud had mostly abandoned the seduction theory and was promoting unconscious fantasies as a cause of neurosis. It was a personal as well as an intellectual journey.

The film goes over much of this territory, it also presents Freud as an innovator with a flaw; that is unresolved issues with his father. Without coming to terms with his father-son complex, the film implies that he cannot achieve heroic status. The movie does cover Freud's time in Paris in 1885 observing Charcot with hysterics, and then on his return his growing partnership with prominent Vienna physician and scientist Josef Breuer. Breuer had a patient named Bertha Pappenheim, who later became a social worker and who in 1904 founded the Jewish Women's Association. In their book on hysteria, Breuer named her Anna O. When going over her various symptoms if Breuer could get Anna O. to talk, he found that the catharsis of reliving the experiences could lead to the disappearrance of that symptom. She called this chimney sweeping. It has often been said that this treatment solely by Breuer was the origin of the psychoanalytic method.

The film renames Anna O. as Cecily Koertner. In Sartre's initial draft she is called Cäcilie, which was the name Freud gave to one of his patients

CHAPTER 2: LETTING LIGHT INTO DARKNESS

discussed in *Studies on Hysteria*. She was in real life a baroness named Anna von Lieben (Appignanesi & Forrester, 1992, pp. 86-87). Freud (1985) told Fliess that "only this woman could have been my teacher" (p. 229). Appignanesi and Forrester (1992) say that Freud's "first personal experience of the possible effectiveness of a talking cure" (p. 87) was with her. They add that "a talented patient needs to exist for a talented doctor to emerge. The talking cure is a collaborative act" (Appignanesi & Forrester, 1992, p. 87). Certainly, the film plays it this way.

A central focus of the movie is Freud's lengthy analysis of Cecily and the processes both go through in their interaction. Cecily is a composite fictionalized character of Bertha Pappenheim, Anna von Lieven, and others. In the film, Montgomery Clift plays an intense yet often reserved Freud, and the 22- year-old willowy blonde British Susannah York is cast as Cecily.

Another important motif, as mentioned, is Freud's feelings towards his father. There are a few fictionalized scenes that illustrate this. Towards the beginning of the movie, just before Freud is to leave to study under Charcot, his father, Jakob Freud, gives Sigmund a watch which had belonged to Jakob's father. He is clearly passing the torch to his son. Soon after Freud drops the watch and it breaks. Clearly, this is to be taken as Freud's unconscious destructive wishes towards his father. In a later scene, Dr. Freud examines a patient who attacked his father. Under hypnosis, the client says his father every night "raped" his mother. And then the adult son sexually caresses and kisses a tunic shaped like a female and he addresses this object as "mother." This unnerves Freud who soon leaves the building. Here is another way the movie is telling the audience that Sigmund has troubling father issues and desires his own mother. The script is setting the stage for Freud's later discovery of the Oedipus complex.

Freud and Breuer disagree about the role of sexuality in causing neuroses, and Breuer declares that sex is not part of Cecily's troubles. To test Breuer's claim, Freud asks if he can treat her. The two physicians go to see Cecily, who is lying in bed. When Breuer questions her about when she first had trouble seeing, Cecily describes a scene where she is in Naples in a hotel room at night. She is called to go to a hospital where her father has died. After Breuer has completed his questioning, he tells Cecily she can now see. But that prediction does not materialize. Freud requests to keep going, and Sigmund then questions her. He gets Cecily to recognize that it was not a hospital where her father's body lies, but a brothel. She then realizes that her father died in the arms of a prostitute. This not only reinforces the sexual theme Freud asserted and Breuer contested, but in itself shows how Freud's more penetrating questioning goes deeper than Breuer's. When Cecily comes out of the hypnosis, she can see. This is presented as evidence of Freud's sexual theories.

The dramatic framework of the film is set. Freud will conduct therapy with the hysterical patient Cecily. How Freud proceeds will reflect the various stages of his own theoretical and personal development. In its own way, the film presents a dialogic interaction between these two main characters. As Freud gets Cecily to recall her life, he uses it to process through his own unresolved dilemmas and discovers the science of the unconscious.

In focusing on one client, Cecily, the film does not present the diversity of patients Freud dealt with and blends into one time frame what took much longer. During Freud's collaboration with Breuer in their jointly authored book, Breuer presented just the therapy with Anna O., while Freud discussed four cases (Breuer & Freud, 1895/1957). The two authors then went their separate intellectual ways. In 1896 publications, Freud cited over a dozen documented cases that confirmed his theory that adults and siblings committed sexual abuse of children. The film slides over the content of the 1896 publications, and goes directly into the next stage of Freud's personal and intellectual development.

In the movie, soon after Cecily's initial breakthrough with Freud, Sigmund's father dies. He declares his love for his father, but interprets a dream to mean that the son shall close the eyes to the sins of the father, Sigmund does not do so and sees this as a sin. He finds himself to be a neurotic hysteric. Sigmund then recounts to Breuer when Jakob tells his son about an anti-Semitic incident where the father acquiesced to being attacked. Sigmund says that from that point on he saw his father less as a God and more as a man. His father issues have returned to his consciousness.

The film returns to Freud's analysis of Cecily. As she brings up memories, he asks for her associations and dreams, which she freely tells him. He now moves away from hypnosis towards these new methods. Cecily has

CHAPTER 2: LETTING LIGHT INTO DARKNESS

told him that at 14 she had fainted and could not walk for two weeks. She recollects that she followed her father to a brothel, and this upset her. Freud gets Cecily to reveal more about her earlier life, including her father touching her. Freud concludes he too needs to examine his early childhood to find out about his own hysteria. He proceeds to question his mother, who tells him about a train journey when he was four years old. The conversation at first is incomplete. Freud then goes to see Cecily who he finds is on a street with brothels. Cecily says that she lied earlier that day about her father touching her, that she did so to please Freud. At the time, Freud thought that his father may have done something untoward with one of his sisters, but could not confirm his suspicions. Cecily's new revelation led Sigmund to examine himself, and to go back to the incidents surrounding that train ride and the night in the hotel. He now recalls that that night in their room he saw his mother with her back towards him but naked to the waist. His mother was going to lay in the bed with him. Instead, his mother went to his father's room.

Freud then declares he was jealous of his father and wished him dead. To justify his bad thoughts, Freud says that he conjured up a crime against his sister committed by his father. He says," I was jealous of my father. I wanted my mother all to myself. I wanted to be rid of him. I am the guilty one. I dishonored my father." A few minutes later, he is talking to his wife and says to Martha, "I deserve to be punished. I invented a theory that dishonored my father. I desecrated his image and the fathers of my patients." He then reflects that when Cecily had said that her father seduced her, this was not a memory. He says, "It was a fantasy." Then he says Cecily loved her father while he loved his mother. She hated her mother, while he hated his father. Sigmund tells Martha that there is sexuality in childhood, even in infancy.

There is an incongruity in the script here. The movie brings out sordid things about Cecily's father, but not Sigmund's. There is no account of Freud's controversial theory that the causes of hysteria are sexual abuse of children by fathers. There is a passing reference to Freud saying he has a vision of something transpiring between his father and a sister, but he then is unable to confirm his suspicion. The movie shows no theory that dishonored Freud's father. In his actual life, Freud did accuse his father of being perverted. What leads the cinema Freud to be so self-accusatory is not presented. Freud certainly went through agonies and turmoil after his father died. In the movie, we see more about Cecily's suffering and discoveries than the internal emotional and intellectual struggles of Sigmund Freud. There is thus a hole in the film at a crucial part.

Freud's assertions in 1897 against his own father and even himself could well have been found by the screenwriters in the works available at the time: in the 1953 Jones (1953, p. 357) biography of Freud and the Freud-Fliess letters (Freud, 1954, pp. 179-180; p. 206; p. 213; & p. 215). Not giving more details here about the charges of paternal perversion is both a dramatic flaw and a biographical evasion. Also, in condensing the path Freud went through in the various stages of his seduction theory, it gives a seriously incomplete account of Freud's path.

After his announcing how he dishonored his father, in another scene Freud talks with Cecily's mother, who tells him that when her daughter was little, she would have dreams that her mother was dead. When he subsequently talks to Cecily, he says that her dreams of her mother being dead was a wish she had that she could not admit to herself. Whatever stands between desire and fulfillment the child wishes away. Freud tells her the wish is love of her father and jealousy of mother. She is not guilty, he says, or your guilt is shared by every human being. He admits to her that he dreamed of killing his own father. Cecily says, then you "were a monster as well." He replies, "no, I was a child." He tells her she still has more work to do, but the day will come when she will face life on its terms.

Freud wants to present his new, striking discoveries to the assembled doctors of Vienna. Breuer advises against it, but Freud proceeds. In the very location where Freud lectured on hysteria, he reports to the congress of doctors on his new theories of childhood sexuality. Shouts and pounding the tables ensue, and many of the doctors walk out of the hall. Echoes of Jimmy Stewart's Mr. Smith in Washington return. The hero is assailed, and so the Hollywood biographical tradition, in part, is upheld.

The movie then shifts to the cemetery where Jakob Freud is buried. As Freud walks through the graves, John Huston speaks, that knowing thyself can be the weapon against man's oldest enemy, his vanity. Huston says this "knowledge is now within our grasp. Will we use it? Let us hope." The implication is that this knowledge derives from Freud's great discoveries.

CHAPTER 2: LETTING LIGHT INTO DARKNESS

The movie ends with Freud appearing to reconcile with Jakob's legacy and to have resolved his father complex. Freud has earned his heroism by going to the depths and finding out sometimes harsh truths about human beings. It is the elaboration of the workings of the unconscious, the interpretation of dreams, and the notion of the Oedipus complex that are the early foundation of Freud's greatness. He, of course, did not rest on his laurels, and developed and expanded these core psychoanalytic components and developed new ones for the remainder of his life. There are substantial reasons why Freud remains among the most cited thinkers and researchers. Yet many of the twists and turns in Freud's journey are left out of the film. To understand Freudian psychoanalysis and Freud the person, we need to go beyond Huston's *Freud*.

REFERENCES

Appignanesi, L., & Forrester, J. (1992). *Freud's women*. Basic Books.

Breuer, J., & Freud, S. (1957). *Studies on hysteria*. (J. Strachey, Trans.). Basic Books. (Original work published 1895).

Consejo Superior de Investigaciones Cientificas (CSIC) (2019). Highly cited researchers according to their Google Scholar citations public profiles. Retrieved 11/9/2019 from https://webometrics.info/en/hlargerthan100

Freud, S., & Bonaparte, M., Freud, A., & Kris, E. (Eds.). (1954). *The origins of psycho-analysis: Letters to Wilhelm Fliess, drafts and notes: 1887-1902*. (E. Mosbacher & J. Strachey, Trans.). Basic Books. doi.org/10.1037/11538-000

Freud, S., & Strachey, J. (Ed. & Trans.) (1962). *The standard edition of the complete psychological works, Volume III (1893-1899)*. The Hogarth Press.

Huston, J. (Director). (1962). *Freud* [Film]. Universal-International.

Jones, E. (1953). *Sigmund Freud: Life and work. Vol. One: The Young Freud, 1856-1900*. The Hogarth Press.

Meyer, J. (2011). The making of John Huston's 'Freud: The secret passion.' *Kenyon Review, 33*(1), 178-199.

Roudinesco, E. (2008). *Philosophy in turbulent times*. Columbia University Press.

Sartre, J-P. (1953). *Being and nothingness. An essay on phenomenological ontology* (H. Barnes, Trans.). Washington Square Press. (Original work published 1943)

Wollen, P. (1999). Freud as adventurer. In J. Bergstrom (Ed.), *Endless night: Cinema and psychoanalysis, parallel histories.* University of California Press.

CHAPTER 3:

GREATNESS AND PARADOX:
SIGMUND FREUD IN THE 1890S AND BEYOND

John Huston's film shows an apparent resolution of Freud's father issues. Yet, a close examination shows that paternal concerns remained important in his life and theories. He does go through an emotional and intellectual crisis after his father died in 1896, which after twists and turns ended up in his great 1897 discoveries. This story of Freud and fathers, in large part, begins earlier with his 1896 theories of hysteria which assert that actual sexual abuse of children leads to this disorder. These finding interconnect the internal and external. In September 1897 and afterwards, he focuses less on actual perpetrators than the child's unconscious fantasies. His writings in this period go from documenting a variety of abusers, to centering on fathers as sexual perverts, to seeing the unconscious and then the Oedipus complex as primary.

To understand anyone's thought it is helpful to see what they argue for and what against. It is not infrequent for a thinker to have a complicated relationship to what they once affirmed and then opposed. As Montaigne writes, "we are, I know not how, double within ourselves, with the result that we do not believe what we believe, and we cannot rid ourselves of what we condemn" (Montaigne, 1943, p. 570).

As Freud moves from the seduction theory to the Oedipus complex, he sometimes argues against what he once championed. An exploration of his reversals and affirmations shows that as Freud is breaking new ground, he also leaves under addressed some of his own intellectual and personal dilemmas. In treating Freud as primarily heroic, Huston's film does not capture Sigmund's full humanity.

One side of Freud's being human is his multi-sided responses to his father. On one hand, he revered him. After his father's death, Freud (1985) wrote about Jakob to his friend, Wilhelm Fliess, a Berlin physician, "I valued him highly...and with his peculiar mixture of deep wisdom and fantastic light-heartedness he had a significant effect on my life....in [my] inner self the whole past has been reawakened by this event" (p. 202). Jakob recognized how bright Sigmund was, and for a period educated his son himself. Yet beyond these powerful kinship bonds, Sigmund harbored mixed feelings about his father. This led to life-long struggles on Freud's part over his attitudes about Jakob and the role of fathers in human psychology. It is the son's ambivalence towards Jakob and fathers, and how it influenced his theories that is the subject of what follows. It is quite a journey.

Sigmund Freud On His And Other Fathers

The concerns Sigmund had about his father are financial and whether Jakob was a sufficient role model. In January 1884, 27-year-old Sigmund wrote his fiancé, about Jakob and his two adult half-brothers: "Yesterday I met Father in the street, still full of projects, still hoping. I took it upon myself to write to Emanuel and Philipp urging them to help Father out of his present predicament" (Freud, 1960, p. 86). This was not a one-time worry. As biographer Louis Breger puts it, Jakob had a "lifelong inability to provide for the family" (Breger, 2000, p. 25). There was no record of Freud's father in either the Vienna Trade Register or the Trade Tax Register, which means he was not a trader of any sort (Clark, 1980, p. 15). It seems that Jakob's family was kept afloat by money sent him by his sons in England and his wife's family, among others (Whitebook, 2017, pp. 62-63). His family's economic struggles left a mark on Sigmund. In his 1925 autobiography, Freud mentioned his "father's generous improvidence" (Freud, 1925/1959, p. 10).

It was not only about money that Freud thought Jakob wanting. In the most well-known incident, Jakob tells his ten to twelve-year-old boy of when a Christian knocked off Jakob's hat and said "Jew get off the pavement." When Sigmund asked his dad what he did, the father replied that he picked his hat up. The son wrote, "This struck me as unheroic conduct" (Freud, 1900, p. 197). In his mind, he contrasted Carthaginian general Hannibal's heroism with Jakob's meekness (Freud, 1900, p. 197). Sigmund sought other paternal models, but he appears to have had some uneasiness over his judgment of Jakob.

Writing in 1936, Freud talks of "a sense of guilt" that "has something to do with a child's criticism of his father." Sigmund writes that "the essence of success was to have gotten further than one's father, and as though to excel, one's father was still something forbidden" (Freud, 1936, p. 247).

CHAPTER 3: GREATNESS AND PARADOX

This discontented son not only sought to go further than Jakob, he expressed wishes to replace his father. Sigmund's two adult half-brothers were about the same age as his mother. In his late teens, Sigmund visited his older half-brother, Emanuel, in England and had a fantasy "of how different things would have been if I had been born the son not of my father but of my brother" (Freud, 1901, pp. 219-220). In 1924, he writes of himself and family when he was about three years-old. Sigmund asserts that his adult half-brother Philipp "had taken his father's place as the child's rival" (Freud, 1901, p. 51). For decades, Sigmund vacillated between appreciating his father, being judgmental, and then feeling guilty for what he thought about Jakob. As important elements of Freud's theories involve fathers and sons, Sigmund's ambivalence about his own father significantly impacted on his theories.

When in 1896 Freud published articles on the origins of hysteria, he focused on sexual misconduct by adults and childhood siblings. Freud listed a number of possible perpetrators of sexual abuse (Freud, 1896b, p. 208). His emphasis on diverse agents initiating abuse of children began to change not long after his father's death on October 23, 1896. As is often cited, Freud declared that the death of the father is "the most important event, the most poignant loss, of a man's life" (Freud, 1900/1953, p. xxvi). Less than two weeks after Jakob died, Sigmund wrote that "the old man's death has affected me deeply... I now feel quite uprooted" (see 11/2/1896 letter in Freud, 1985, p. 202).

This being shaken up by Jakob's demise soon took some unusual paths. Just six weeks after his father died, on December 6, 1896, Sigmund wrote Fliess that more and more the perverse seduction that results in hysteria is enacted by the father (see 12/6/1896 letter in Freud, 1985, p. 212). Then on February 8, 1897, Freud told Fliess, "My own father was one of those perverts and is responsible for the hysteria of my brother (all of whose symptoms are identifications) and those of several younger sisters" (Freud, 1985, pp. 230-231). How does Freud know this? He gives no indication that there is evidence that his father actually abused his siblings. As psychoanalyst Kurt Eissler (2001) writes, Freud "equated identification and seduction" (p. 163). He views Freud's accusations against his father as containing improbabilities that make it "an unsolved conundrum" (Eissler, 2001, p. 163). Sigmund's accusations against Jakob are a great unexplained leap. How Freud can find that identification by a child is equivalent to the act of abuse by the father remains a puzzlement. Still, from December 1896 to August 1897, Freud is enthralled by the paternal etiology thesis.

This includes that the supposed hysteria is not limited to his brother and some of his sisters, "I have been through some kind of neurotic experience," Freud writes to Fliess on June 22, 1897 (Freud, 1985, p. 254). On August 14, 1897, Freud talks of "My little hysteria" (Freud, 1985, p. 261). Then on September 21, 1897, Freud makes another leap. He tells Fliess of his "surprise that in all cases, the *father*, not excluding my own, had to be accused of being perverse" (Freud, 1985, p. 264).

As Freud moved from multiple types of sexual abusers towards primarily fathers, including his own, the issue of the causes of hysteria became both personal and troubling. On May 31, 1897, Sigmund interprets a dream of his as indicating that he "had over affectionate feelings for Mathilde," his eldest daughter. He then writes to Fliess that this dream fulfills his wish to catch fathers as "the originator of neurosis" and his interpretation of the meaning of the dream "puts an end to any ever-recurring doubts" (Freud, 1985, p. 249). That Freud believes he had desire for his child then adds another complex dimension.

If in all cases hysteria is a product of abuse by the male parent and the hysteria of Freud's siblings was caused by Jakob's perversions, would not it follow that Sigmund's little hysteria would be caused by the sexual abuse of his father? If true, is this something Freud can live with? Also, how easy it would be for Sigmund that he might have desires for his own female child, especially when he was accusing his father of being abusive with his own siblings? When Freud's 1936 statement that criticizing the father leading to guilt is applied to him in 1897, he may have had much regret for saying Jakob was a sexual pervert.

Just six weeks after the August 1897 declaration of his own hysteria, Sigmund begins trying to convince himself that fathers are not culpable. His writings take various psychological paths in pursuit of this effort. For starting in September 1897, Freud tries in different ways to turn away from the responsibility of fathers. He begins arguing with himself against what he formerly and boldly asserted.

CHAPTER 3: GREATNESS AND PARADOX

Freud wrote to Fliess on September 21, 1897 replacing his sexual seduction theory with one where it is not actual abuse but the child's fantasies that are the causal factors. He said that "there are no indications of reality in the unconscious," and so "one cannot distinguish between truth and fiction that has been cathected by affect." Hysterics have unconscious reasons to accuse their elders, and so "sexual fantasy invariably seizes upon the theme of the parents." He also asserts that actual "widespread perversions against children are not very probable." Freud in the same letter, as mentioned, said that his prior descriptions meant that in all cases the father had to be accused of being the abuser (Freud, 1985, 264-265). How can Freud be sure that sexual abuse of children is not widespread? His assertion that in every case it is the male parent who needs to be suspected of being the abuser contradicts his finding from 1896 of diverse perpetrators. Freud is making bold claims, jumping to conclusions without seeking outside documentation.

As well, there is something curious about the reasoning in this letter. Just because there is unconscious fantasy, of course, does not mean that sexual abuse is absent. On one hand, Freud said the unconscious blurs the line between fantasy and reality, and, on the other, in the 1896 hysteria articles, Freud claimed to have obtained evidence on who the abusers were.

In his first of these papers, he claimed to have carried "out a complete psycho-analysis in thirteen cases of hysteria." His findings then did not point primarily to fathers. Instead, Freud reports that in "seven out of the thirteen cases the intercourse was between children on both sides." Usually a girl and her brother (Freud, 1896a, p. 152). This would indicate that seizing on the parents may not always be the case.

Later in 1896, he says he now had treated eighteen cases of hysteria, and finds three categories of perverted abusers: assaults on female children by strangers, abuse by adults looking after the child, a nurse, governess, tutor, or close relative, or the aforementioned sexual relationship between a brother and sister. He also reported that "in most of my cases I found two or more of these etiologies were in operation together," for regularly "sexual experiences" for these exploited children were "coming from different quarters" (Freud, 1896b, pp. 207-208). This means that there were more often at least two different perpetrators acting independently of each other. So, when in September 1897, he says it was always fathers that had to be suspected of sexually abusing children, something seems askew. In the autumn of 1897, Freud seems to have discarded his earlier research on who sexually abused children; he ignores, forgets, or denies his own prior findings.

As well, when in September, 1897, he downplayed the paternal etiology thesis, this could not only let fathers off the hook, but mean that his father was not an abuser. From this September letter on, Freud remains quite divided about the responsibility of fathers in general and his father in particular. On one hand he seeks to absolve fathers, including his own, and on the other hand, his discontent with Jakob Freud remains. Some of his writings shifts responsibility away from male parents and others specifically point up Jakob's failings.

What we have in the September 21, 1897 letter is a complex maneuver. The declaration of the primacy of the unconscious is inseparable from downgrading the frequency of sexual abuse, from discounting the previous accusations that fathers are the perpetrators, and finally acting as if the 1896 findings on hysteria did not exist. For if sexual abuse of children and unconscious fantasies can co-exist then fathers could be perpetrators. From the September 21st letter on, Sigmund Freud was actively pursuing finding ways that fathers could be absolved.

While he says that it is unconscious fantasy rather than paternal perversion that leads to hysteria, in his letters to Fliess he sometimes ignores that conclusion. For instance, as part of his 1897 self-analysis, Freud tried to find what led him to become a hysteric. In this search, even though he wrote that he no longer believes in his seduction theory, he does not focus on internal fantasies but is looking for an actual abuser. On October 3rd and 4th of 1897, Freud reports "that in my case the 'prime originator' was an ugly, elderly but clever woman," his nannie. He describes her as being "my teacher in sexual matters," and gives specifics. Instead of fantasy, he has now found a culprit who acted sexually with him when he was under three years old. This allows him to declare "that the old man plays no active part in my case" (Freud, 1985, pp. 268-269). Wait a minute. Freud had previously found that in most cases there was more than one perpetrator. He now ignores that claim in a rush to exclude the possibility that his father was sexually abusive. That Sigmund now acquits his father

CHAPTER 3: GREATNESS AND PARADOX

in his own case indicates that the son had suspected that his father may have been the originator of his hysteria.

If his father in relation to him was not a pervert, what about with his younger siblings? Oddly enough, Freud makes no further reference to the earlier claim that his father abused his younger brother and some sisters, nor in the letters to Fliess is there any further reference to Sigmund's over affectionate feelings towards Mathilde. The subject of his sibling's hysteria and sexual interest in Mathilde are dropped. After all, they are now psychological hot potatoes.

His next major assertion in this extraordinary journey also downplays paternal perversions. In the same month that Freud found his own hysteria was not caused by his father, he announced the Oedipus complex to Fliess. This new idea also grew out of his self-analysis. In particular, in October, 1897, Sigmund asked his mother if she remembered this nurse whom he had claimed was his sexual teacher. His mother did, and this led Freud to recall that this elderly woman had been removed from his life when he was a youngster of three or under in Freiberg. Part of this memory was that Sigmund had been afraid that as his nannie was missing and once he found that his mother too was absent, he became very upset. "I was crying in despair." He called on his adult half-brother Philipp to help, which he did. When his mother showed up "slender and beautiful," the boy was relieved. In recounting to himself these memories, a light bulb went off in Sigmund's head. He tells Fliess, "A single idea of general interest dawned on me. I have found in my own case too [the phenomenon of] being in love with my mother and jealous of my father, and I now consider it a universal event in early childhood." Freud then proceeds to connect these feelings to Sophocles' drama, *Oedipus Rex*. "Everyone in the audience was once a budding Oedipus in fantasy" (see 10/15/1985 letter in Freud, 1985, pp. 271-272).

And so was born the idea of a universal Oedipus complex. It remained a cornerstone of psychoanalysis from its inception to Freud's death and beyond. As philosopher Patricia Kitcher (1992) concludes, "Nothing was more central or more original in psychoanalysis than the postulation of the Oedipus complex" (p. 107). Freud (1939) himself declared: "I venture to say that if psycho-analysis could boast of no other achievement than the discovery of the repressed Oedipus complex that alone would give it a claim to be included among the precious new acquisitions of mankind" (pp. 192-193). When in 1900, Freud first publicly proclaimed this discovery, these incestuous wishes of love of mother and jealousy of father, he wrote that they "have been forced upon us by Nature" (Freud, 1900, p. 263).

The way that Freud formulated this newly discovered complex reversed his sexual seduction thesis. With the Oedipal theory, the adults and siblings were basically acquitted and the boy's desires and jealousy were to blame. To reach his bold conclusion Freud was highly selective in what he included and omitted from the full myth of Oedipus. To avoid a prophecy Oedipus's father, Laius, had unsuccessfully acted to cause the death of his infant son. Freud recognized this aspect of the father's role in the Oedipus myth, yet he did leave out a crucial element in this tale. The prophecy against Laius came following Oedipus's father earlier rape of the boy Chryssipus. "Laius was deemed to have been the inventor of pederasty," writes anthropologist and psychoanalyst George Devereux (1953/1988, p. 100). This made Oedipus's father a sexual pervert who committed the very sexual abuse that Freud had previously said was the cause of hysteria. We do not know if Freud was cognizant of this part of the story, still he was aware of Laius acting to cause the death of Oedipus. This latter makes curious his choice of the Oedipus myth as grounds for focusing on the child's desires and leaving out crucial parts of the father's actions.

Psychoanalyst John Munder Ross writes "it is remarkable that Freud should have ignored Laius' active part in the narrative," and adds that few later analysts "fill in the gaps. The blind spots are reminiscent of Oedipus' own assumption of the entire burden of guilt… as if exculpating the dead father altogether" (Ross, 1994, p. 98). The question of the causes of neuroses had become highly personal to Freud. As Ross says, in moving from paternal etiology to the child's dynamics Freud sought to absolve fathers from being either murderous towards their child and/or sexual perverts.

This echoes Devereux's declaration that the "Oedipus complex is rooted in the adult's deep-seated need to place all responsibility for the Oedipus complex upon the child and to ignore, whenever possible" the role of the parents in this phenomenon (Devereux, 1953/1988, p. 98). Freud's

CHAPTER 3: GREATNESS AND PARADOX

omissions are telling. What he leaves out returns to the phenomenon of fathers as attempted murderers or sexual abusers. This takes place in the very assertion that it is the child's feelings and wishes rather than parental aggression or perversion that leads to neurosis. The complete Oedipus myth then gives ground to affirm the perversion of fathers that Freud now seeks to disconfirm. At the same time as Freud is opening doors, he is trying to run away from something.

He has gone from one extreme to another; from proclaiming adults and siblings were perpetrators and children were victims, to fathers as abusers, to children as desiring agents while the parents' actions mostly fade into the background.

From December 1896 to October 1897 Freud has gone from indicting to acquitting fathers as sexual abusers. The absolving occurs by finding ways to downplay real psychologically threatening events. Freudian psychoanalysis was largely built on the unconscious over the actual, rather than a synthesis of the real and the imaginary. Keeping the distance between the two enabled dismissing his own charges against fathers.

From the complete Oedipus myth, one case can be made that the origin of neurosis is in the sexually abusive and murderous intent of the father towards his child. Just as strong is the case that possessiveness towards the mother and hostility towards the father is a universal event of childhood. Sigmund Freud could also have developed a theory that integrated the desires of the child and the intent and actions of the father. But, of course, he did not; he did not choose to connect the centrality of parental fantasies with childhood fantasies, and how they intersect. A central focus of his thought in late 1897 was to move attention away from fathers and towards sons, and so he omits much.

He also has a tendency to make extraordinary leaps. His path from the 1896 articles on hysteria to the next year's declaration of the Oedipus complex are filled with puzzlements and quandaries. As innovative as Freud's assertions are, each step following the 1896 hysteria papers is filled with a paucity of evidence, a rush to judgment, and an eagerness to be free of something that troubles Freud's uneasy conscience.

Freud's Oedipal theories grew out of his personal experience, and yet, as mentioned, he leaped to universalizing his own psychology to all humanity. Writing about Freud's initial Oedipal formulation, psychologist Robert Holt (1989) says, "it seems audacious to the point of foolhardiness to jump from self-observation to a general law" (p. 53). Freud's great leaps, of course, led to innovative notions that have altered the conceptions of many of what it is to be human. His version of the Oedipus myth served its psychological function of discarding the paternal etiology thesis.

Freud's rush to judgment about fathers as sexual abusers, his later absolving fathers, and the universality of love of mother and jealousy of father are not disinterested observations. They are all connected to the very personal nature of Freud's struggles between Jakob's 1896 death and the 1900 publication of *The Interpretation of Dreams*. His emerging doctrines were inseparable from his own preoccupation with the sins of the fathers and his own self-described neurosis and hysteria. We cannot understand the ways Freud structured his ideas separate from his internal divisions. With the discovery of the unconscious, the abandonment of the "seduction theory," and the proclamation of the Oedipus complex the internal dynamics of Freud's psyche and his doctrines are all interconnected. His great discoveries are part and parcel of his psychological struggles.

There is another aspect of these divisions. In moving from adult and sibling abuse to the Oedipus complex, Freud is shying away from integrating the internal and external, fantasy and reality. Here the Freudian internal refers to the thoughts, wishes, and desires of the child, plus the internal images he or she has towards other persons and objects. The external is material reality and others' actual personages. His challenges with the relationship of the internal and external are noticed by others. Peter Gay in discussing the famous September 21, 1897 letter admits that if "the ground of reality had been lost, that of fantasy had been won" (Gay, 1989, p. 96). Physician and psychoanalyst Willard Gaylin (1990) finds that Freud "tended to ignore the environment in which the isolated self would be nurtured or deprived" (p. 114). Hans Loewald (1951/1980) writes that Freud views "external reality…in the aspect of a hostile, threatening power" (pp. 3-4) for the ego. Philosopher and psychoanalyst Joel Whitebook (2017) wrote that "Freud's position in 1900… suffered from a degree of perhaps unavoidable one-sidedness" (p. 223).

CHAPTER 3: GREATNESS AND PARADOX

If the impact of the external can be downplayed, the fear of the father's actions and the guilt over making such severe accusations against Jakob can be attempted to be swept under the psychological rug. In 1897 when Freud was intent on universalizing fantasy over reality, was he was also hiding his guilt over his destructive impulses towards Jakob and uneasiness of his own desires towards his daughter? We have in the twists and turns of his 1897 correspondence a Freudian paradox: he combines self-deception with his revelations about the unconscious that show exceptional insight. In addition, his one-sidedness in not more fully interconnecting the internal and the external makes his findings an incomplete portrait of the unconscious.

Another paradox: a good deal of these 1897 revelations emerged out of his self-analysis. Towards the end of his life Freud came to doubt self-examination. He writes, "in self-analysis the danger of incompleteness is particularly great. One is too soon satisfied with a part explanation, behind which resistance may easily be keeping back something that is more important perhaps" (Freud, 1935, p. 234). To me, Freud's struggles with his guilt over his criticisms of his father and his own wayward desires are connected to his omissions and self-deception. How so? The way Freud turns away from accusations against fathers leads him to disconnect the internal and external, fantasy and reality. Another sign of Freud's uneasiness and incompleteness is that at times, he distorts his own writings.

In 1933, recalling the period when he saw hysteria as caused by a variety of sexual abusers, Freud says that "almost all my women patients told me that they had been seduced by their father" (Freud, 1933, p. 120). Analyst Kurt Eissler (2001) comments on Freud's statement, saying, "Nowhere in his publications of that period does one encounter women accusing their fathers" (p. 216). Eissler (2001) assets that this applies to both the 1895 *Studies on Hysteria* and to the papers on hysteria published in 1896. What Freud's 1933 misrepresentation of his own writings enables him to do is to claim that "these reports were untrue" and were "derived from phantasies and not from real occurrences" (Freud, 1933, p. 120). Of course, Freud is saying that these fantasies are aimed at parents. This claim does not fit with his 1896 reports that it was siblings more than fathers who sexually abused children.

Of course, it was Freud's finding of fantasy over his earlier reports of actual abuse that, in part, enabled Freud to acquit fathers. From the 1897 declarations on father's perversions to 1933, Freud chose to ignore that he had reported that the sexual misconduct he reports comes from a variety of perpetrators. These findings of multiple types of abusers make it more of a challenge to conclude that all these reports were false, as the majority of cases were not directed at parents.

Some Perplexities In Freud's Thought

Then there is another Freudian perplexity: why in September and October 1897 are unconscious fantasies of a sexual nature primarily attributed to children? Why are not adult fantasies included? All of a sudden for Freud the wishes and actions of male parents are not as relevant as youngsters. Do not fathers have sexual wishes towards children, and are they not pertinent in discussing the causes of hysteria? Would not this include Sigmund Freud himself, and his dream of feeling over affectionate towards his oldest daughter? Freud's downplaying of adult sexual fantasies towards children reveal that his frequent one-sidedness is connected to a personal meaning he evades.

In relation to his father, whether Freud was motivated by guilt and remorse or something else, in his effort to absolve fathers, including within his own family, the die is cast. His acquittal of fathers is accompanied by an underplaying of the impact of real events in the unconscious. For the rest of his career, he does not sufficiently connect the real and the imagined. He thus leaves a major gap in his theoretical structure.

At times, Freud goes so far as to declare that the actual events of someone's life were not as important as a particular biologically derived internal dynamic. To him, the phylogenetic inheritance is when the earlier experiences of humanity takes over an individual's psyche. Freud says that *"primal phantasies*...are a phylogenetic endowment. In them the individual reaches beyond his own experience into primeval experience at points where his own experience has been too rudimentary" (Freud, 1916-1917, p. 371). He adds, "Wherever experiences fail to fit in with the hereditary schema, they become remodeled in the imagination" (Freud, 1918, p. 119). For "what the subject himself has really experienced" may "seem unjustified in the individual case and only make sense phyloge-

CHAPTER 3: GREATNESS AND PARADOX

netically – by their connection with the experience of earlier generations" (Freud, 1939, p. 99). Humanity's primeval experience reshapes actual life experiences to fit into the inherited pattern; the internal trumps the external. This doctrine of the phylogenetic inheritance can be used to justify sometimes giving short shrift to actual life experiences.

Freud is aware that this effort to discount the external has problems. He says that his "position…is made more difficult" in that "biological science… refuses to hear of the inheritance of acquired characteristics by succeeding generations… nevertheless I cannot do without this factor" (Freud, 1964, p. 100). Freud says, "I am not an ethnologist but a psychoanalyst. I had a right to take out of ethnological literature what I might need for the work of analysis" (Freud, 1964, p. 131). Freud had asserted that "psycho-analysis must keep itself free from any hypothesis that is alien to it, whether of an anatomical, chemical or physiological kind" (Freud, 1916, p. 21).

It is this doctrinaire side of Freud that allows him to override research findings in order to promote his particular version of psychic reality. It is not that internal reality is not central to being human, it is not integrating the internal with the external that makes Freud's thought too often one-sided. By discounting experience and underplaying the parents' fantasies and actions in relation to the child, his science of the unconscious is necessarily highly partial. Again, it should not be forgotten that this pitting the unconscious over the empirical began, in part, as an effort to turn away from his version of the seduction theory where fathers were responsible for causing hysteria, including Sigmund's own.

Freud's Attempts To Connect
The Internal And External

It can be countered that what I have described is only part of the story, and that Freud writes throughout his career on material as well as psychological reality. I will look at three topics to see to what extent Freud is seeking to interconnect the real and the imagined.

Totem and Taboo from 1913 to Freud is a "just-so-story" that he finds credible (Freud, 1921, p. 122). The book contains sort of a creation myth, a psychoanalytic version of Genesis, applying elements of the Oedipus complex to the creation of civilization. Freud imagines an ancient primal horde dominated by an oppressive father who monopolizes all the sexually available women and subordinates the sons. These younger men rise up and slaughter their father. Then out of guilt and remorse renounce their murderous act and establish rules limiting sexuality (Freud, 1913). This is a version of the origins of human social life. To Freud (1921), "the beginnings of ... social organization" is due to killing the father then the "transformation of the paternal horde into a community of brothers" (p. 122).

Freud's mythic creation primarily focuses on the psychic element of human relations. Certainly, in the early stages of humanity's history, danger would come not only from the father suppressing his sons; it would also come from predators aiming to slay fathers and sons. Not surprisingly, external threats are not incorporated into the dynamics of Freud's just-so story.

Another Freudian account of applying psychoanalysis to material reality followed the 1914-1918 Great War. The horrors of trench warfare, with their astounding casualty rates transformed Western culture's perspective on itself. In addition to the millions of deaths was the psychological toll of the deadly violence for the combatants. This was called shell shock at the time. In two lesser-known writings from 1919 and 1920 Freud addresses the war neurosis of soldiers.

In 1919, he says that the neurosis of war has been "made possible" by "a conflict in the ego" (Freud, 1919, p. 209). The next year, he says: "... the immediate cause of all war neurosis was an unconscious inclination... to withdraw from... active service. Fear of losing his life, opposition to the command to kill other people" and rebellion against military obedience "were the most important affective sources" (Freud, 1920, pp. 212-213). Experiencing the actual terrors of combat are not included in this litany. Freud then adds: "with the end of the war the war neurotics too, disappeared." This to Freud is "impressive proof of the psychical causation of their illnesses" (Freud, 1920, p. 215). The evidence from World War I and earlier wars is that many shell-shocked soldiers had symptoms for a long time after their war ended.

CHAPTER 3: GREATNESS AND PARADOX

In Freud's articles, as mentioned, the actual experience of combat has faded into the background and internal motivation has taken over. He did not seek to understand the impact of the violence and horrors of war on the soul and body. Freud had significant blind spots as to what brings psychological disorder to many who faced the brutalities of combat. Once again, he focused much more on the internal psyche than how horrifying material reality may be instrumental in bringing on long-lasting traumatic disorder.

Freud's most serious grappling with the intersection of the internal and external is in *Civilization and Its Discontents* from 1930. Civilization, he said, serves the purposes of distinguishing humans from other animals, and "to protect men against nature and to adjust their mutual relations." This includes the "cultural" phenomenon of inventing tools, controlling fire, and constructing dwellings. These activities are "useful to men for making the earth serviceable to them" (Freud, 1930, pp. 89-90). Another purpose is that "civilization is built up upon a renunciation of instinct" (Freud, 1930, p. 97).

It is not only the vicissitudes of the drives that concern Freud in this work. Over the last few generations, he writes, humankind has established a "control over nature in a way never before imagined." This has been done through science and technology. Freud mentions the railroad, telephone, how the advances of medicine have reduced infant mortality and lengthened the human life span. Still, all these advances have not made humans "feel happier" (Freud, 1930, pp. 87-88). Nevertheless, Freud finds that civilization encourages "man's higher mental activities – his intellectual, scientific and artistic achievements – and the leading role it assigns to ideas in human life" (Freud, 1930, p. 94). Here Freud is giving due place to external reality in the ways human life has been enhanced by our higher capacities and the material advances promoted by science and technology.

Certainly, how we have created art, rigorous science, intellectuality, and technology are central issues. Not surprisingly, Freud attributes these higher activities to psychoanalytic notions. He finds that the ways in which civilization discourages direct satisfaction of the sexual instinct leads to sublimation, which entails finding substitutes for the restrictions on instinctual primal pleasure. For sublimation is based on "an abandonment of sexual aims, a desexualization" (Freud, 1923, p. 30). Freud declares that "Sublimation of instinct...is what makes it possible for higher psychical activities, scientific, artistic or ideological, to play such an important part in civilized life" (Freud, 1930, p. 97). How to Freud does sublimation facilitate these accomplishments? To him sublimation takes "place regularly through the mediation of the ego" (Freud, 1923, p. 45).

What is this ego and how does the ego facilitate sublimation? To Freud, on one hand, the ego entails the "coherent organization of mental processes" (Freud, 1923, p. 17). On the other hand, "the ego is that part of the id which has been modified by the direct influence of the external world." The ego seeks to bring the influence of the external world on the tendencies of the id, and wishes to "substitute the reality principle for the pleasure principle...The ego represents what may be called reason and common sense" (Freud, 1923, p. 25).

As the id is modified by reason and the reality principle, where do "reason" and the "reality principle" originate, and how do they lead to human excellence in mental life and advanced technology? Freud's treatment of the ego and of sublimation are eventually integrated into his tri-partite theory of mind with the id, ego, and super-ego. Yet in expounding on sublimation, Freud does not fully address the central question of why in some periods sublimations leads to advanced high culture and in other periods it does not. Sublimation, as Freud presents it, remains a general term more an internal activity rather than one connecting the internal to the external. Again, he does not clarify what in culture and history has led to extraordinary achievements in technology, science, art, and other intellectual activity and what does not.

Freud does not seriously explore other explanations for high culture distinct from his psychoanalytic notions of sublimation, the reality principle and reason. Even when recognizing the achievements of civilization, he mostly stays within his psychoanalytic theories rather than incorporate other approaches into the study of the material and intellectual transformations.

Freud in *Civilization and Its Discontents* is recognizing external reality in ways beyond what he typically focuses on. Still, his attempts to have advanced accomplishments derive from psychoanalytic notions still too much focuses on the internal over the external. Freud is much better at showing the discontents than the achievements of civilization.

Conclusion

Sigmund Freud is in some ways a great paradox. Not that many others in the history of Western thought have been as willing to plunge the depths of the human heart. Yet he also made decisions that created significant blind spots and omissions in his theories. He also denied and distorted his own intellectual history as a way to not face what he wishes to evade about himself and his doctrines.

All of us need to recognize how views we once affirmed but now oppose may have some lingering hold on us. John Huston at the end of his *Freud* film said it is self-knowledge that is our goal. Self-deception may be our demon. Even Freud, who went deep into the unconscious, evaded some of his own psychological dilemmas and divisions. The Freud of the 1890s and afterwards both developed psychoanalysis into an invaluable enterprise, and regularly sought to deny what he had earlier affirmed. His divided internal dialectic was fully present in his thought.

It is not unusual in human endeavors for great discoveries to contain denials, gaps, and blind spots. Freud evolved into one of the boldest, most innovative, and fertile thinkers that Western culture has ever seen. At the same time, he retained an internal dialectic, an argument within himself that left his doctrines one sided and incomplete. Like many of us, Freud was a mixture of opposites. We do him justice as a fellow human in recognizing his struggles and evasions along with his genius.

REFERENCES

Breger, L. (2000). *Freud: Darkness in the midst of vision.* John Wiley & Sons.
Clark, R. (1980). *Freud: The man and the cause* Random House.
Devereux, G. (1988). Why Oedipus killed Laius: A note on the complementary Oedipus Complex in Greek drama. In G. Pollock & J. M. Ross (Eds.), *The Oedipus papers* (pp. 97-116). International Universities Press. (Original work published 1953)

Eissler, K. R. (2001). *Freud and the seduction theory: A brief love affair.* International Universities Press.

Freud, S. (1960). *Letters of Sigmund Freud* (E. Freud, Ed., & T. & J. Stern, Trans.). Basic Books.

Freud, S. (Ed.) (1962). *The standard edition of the complete psychological works (SE), Vol. III (1893-1899)* (J. Strachey, Ed. & Trans.). The Hogarth Press. (Original work published 1896)

Freud, S. (1953). *SE, Vol. IV* (J. Strachey, Ed. & Trans.). The Hogarth Press. (Original work published 1900)

Freud, S. (1960). *SE, Vol. VI* (J. Strachey, Ed. &Trans.). The Hogarth Press. (Original work published 1901)

Freud, S. (1957). *SE, Vol. XI* (J. Strachey, Ed. & Trans.). The Hogarth Press. (Original work published 1910)

Freud, S. (1955). *Totem and taboo.* In J. Strachey (Ed. & Trans.), *SE, Vol. VIII* (pp. 1-162). The Hogarth Press. (Original work published 1913)

Freud, S. (1963). *SE, Vol. XVI (1916-1917)* (J. Strachey, Ed. & Trans.). The Hogarth Press. (Original work published 1916-1917)

Freud, S. (1955). *SE, Vol. XVII (1917-1919)* (J. Strachey, Ed. & Trans.). The Hogarth Press. (Original work published 1918)

Freud, S. (1955). Introduction to psycho-analysis and the war neuroses. In J. Strachey (Ed. & Trans.), *SE, Vol. XVII* (pp. 205-210). The Hogarth Press. (Original work published 1919)

Freud. S. (1955). Memorandum on the electrical treatment of war neurotics. In J. Strachey (Ed. & Trans.), *SE, Vol. XVII* (pp. 210-215). The Hogarth Press. (Original work published 1920)

Freud, S. (1955). Group psychology and the analysis of the ego. In J. Strachey (Ed. & Trans.), *SE, Vol. XVIII* (pp. 69-143). The Hogarth Press. (Original work published 1921)

Freud, S. (1961). The ego and the id. In J. Strachey (Ed. & Trans.), *SE, Vol. XIX (1923-1925)* (pp. 1-66). The Hogarth Press. (Original work published 1923)

Freud, S. (1961). *SE, Vol. XIX (1923-1925)* (J. Strachey, Ed. & Trans.). The Hogarth Press. (Original work published 1925)

Freud, S. (1961). Civilization and its discontents. In J. Strachey (Ed. & Trans.), *SE, Vol. XXI* (pp. 64-145). The Hogarth Press. (Original work published 1930)

CHAPTER 3: GREATNESS AND PARADOX

Freud, S. (1964). *New introductory lectures on psycho-analysis.* In J. Strachey (Ed. & Trans.), *SE, Vol. XXII (1932-1936)* (pp. 5-182). The Hogarth Press.(Original work published 1933)

Freud, S. (1964). The subtleties of a faulty action. In J. Strachey (Ed. & Trans.), *SE, Vol. XXII (1932-1936)* (pp. 233-235). The Hogarth Press. (Original work published 1935)

Freud, S. (1964). A disturbance of memory on the Acropolis. In J. Strachey (Ed. & Trans.), *SE, Vol. XXII (1932-1936)* (pp. 239-248). The Hogarth Press. (Original work published 1935)

Freud, S. (1964). *SE, Vol. XXIII (19137-1939)* (J. Strachey, Ed. & Trans.). The Hogarth Press. (Original work published 1938, 1940)

Freud, S. (1985). *The complete letters of Sigmund Freud to Wilhelm Fliess, 1887-1904.* (J. Moussaieff-Masson, Ed. & Trans.). Harvard University Press.

Gay, P. (1989). *Freud: A life for our time.* W. W. Norton & Company.

Gaylin, W. (1990). *On being and becoming human.* Penguin Books.

Holt, R. (1989). *Freud reappraised: A fresh look at psychoanalytic theory*. The Guilford Press.

Jones, E. (1953). *Sigmund Freud: Life and work. Vol. One: The young Freud 1856-1900.* The Hogarth Press.

Kitcher, P. (1992). *Freud's dream: A complete interdisciplinary science of mind.* The MIT Press.

Loewald, H. (1980). *Papers on psychoanalysis.* Yale University Press.

Montaigne, M. (1943). *The complete works* (D. Frame, Trans.). Everyman's Library.

Ross, J. M. (1994). *What men want: Mothers, fathers and manhood.* Harvard University Press.

Whitebook, J. (2017). *Freud: An intellectual biography.* Cambridge University Press.

CHAPTER 4

SARTRE AND PSYCHOANALYSIS: *THE FREUD SCENARIO*

While John Huston's *Freud* is an intriguing movie, the first version of Jean-Paul Sartre's *The Freud Scenario,* within its' limits, is a masterpiece. The French Nobel Prize Winner captures how Freud's innovations emerge from his psychological turmoil and changing relationships within his inner circle.

It was long known that the Frenchman had composed a screenplay for this proposed movie, and that his name was not listed as screenwriter when the movie appeared in 1962. It was only following Sartre's death in 1980 that his various written drafts were discovered, translated, and published in English in 1986.

When John Huston hired the eminent Parisian in 1958 to draft a script for a proposed movie on Sigmund Freud, this was not the first venture by the philosopher into screen writing. Sartre had composed the script in 1943 for a French movie *Les Jeux Sont Faits,* and adapted Arthur Miller's *The Crucible* for a 1957 European produced film. Internationally, he was recognized as an accomplished playwright. These were not the only areas with which this prolific writer was engaged. He was a novelist, philosopher, short story writer, founding co-editor of the journal Les Temps Modernes, and had written biographical portraits of writers, including Baudelaire and Andre Gide. Throughout his career, Sartre had a talent for showing the character of important literary and philosophical figures.

In relation to Freud, Sartre follows quite an intellectual journey. He went from being highly critical to being more receptive. Placing the Freud scenario in the context of Sartre's views helps us better understand its' meaning. In the 1940s, Sartre the existentialist was skeptical concerning the notion of the unconscious. In 1946, he had written, "man is condemned to be free: condemned, because…once cast into the world he is responsible for everything he does" (Sartre, 1946/2007, p. 29). This view differs from Freud who declared that "the ego is not master in its own house." For "mental processes are in themselves unconscious… [and only become conscious] … through incomplete and untrustworthy perceptions" (Freud, 1917, p. 143). How can we be responsible for all our actions, if much of what we do is influenced by our unconscious and we are not in control of ourselves?

Sartre, in upholding his particular conception of freedom, seeks to undermine the notion of the unconscious. He writes, "By the distinction between the 'id' and the 'ego,' Freud has cut the psychic whole into two. I *am* the ego, but I *am not* the *id"* (Sartre, 1943/1953, p. 91). He calls this maneuver of Freud's a "materialistic mythology" (Sartre, 1943/1953, p. 93). Not only to Sartre is the psychoanalyst positing a "magic unity" that contains an "inferiority in principle," but his formulations do "not avoid the coexistence" of "the unconscious" and "consciousness" (Sartre, 1943/1953, p. 95). For to Sartre repression and the censor exist at the conscious level (Sartre, 1943/1953, p. 94). He concludes that the psychoanalytic conception of "the unconscious...cannot account for the facts which at first sight it appeared to explain" (Sartre, 1943/1953, p. 96). In contrast, for Sartre, there is in "essence the unity of a *single* consciousness" (p. 89). He writes that "fear, forgetting, dreams exist really in the capacity of concrete facts of consciousness" (Sartre, 1943/1953, p. 90). Then, Sartre (1943/1953) declares: "All knowing is consciousness of knowing" (p. 93). As mentioned, to the Sartre of the early 1940s the Freudian idea of the unconscious is a mythology that is inferior in principle and actuality, for there is no real difference between what is conscious and what not. In 1949, Sartre made an additional distinction. The "secret of man is not the Oedipus complex, or inferiority complex, it is the very limit of his liberty, it is his power of resistance to torture and death" (Roudinesco, 2008, p. 35). It is not our psychology which is paramount but freedom and resistance. To this philosopher, Freud is off-base.

Sartre's assessment of psychoanalysis begins to soften as his overall outlook evolves. After World War II, he became drawn to communism. He went so far as to declare in 1957 that "Marxism is... the philosophy of our time" (Sartre, 1957/1963, p. 30). Is Sartre here displacing the existentialist philosophy which he had embodied and championed? Marxism focuses on defined economic classes and specific periods of history that shape, even determine an individual's existence, while Sartrean existentialism celebrates an individual's freedom and autonomy. Sartre in the mid to late 1950s recognized the tensions between his existentialist and Marxist allegiances. He sought to mediate between the

CHAPTER 4: SARTRE AND PSYCHOANALYSIS

two philosophies in his 1957 *Search For A Method*, and found psychoanalysis to be useful in this endeavor.

Sartre (1957/1963) writes: "Psychoanalysis alone allows us to discover the whole man in the adult" (p. 60). For it is "the psychoanalytic method which discovers the ways there is "a mediation between the universal class and the individual" (Sartre, 1957/1963, p. 62). In seeking to bridge the chasm between Marxism and existentialism, Sartre finds that psychoanalysis can bring understanding and insight into this intellectual challenge. One of Sartre's existentialist goals is to capture "the profundity of the lived" for "profundity comes to the world through man" (Sartre, 1957/1963, p. 145). How to Sartre do humans bring about this profundity? "Man defines himself by his project" (Sartre, 1957/1963, p. 150). Out of human freedom, an individual finds a sense of self and identity through developing and pursuing a project which concentrates the person's efforts. As a depth psychology, profundity and psychoanalysis are not strangers. By showing the whole person in adults, psychoanalysis can assist free persons in discovering their central direction.

As well, throughout his career Sartre discussed the lives of French writers. He seems to be both celebrating these individual's paths and reconfirming the importance of his own theory of the project. A film about how Freud became Freud could also be subtitled how Freud found his project. Becoming immersed in writing about Freud left its mark on Sartre. Imagining being in Freud's shoes led him to reconsider himself through his own version of a Freudian lens. A few years after composing the scenario, in his own autobiography, the influence of psychoanalysis is evident. The commission to write on Freud coincided with Sartre's own evolution.

A virtue of Sartre's script is that he reveals – better than does Huston film – Freud's character and how his interpersonal dramas were connected to his theoretical developments. As will be evident in what follows, there is both much overlap and remarkable differences between Huston's film and Sartre's scenario. To begin, for whatever reason, when the transition was made from Sartre's screenplay to Huston's film, Berlin physician Wilhelm Fliess was cut from the script. This was a serious omission. For not only for Sartre is Fliess the catalyst that propels the drama, but the actual dialogue in letters between this German doctor and his Viennese counterpart was crucial in Freud's own development. It is in their correspondence throughout the 1890s that Freud discussed his own psychology and first revealed his innovative ideas. An expurgated version of these letters was published in 1954, and Sartre relied on them and the first volume of Ernest Jones's Freud biography in putting together his screenplay (Pontalis, 1986, p. xi). Leaving Fliess out then detracted from the aim of showing how Freud became Freud, including that Fliess plays a central role in the interpersonal dramas between Freud and Breuer and he and his wife, Martha.

Understanding the character of the Freud-Fliess relationship, as well as Fliess himself is thus indispensable. Fliess was a charismatic figure and an adventurous thinker. Some of his ideas such as bisexuality and biorhythms have had followers, and others such as the sexual significance of the nose might be considered medical quackery. What made him a model for Freud is that Fliess was a bold thinker. The closeness of the two men provided Freud with a receptive audience for his own innovative conceptions. Where Breuer was not always sympathetic to what he called Freud's "psychical need" to make "absolute and exclusive formulations" (Holt, 1989, 50-51). Fliess had the very same tendency as Freud. For a good amount of time, Freud and Fliess were a good match for each other. As Sartre's drama unfolds, we get to see how crucial Fliess was for Freud evolving into a psychoanalyst.

Freud's character is also central to this unfolding drama. What distinguishes Sartre's version from Huston's film is the playwright and novelist's gift for psychology. In relation to Sigmund, Sartre shows early on how the obscure Austrian physician had both an elevated and troubled conception of himself. Sartre has Freud telling his fiancé, Martha, that he is burning fourteen years of his diary. The reason being that "I want to give my future biographers a hard time. They'll shed tears of blood" (Sartre, 1986, pp. 24-26). This echoes what Freud (1960) actually wrote to Martha on April 28, 1885, that in relation to "the biographers… I am already looking forward to seeing them go astray" as they write on "'The Development of the Hero'" (p. 141). He already sees himself in heroic terms. Another example of Freud's ambitious self-importance is that after returning from Paris with Charcot, Freud prepares to address a gathering of Viennese physicians where he intends to reveal to them the secrets of hysteria he has learned in France. Sartre has him say to Martha, that in an

CHAPTER 4: SARTRE AND PSYCHOANALYSIS

hour he will address the Medical Society about "male hysterical patients and will propose a new therapy." He will receive "general acclamation... By tomorrow the story of his triumph will be all over town" (Sartre, 1986, pp. 70-71). In Sartre's version, Sigmund's expectation of adulation at this lecture did not materialize. His report was generally met by disdain and skepticism. Freud's elevated self-assessment was not matched by his ability to accurately read his audience.

Sartre presents another side to Freud. Martha once found him in a disoriented state. He then tells her that doctors cannot help him as his troubles lie in his own head. "Yesterday, I was no longer in control of myself. I'd have blown up the whole world." He says to his fiancé, "There's no one but you who can cure me... I love you more than anything" (Sartre, 1986, pp. 45-46). It is in portraying Freud as a person of both great highs and lows that Sartre shows character traits that are later paramount when Freud's inner crisis leads to his extraordinary discoveries that have altered our ideas of what it means to be human. This last cited exchange between Freud and Martha also illustrates another important element within Sartre's drama and Freud's character: how in this period of his life, Freud's psychic and intellectual well-being are entangled in his close personal relationships. He is psychologically interdependent with a select few people. It is through his close relationships that Freud enacts his inner turmoil, gets support, and finds his way intellectually and emotionally. He needs a receptive audience; his inner path is not reached in isolation.

On May 7,1900, he writes Fliess, "no one can replace for me the relationship with the friend....inner voices to which I am accustomed to listen suggest a much more modest estimate of my work than that which you proclaim" (Freud, 1985, p. 412). He elaborates on August 7, 1901: "my life, as you know, woman has never replaced the comrade, the friend" (Freud, 1985, p. 447). If this was ever an accurate view of himself, the evidence of his letters to Martha when they were engaged shows that for a good while a particular woman was paramount to him. It was within this relationship that Freud revealed his inner thoughts and fears. In a close reading of Sigmund and Martha's correspondence, literature professor Madelon Sprengnether writes how in the letters Freud "bares his soul, confiding his anxieties, his ambitions, and love." When he alienates Martha, "Freud feels anxious and bereft, a condition of inner desolation from which only she can rescue him" (Sprengnether, 2018, pp. 45 & 47). Sprengnether quotes a June 30, 1884 letter in which Freud confesses to his fiancé, "I really think I have always loved you much more than you me" (Freud, 1960, p. 117). Given how important Martha then was to Sigmund, it was not only males that were crucial to his sense of self.

Sartre shows Freud's psychological need for interdependence, and how in the beginning of this period how loyal and supportive Martha is to Sigmund, though she clearly recognizes his imperfections and peculiarities. Martha played the role of buttressing Sigmund when he had a more modest view of himself; a role also played by Breuer and Fliess. Part of Sartre's insight is to delineate how Freud depended on select others to keep him afloat and to unleash his ambitions and creativity.

It was not only Martha who was central to Freud in the early period of this scenario but, as just mentioned, so did esteemed Vienna physician and physiologist Josef Breuer. As with Martha, Sartre's drama shows how this once important relationship is transformed through both their internal dynamics and Sigmund's relationship with Fliess. Breuer was 14 years older than Freud, and became the younger man's mentor, collaborator, and backer. Besides their close friendship, Breuer sent patients to his younger colleague when Freud first established his medical practice, and also loaned the struggling Freud a good amount of money (Gay, 1988, p. 53; Clark, 1980, p. 58). In Freud's scuffling years, there was no one who did more for him than Josef Breuer, he was supportive, welcoming, and generous.

As well as having a successful private medical practice, Breuer moonlighted doing scientific research in the evenings, and made important discoveries in how wound fever is transmitted, in the regulation of respiration, and how the functioning of the inner ear becomes balanced. The Hering-Breuer reflex is named for a reflex they found how the vagus nerve played a role in the depth and rhythm of breathing (Breger, 2009, pp. 23-24).

A turning point for both Breuer and Freud became the older man's treatment in German speaking Vienna of a young hysteric named Bertha Pappenheim. She had a variety of extreme symptoms including for a time only being able to talk in English. Breuer began treating Bertha in 1880,

CHAPTER 4: SARTRE AND PSYCHOANALYSIS

and by 1883 at the latest was sharing this case with Freud (Gay, 1988, pp. 63-64). These conversations preceded Freud's going to Paris in 1885 to study hysteria in Charcot's clinic.

After Sigmund's return with his stronger involvement with hysterics, Breuer and his collaboration increased with this shared interest. Sartre's scenario also focuses on this therapy and the tangles it weaves. When the jointly authored collaboration resulted in the 1895 publication of *Studies on Hysteria* Bertha is called Anna O. and in Sartre's work, she is a composite character called Cäcilie, based not only on Ms. Pappenheim, but other clients. Bertha or Cäcilie, in Sartre's version, is no ordinary client. The frequency of Breuer's tending to her has caused tension in his marriage. His wife, Mathilde, calls Cäcilie "an enchantress." When it is set up for Freud and Fliess to accompany Breuer to Cäcilie's home, Mathilde tells Martha Freud, "You'd better watch out" (Sartre, 1986, 140). Mathilde has found Cäcilie a rival for her husband's attention and affecttion. Breuer's wife knows that her husband has come under his patient's spell. Even before Freud and Fliess become entangled with Cäcilie a jealous triangle is already in place.

Yet for both Breuer and eventually Freud this emotionally complex case was transformative; it is often mentioned as the first case of a psychoanalytic treatment. Breuer found that when he could get Bertha to talk about what preceded the origination of a particular problem that then the symptom would disappear. She called it chimney sweeping and the talking cure (Breuer, 1895/1957, p. 30). From that time to this, central to psychoanalysis is healing through speaking. Integral to these therapeutic efforts is not only the catharsis of talking but the initial questions that are asked of the client and then the follow ups after the answers are given. The inquiries made are connected to the perception and orientation of the questioner.

Breuer, Freud, and Fliess go see Cäcilie. In Sartre's fictional account, Fliess sits outside her bedroom while the other two enter. Cäcilie is having trouble hearing and has lost her sight. Breuer asks when her problems with sight began. She weaves a tale of doctors coming to tell her that her father is ill. She says they then escorted her to a hospital where music is playing for the patients, nurses are present, and her father has died. After Cäcilie relayed this account, Breuer expects the talking cure will work. He tells her that her sight will be restored. But it is not. Something is missing.

Freud asks if he may question Cäcilie. Breuer resists, then consents. Freud has noticed certain improbabilities in her story. Through his pointed questioning, he gets her to admit that it was police and not doctors; it was a brothel not a hospital, and there were no nurses, but whores. One of these ladies of the night had left a lipstick mark on her father's cheek. Where Breuer had accepted at face value what Cäcilie said, Freud did not; where Breuer had omitted the sexual, Freud had uncovered it. When Freud finished his examination, Cäcilie can see and hear (Sartre, 1986, pp.148-163). Sartre here has created a fictional scene that affirms Freud's perspective over Breuer's. Sartre shows how central is the therapist's ability to move the client from bad faith to a truer recollection of events.

After this session, the three doctors are riding in a cab together. Breuer berates Freud for being so firm and pushy with Cäcilie. Sigmund blurts out, "All neuroses have a sexual origin." Breuer is taken back: "That's the first I've heard about it." Breuer then exits the vehicle. Soon after, Fliess tells Freud, "It's necessary *first* to generalize." Freud says, "I owe him everything." Fliess responds, "He's not your father; he doesn't have the right to reprimand you." Then he says that he is in full agreement with Freud about the sexual origin of neuroses, and adds: "You and I, we're of the same breed. We're visionaries." Fliess encourages Freud: "Freud, you're on your way. Don't let yourself be stopped by Breuer's inhibition… Sex: that's what produces the world and what drives it" (Sartre, 1986, pp. 168-172). The die is cast: sexuality is front and center. Fliess interposes himself between Freud and Breuer, and seeks to have Freud align with him against the Breuer to whom Freud says he owes everything.

Not long afterwards Sartre presents a lunch that includes Sigmund, Martha and Fliess. The Berlin doctor encourages a reluctant Sigmund to have it out with Breuer. After Fliess departs, Martha says, "I don't like that Fliess of yours… He doesn't like Breuer… Fliess… frightens me. You're like a little boy in front of him" (Sartre, 1986, pp. 183-185). Sartre has established Fliess as a provocateur, as the great disrupter of Freud's most important personal relationships. Martha has immediately perceived the threat. This is just the beginning.

CHAPTER 4: SARTRE AND PSYCHOANALYSIS

Freud goes to the Breuers. Mathilde is still upset with her husband over his infatuation with Cäcilie. He has told her that he is no longer seeing this patient, but he still was. Breuer and Freud then go to Cäcilie's where Breuer turns over the treatment to Freud, and tells the young woman he will no longer be seeing her.

As Breuer withdraws from the field and Freud follows his mentor's method of therapy with young adult female patients, Martha has an issue. Sartre has her telling Sigmund that he is making women fall in love with him as a method of curing them. "I find that unsavory," Martha says. She later adds that the way Sigmund exploits these false loves is dirty. "I'm a decent woman" and "I'm revolted by what goes on in your doctor's consulting-room. It's not jealousy, it's disgust…are you sure a woman can live with a husband whose occupation disgusts her?" (Sartre, 1986, pp. 228 & 230). Martha Freud actually once told a visiting analyst that her husband's work was "a form of pornography" (Laforgue, 1973, p. 342). A variation on what divided Josef and Mathilde Breuer is doing the same to the Freuds. Martha implores her husband to give up his newer methods of treatment. "In the old days you used to tell me everything… Now you keep silent… For the sake of our happiness," Martha says. Sigmund's reply is, "No, Martha. Not even for the sake of our happiness." He has laid down the gauntlet, and his wife is not to talk to him about his work. The two of them, Martha says, will still share their house and children, but not the details of his therapeutic work (Sartre, 1986, pp. 230-231).

Sartre's Breuer too wants him to abandon his new approach after hearing one of Freud's patients jumped out a window, but survived. Freud says, "It's your method," and reports that he has thirteen cases where neurosis was caused by childhood sexual abuse. The senior physician says, "You see sex everywhere and I can't follow you" (Sartre, 1986, pp. 254-256). Earlier Fliess pushed Freud to continue to expand on Breuer's method and criticized Breuer for trying to hold Freud back. Sigmund says I used to obey Breuer as a child, and I needed a tyrant. Now Freud follows Fliess's lead and overcomes his own reluctance to go beyond Breuer (Sartre, 1986, pp. 216-219). Freud is transferring allegiances and this holds great promise for his intellectual development, but is simultaneously unsettling established relationships, as both his wife and mentor seek to derail Freud from his embrace of the centrality of sexuality.

In the scenario, when Fliess says to Sigmund, "Today, 13 July 1892... there stand two men who are the only ones to know Nature's secret sexuality drives the world," Freud is hesitant. "I'm afraid of losing Martha... I love her because she's like me, strict and chaste." Fliess completely ignores Freud's worries, and says "In ten years, we shall be able to govern men....we must be as close as brothers" (Sartre, 1986, pp. 234-235). In a later scene, Freud explains to Fliess about how the psychological impact of sexual abuse in childhood is delayed until adolescence, and then can lead to hysteria (Sartre, 1986, pp. 265-266). This is, for some unexplainable reason, what has become known as the seduction theory. Freud published articles in 1896 promoting this position. Sartre includes it while these papers of Freud's do not play much part in Huston's film. It is Freud's later elaborating on this theory and then renouncing it that led to his further focus on unconscious fantasy and soon after the announcement of the Oedipus complex. Following his initial publications on the etiology of hysteria, what stimulated his expansion then reconsideration of these notions related to his own father.

Sartre has Freud visiting his father, Jakob, whom his son has been avoiding. The screenwriter then flashes back to when anti-Semites knocked Jakob's hat off and he did not resist and humbly went into the street and picked his hat up. An account of this was later given by Freud, who said it changed his view of Jakob. Sartre then creates a scene where a six-year-old Sigmund proclaims, "I shall avenge all Jews. I shall never retreat. I shall never go down into the roadway" (Sartre, 1986, pp. 284-287). It is clear to Sartre that as an adult Freud remains uneasy around his father. He leaves the house, and his mother wonders if Sigmund loves Jakob. Martha replies "apart from you, Mama, I wonder if he loves anybody" (Sartre, 1986, p. 288).

He wishes to resume treating Cäcilie. Freud tells her mother that he has ideas about neurosis and wants to verify them, and that her daughter is the most intelligent patient he has known (Sartre, 1986, p. 292). With Cäcilie he abandons Breuer's use of hypnotism and substitutes free association and her recounting her dreams. He is coming into his own in some ways, and in others he is too eager. From inconclusive things Cäcilie tells him, he concludes her father abused her. Freud wishes to present this and other cases to the medical society. Breuer objects as this was his patient and his reputation is at stake, and also because he does not concur with Freud.

CHAPTER 4: SARTRE AND PSYCHOANALYSIS

Sartre has Sigmund later writing to Fliess he has broken things off with Breuer. The alliance with Fliess has given Freud the courage to confront his mentor. As usual, Freud needs the backing of someone to keep on his path. Fliess has been pushing Freud to leave Breuer behind, and now the shift of allegiances has taken place.

Returning to Cäcilie, she says she now remembers things and her father was not seducing her, but having an affair with a housekeeper. Freud says that he forced this sexual memory on her, and that he was mistaken (Sartre, 1986, pp. 334-335). After this realization, Freud's father dies. The two circumstances of treating Cäcilie and Freud's agony over his father's dying end up converging. In Sartre's account, when Freud recognizes that with Cäcilie he has manufactured evidence to confirm his theories. He turns inward, and begins to examine himself as he would a patient. Surprisingly soon after the funeral, Sartre has Fliess show up in Vienna. Sigmund talks about his father. "His death is driving me mad... I wonder if I loved him... Sometimes I thought I hated him... I ought to apply my own method to myself... If I want to analyze myself, I must speak in someone's presence" (Sartre, 1986, pp. 341-343). Freud then recounts an incident, and believes he is repressing something from his consciousness, and wishes to recover the memory (Sartre, 1986, p. 344). In response, Sartre has Fliess telling him, "don't dig down into yourself any more. You'll go mad if you try to know yourself" (Sartre, 1986, p. 386). In Sartre's imagined scene, as with Breuer and Martha, Freud's drive to know has gone farther than the other can support. His relentlessness pushes his intimate associates too far. Freud can endure what they turn away from.

With Fliess warning him to stop as had Breuer and Martha, as he still needed to play off someone, Sartre has Freud returning to Cäcilie. But one gets the sense that this treatment will be as much about Freud's self-analysis as about Cäcilie's well-being. With her, Freud almost acts as if he is the patient rather than the therapist. He asks Cäcilie if she is mad at him. Then Sartre has Freud confessing to her, "I think I'm sick myself. I project my own sickness onto my patients." He has once again returned to needing others to find himself. Referring to his patients, Freud says, "I won't be able to...understand myself until I understand them. I must discover in them what I am." Cäcilie immediately picks up what Freud wants. "It's a collaboration that you're asking of me?...You want us to be cured together." Freud responds, "Yes. And by one another" (Sartre, 1986, p.

348). In asserting this, Sartre has Freud tempting Cäcilie to recreate with him the symbiotic relationship she had with Breuer. He is also seeking from Cäcilie what Sartre had him once wanting from Martha. He then said that he needed Martha to cure him, now he is saying to Cäcilie he cannot find himself without her assistance. Sartre is having Freud seek autonomy and authentic self-knowledge through being co-interdependent, of being a free agent pursuing a project while simultaneously acting like a dependent child. Sartre presents Freud as once needing his fiancé, and now needing his patient, to act towards him as a nurturing mother might, to cure him when he is ill.

With Cäcilie, he gets her to talk about her father, his mistresses, his being drawn to prostitutes, that her father treated Cäcilie when a young girl as a substitute wife when his actual spouse was away, that the woman he married was a former lady of the evening. Her mother talks honestly to Freud about her own past, her husband's dalliances, and the conflicts between mother and daughter.

Freud remains with Cäcilie overnight as she is troubled. In response to what Cäcilie has told him, he dreams that his own daughter, Mathilde, is both his daughter and wife. This resembles but does not quite match a dream about Mathilde that Freud reported to Flies on May 31, 1897, where Freud said that this sexual interest towards his daughter confirmed his wish to find fathers as the causes of neurosis (Freud, 1985, p. 249). Sartre handles this dream somewhat differently. First, he has Freud declaring, "If I feel desire for my daughter, that means all fathers do. I dreamed I was committing that sexual assault because I wanted my theory to be true." Then Sartre has Freud making other assertions that in real life took Freud four months to assert. He has Freud saying this theory is "certainly false… I wanted to sully my father's name. To degrade him." Freud continues this inner dialogue and asks himself about the thirteen cases of females being sexually abused. He then asserts that all of them "were entertaining unconscious desire… Cäcilie was in love with her father." Then Sartre has Freud recalling a variation of a tale Freud tells about seeing his mother nude, but in this instance Sartre has a two-year-old Sigmund sharing a hotel room with his mother while his father is in an adjoining room. Jakob induces his wife to leave their young boy alone and join him for a while in her husband's room. Sartre is portraying an imagined version of the infamous primal scene (Sartre, 1986, pp. 366-369).

CHAPTER 4: SARTRE AND PSYCHOANALYSIS

Cäcilie suddenly awakens, and asks if she tried to murder her own mother. Freud can confirm that as a child she did. She says then I "was a little monster." Freud says no you were a child, that is all. Freud then says to her, "Thanks to you, I think I understand both of us. And that I can cure us." He then asks if she knows the story of Oedipus. She tells the outlines of the myth. Freud responds by saying, "Oedipus is everybody." Then again Sartre has Freud confessing to his patient as if she were Fliess, "In neuroses, I've viewed the parents as guilty and the children as innocent. That was because I hated my father. It's necessary to reverse the terms." Cäcilie interjects that is then the children who are guilty. Freud responds that no one is guilty, but children have desires. He then talks about his love and desire for his mother, and that he was jealous of his father who possessed his mother. "I loved him and hated him at the same time." Then Sartre has Freud going beyond both the Oedipus complex and what Freud actually said. "I searched for other fathers," but when "they gave any sign of weakness, I'd abandon them. It was his weakness that I hated in them" (Sartre, 1986, pp. 370-371). His self-analysis has reached its zenith. He has renounced the seduction theory, asserted children's unconscious desire as a reversal, announced the Oedipus complex, and appears to have come to terms with his complex responses to his imperfect father. Freud has made breakthroughs that became the backbone of psychoanalytic theory. A Sartrean project has not only begun has reached beyond what most other humans achieve. But six months later, when Freud and Fliess meet, the latter is still dissenting. The German physician still holds on to the seduction theory. Fliess then adds, "Your patients lie down on your couch, they tell you whatever they like, and then you come along and project onto their heads whatever ideas you've got in yours" (Sartre, 1986, p. 375).

According to what Freud wrote on August 7,1901, Fliess had written to him exactly that "the reader of thoughts merely reads his own thoughts into other people" (Freud, 1985, p. 447). But Sartre's Fliess has more to add: "Where does Science come into all that? It's nothing but cock-and-bull stories. Thinking means measuring" (Sartre, 1986, p. 375). He asks Freud if he has established "quantitative measures." When Freud says he did not, Fliess says "Then it's all quackery" (Sartre, 1986, p. 375). It is not clear how much of this on Sartre's part are his own views on psychoanalysis and how much just skilled dramatic writing. Still, Sartre's Freud is not without resources in this exchange. "You can talk of nothing but figures... I wonder whether you don't tailor your calculations to produce whatever final results you've been aiming at from the outset" (Sartre, 1986, p.375).

Then the question turns as to whether they will remain close intimates. Fliess remains skeptical of Freud's concepts and whether they can collaborate. Sartre has Freud saying "You're my friend, Fliess." Fliess says we are friends if you believe in my ideas, and Freud acknowledges he no longer does. The Berlin doctor says, "You had only one father left, Sigmund. And I wonder whether you didn't come here with the intention of liquidating him." Freud says, "Perhaps." Flies responds, "…it's done. Farewell" (Sartre, 1986, p. 377). With that father replacement for Freud finished, Sartre has Sigmund go to the cemetery to visit his father's resting place and lay a wreath on Jakob's gravestone. There he runs into his previous father substitute, Josef Breuer, and his wife, Mathilde. Speaking about his and Breuer's relationship, Freud admits, "It's all my fault." Breuer says, "I saw myself as your spiritual father" but turned "against you and your ideas" when you went beyond me. In return, Freud says, "I've applied your method to myself, Breuer… I loved my father, but I was jealous of him" and found within myself towards him "a terrifying aggressiveness" (Sartre, 1986, pp. 381-382).

A little bit later, Breuer asks about Fliess. Freud responds, "A mirage. I took him for the Devil; he was just a book-keeper. No matter I respected his strength." Breuer thoughtfully answers, "What a lot of fathers! Most of the time, you had two of them at once." Freud says, "Yes, I was afraid of myself… I was taking all those fathers to protect myself against myself." Breuer acknowledges this and recognizes they will not be seeing much of each other, and adds you have "won the right to be alone." Freud says, "I'll be my sole judge and my sole witness" (Sartre, 1986, pp. 381-382). This last sounds as much like Sartre' own individualism as the way Freud conducted his life, and this scene neither accounts for Freud's continuing need for intimate others nor the centrality of females in his psyche and life. It is ironic here that Sartre who has presented how important Martha and Cäcilie have been for Freud, does not bring them into this part of the exchange. But then Freud tells Breuer and Mathilde, "I don't want my wife to be the victim of that solitude. She isn't happy, she worries me… I can't imagine it's much fun being the wife of Sigmund Freud." He asks the Breuers to welcome Martha back into their fold. Breuer says his wife will write to Martha today. The Breuer's and Freud

CHAPTER 4: SARTRE AND PSYCHOANALYSIS

say goodbye. Sartre had Martha once wonder if Sigmund loved anyone besides his own mother. Freud's remarks about Martha give Sartre's answer about Sigmund's feelings toward his wife. He then stands before his father's grave, and tears roll down his cheeks. When he leaves the cemetery, his eyes remain moist (Sartre, 1986, pp. 382-383). And that is how this screenplay poignantly ends.

Breuer and Freud's relationship did not conclude as amicably as Sartre presents. On March 24, 1898, Sigmund writes to Fliess about Breuer's "underhandedness" and says, "Again and again I am glad to be rid of him" (Freud, 1985, pp. 304-305). This separation from Breuer continued. Breuer's daughter-in law says that towards the end of his life, on a walk, Breuer saw Sigmund nearby and went to greet him with open arms, and Freud kept on walking as if he was not aware that Breuer was right in front of him (Breger, 2009, p. 84). Freud's relationship with Fliess, Ronald Clark writes, "dissolved in bitterness" (Clark, 1980, p. 224). Fliess himself describes he and Freud's last face to face meeting in 1900: "I detected a personal animosity against me on Freud's part" (Clark, 1980, pp. 221-222).

Sartre presents a Freud who both depends on and plays off of others. Sigmund both counts on them to back and encourage them, and yet pushes some of them farther than they can go. In this script and in his life, Sigmund over and over again forms an intimate alliance with another, implicitly seeks from them unquestioning support, does things that tests their limits, and with those who are males, breaks away from them, and makes a complete cut off. He often retains an intense hostility to them for the rest of his life. Freud has some recognition of what he might call a repetition compulsion. In 1900, he says, "My emotional life has always insisted that I should have an intimate friend and a hated enemy ... and it has not infrequently happened ... that friend and enemy have come together in a single individual" (Freud, 1900/1953, p. 483). With men he was close to and then the friendship ended, Freud's narcissistic wound is manifest as hostility. The list of such close male relationships followed by no further contact is long.

There is one modification of this pattern; it is with his wife. In Sartre's account, she draws the line with him, yet he both goes his own way and values the family and marriage they created together. **The concern and** caring that Sartre has Freud showing for his wife is plainly evident in the letters Sigmund sends to his daughter Anna, as is how much he treasures his family as a whole and his six children (Meyer-Palmedo , 2014). His letters to Anna reveal the family side of Freud in ways that are not as present in most of his other published correspondence.

As for his career, Freud blossomed from his discoveries of 1897 and after. Sartre has him determined to go on his own. After 1900, Freud combined independence, being extraordinarily fertile, and interdependence with others. His creativity lasted for the rest of his life, and he was able to find colleagues, collaborators, and followers that evolved into an international movement. His extensive correspondence helped keep his network going.

Sartre's scenario focuses on Freud's issues with his father and substitute father figures. At some point, Freud himself became the father figure for others. There is a paradox in this. Otto Rank writing in 1932 says that the founder of psychoanalysis "is a rebellious son who defends the paternal authority, a revolutionary who, from fear of his own rebellious son-ego, took refuge in the security of the father position" (Rank, 1932, pp. 191-192). Internal divisions in Freud's psyche about fathers and sons remained and were reflected in aspects of psychoanalytic organizations. Leaders of some movements have been less likely to suffer from as fierce factionalism as characterized psychoanalysis under Freud's direction. Yet for all its ups and downs, its waxing and waning in cultural influence, psychoanalysis remains both vital and full of intellectual dilemmas and divisions.

As for Sartre, his immersion in Freud and psychoanalysis as he was writing *The Freud Scenario* seems to have had some lingering, if unusual, impact on him. A few years later in his autobiography, *The Words,* psychoanalysis and the issue of fathers is mentioned. Sartre's own father died when the boy was two, and he was raised for years by his mother and her parents in their home. He writes, "my father's early retirement left me with a most incomplete 'Oedipus complex.' No Superego… no aggressiveness either. My mother was mine; no one challenged my peaceful possession of her… I was spared the hard apprenticeship of jealousy" (Sartre, 1964, p. 26). Sartre maintains that not having a biological father around was a good thing "There is no good father, that's the rule… Had my father lived, he would have lain on me at full length and would have crushed me… I readily subscribe to the verdict of an eminent psychoanalyst: I have no

CHAPTER 4: SARTRE AND PSYCHOANALYSIS

Superego" (Sartre, 1964, p. 19). While there is much to be skeptical of in Sartre's assertions about fathers, the Oedipus complex and a super-ego, he clearly is incorporating Freudian concepts into his own self-analysis. While Sartre and Freud seem an odd pairing, the philosopher was able to find in Freud's struggles echoes of the search for an all-encompassing project that remained central to his own preoccupations. Using a mixture of surviving evidence, his own ideological lens, and a dramatist's imagination, Sartre convincingly presents an account that in some ways is beyond evidence and in others captures the interpersonal dynamics in Freud's life that have fallen through the historical cracks. An imaginative account can provide a perspective that can then be mined in biographical and historic investigations.

REFERENCES

Breger, L. (2009). *A dream of undying fame: How Freud betrayed his mentor and invented psychoanalysis.* Basic Books.

Breuer, J. (1957). Fraulein Anna O. In J. Breuer & S. Freud, *Studies on hysteria.* (J. Strachey, Ed and Trans.). Basic Books. (Original work published 1895)

Clark, R. (1980). *Freud: The man and the cause.* Random House.

Freud, S. (1953). *The standard edition of the complete psychological works, Vol. V.* (J. Strachey, Ed. and Trans.). The Hogarth Press. (Original work published 1900)

Freud, S. (1955). *SE, Vol. XVII (1917-1919)* (J. Strachey, Ed. & Trans.). The Hogarth Press. (Original work published 1917-1919)

Freud, S. (1960). *Letters of Sigmund Freud* (E. Freud, Ed., T. & J. Stern, Trans.). Basic Books.

Freud, S. (1985). *The complete letters of Sigmund Freud to Wilhelm Fliess, 1887-1904* (J. Moussaieff-Masson, Ed. & Trans.). Harvard University Press.

Gay, P. (1988). *Freud: A life for our time.* W. W. Norton & Company.

Holt, R. (1989). *Freud reappraised: A fresh look at psychoanalytic theory.* The Guilford Press.

Laforgue, R. (1973). Personal memories of Freud. In H. M. Ruitenbeek (Ed.), *Freud as we knew him* (McConchie, Trans.) (pp. 341-349). Wayne State University Press.

Meyer-Palmedo, I. (Ed.) (2014). *Sigmund and Anna Freud: Correspondence 1904-1938* (N. Somers, Trans.). Polity Press.

Pontalis, J.-B. (1986). Editor's preface. In J.-P. Sartre, *The Freud scenario* (pp. vii-xviii). University of Chicago Press.

Rank, O., & Moxon, M. (Ed.) (1932). *Modern education: A critique of its fundamental ideas.* Alfred A. Knopf.

Roudinesco, E. (2008). *Philosophy in turbulent times* (W. McCuaig, Trans.). Columbia University Press.

Sartre, J.-P. (1953). *Being and nothingness: An essay on phenomenological ontology* (H. Barnes, Trans.). Washington Square Press. (Original work published 1943)

Sartre, J.-P. (2007). *Existentialism is a humanism* (C. Macomber, Trans.). Yale University Press. (Original work published 1946)

Sartre, J.-P. (1963). *Search for a method* (H. Barnes, Trans.). Vintage Books. (Original work published 1957)

Sartre, J.-P. (1964). *The words* (B. Frechtman, Trans.). Vintage Books.

Sartre, J.-P., & Pontalis, J.B. (Ed.) (1986). *The Freud scenario* (Q. Hoare, Trans.). The University of Chicago Press.

Sprengnether, M. (2018). *Mourning Freud.* Bloomsbury.

CHAPTER 5

A DANGEROUS METHOD: FILM REVIEW

All quotations in this chapter are from
Hampton, C. (2002). *The talking cure. Faber and Faber.*

The film *A Dangerous Method* is an imaginative recreation of the relationship of the Swiss doctor Carl Jung and his Russian patient Sabina Spielrein. Christopher Hampton wrote the screenplay, which closely follows his 2002 stage play, *The Talking Cure*. Since the screenplay to the film is unavailable, the published text to the same author's play is used, as the same language is used in both. The film is about the transformative power of sexual relationships, although no actual record of the character of Carl and Sabina's sexual relationship actually exists.

A hysterical Spielrein benefits from Jung's employment of the psychoanalytic method. As she starts to improve, Jung helps her get into medical school, and an alliance develops between them. The connection with Spielrein dovetails with other advances in Jung's life. At his wife's encouragement, Jung contacts and then forms a strong bond with Freud, who asks Jung to take on the disturbed but brilliant psychoanalyst Otto Gross as a patient.

Gross may be the first analyst to embody what Paul Robinson called the Freudian left, a combination of psychoanalysis and radical politics. In the film, the political side of Gross's thought is omitted in favor of sexual radicalism. In what seems less like therapy than college bull sessions, Gross preaches sexual liberation to Jung, who responds that "sexual repression" is necessary "in any rational society." Gross then says, "if there's one thing I've learned... it's this: never repress anything!" (pp. 38-39), Otto asserts, "The story of our life is essentially the story of our sexuality... To repress yourself must be to condemn yourself to realize no more than a fragment of your full psychic potential." Jung immediately replies, "Not to repress yourself is to unleash all kinds of dangerous and destructive forces" (pp. 44-45).

Soon after, Jung starts a sadomasochistic sexual relationship with Spielrein. She tells Jung that her father's threats to beat her led her to masturbate. Spielrein asks Jung to be "ferocious," and "to punish me," which he does. Afterwards, she says as a doctor she wants "to give people back their freedom by curing them, the way you gave me mine." Sounding like Otto Gross, Jung responds, "This is what freedom is: no constraints, no chains, where love isn't a means to an end, it's an end in itself" (p. 47). Gone are Jung's assertions that destruction and danger accompany abandoning repression.

Emma Jung is aware of her husband's affair and writes anonymously to Spielrein's mother. This activates exchanges that lead to Jung trying to break off his sexual relationship with Sabina. Word gets back to Freud, and initially Jung deceives Freud. Eventually, Spielrein convinces Jung to confess to Freud what he has done, and then Jung retreats. He acknowledges that although he wants to leave his wealthy wife, home, and children for Sabina, he is ultimately a "complacent coward" and a "philistine Swiss bourgeois" (p. 75). Jung embraces constraints and chains, and unlike Spielrein, he does not have the courage of his experience. She turns acting out her sexual fantasies with Jung into psychoanalytic theory, and becomes the first to formulate the notion of the death instinct.

She also tells Jung that if "we think of sexuality as fusion, losing oneself...in the other, destroying one's individuality" then "the ego in self-defense" will "automatically resist and repress that impulse...true sexuality demands the destruction of the ego" (p. 73). Yet Spielrein acknowledges she gained her freedom through Jung; her ego was restored, not destroyed. Jung remains stuck, repeats his relationship with Sabina in other affairs, and courts emotional and professional disaster by defying Freud. When Freud retaliates by cutting off their relationship, Carl has a breakdown.

It is when Jung is despondent that a married and pregnant Spielrein visits Jung and his wife. The two former lovers talk. Jung says, "My love for you was the most important thing in my life. It made me understand who I am, for better or worse." Touching Sabina's stomach, he adds, "This should be mine." She agrees. A rueful Jung says, "Sometimes you have to do something unforgivable just to be able to go on living" (pp. 86-87). These are the film's last words.

CHAPTER 5: *A DANGEROUS METHOD* – FILM REVIEW

As powerful as this line is, it raises questions. Except for the philistine scene, the viewer has not witnessed enough despair in Jung to drive him to cross certain lines. It is not that Jung did not have a traumatic past – his father died young, his mother was erratic, he was raped by a revered male adult – but that Hampton does not include these troubled aspects of Jung's biography. What internal forces draw him to the volatile sexual expressions with Spielrein are not disclosed. The film's flaw, then, is in Jung's character development – the line about crossing moral boundaries is not given the proper dramatic foundation.

The Jung of *A Dangerous Method* clearly is destructive and self-destructive. It is Spielrein, through unleashing Jung's violence, who discovered the psychoanalytic doctrine of the death instinct, not the man who enacted the violence with her. He continued his unconscious path. His illicit sexual life threatened his marriage and career, and how he dealt with Freud also shows how he risked himself. On one hand, Jung had real disagreements with Freud; on the other, an Oedipal Jung wished to knock his self-appointed father figure off the throne. When Freud perceived these death wishes from Jung toward him, he twice fainted, then later struck back and effectively excommunicated the wayward rebel.

This brings us back to the closing line of the play and film. The line itself is self-centered; Jung is less concerned about its effect on treasured relationships than how it can liberate the self. Doing the unforgivable to live does not occur in a vacuum. The power dynamics of the various relationships will determine if such overstepping helps one keep living or presents other obstacles. With his wife, Jung continued to do the unforgivable and she deferred to him. His death instinct towards the founder of psychoanalysis led to a counterattack that paralyzed Jung for years.

The closing line is an affirmation of Gross's self-centered sexual radicalism. As a psychoanalytic doctrine it is too narcissistic, too removed from power dynamics and the benefits of mutuality. The last line affirms a dangerous method more than an authentic talking cure.

CHAPTER 6

ROMAN POLANSKI'S *CHINATOWN* IN ITS TIME AND OURS

Not long before the WWII started, Bertolt Brecht wrote: "Truly I live in dark times!.. What kind of times are these... All roads led into the mire in my time" (Brecht, 2003, p.70). It was not as ominous in 1974 when the film *Chinatown* opened as when Brecht wrote, but politically in America it was quite dark. The United States was at the tail end of a cycle of liberalism and radicalism. Civil rights activism and student radicalism had ascended in the 1960s, but later fragmented and dissipated. The grand hopes of Martin Luther King Jr.'s 1963 "I Have a Dream" speech was partially fulfilled but then stalled. Opposition to the Vietnam war had galvanized many, but after 1970, the anti-war movement diminished. As the sixties turned into the seventies, for many liberals and radicals hope turned into disillusionment, some stayed the course, others turned from political activism to personal fulfillment, and some ended up adhering to the values they had opposed. In 1972, an anti-radical President Nixon won a landslide re-election over an anti-war Democrat, marking the end to any realistic hope that the radical and liberal visions that had seemed a real possibility as recently as 1968 before the assassinations of King and Robert Kennedy.

But Nixon's triumph was short lived. In 1973, the Watergate scandal became a public preoccupation, leading to further disenchantment. Many Americans across the political spectrum worried that Nixon was a crook, and that our political system was corrupt beyond repair. Then after the autumn 1973 Arab-Israeli war, OPEC countries rationed oil, massive gas shortages appeared, in two months, world oil prices increased by 400% (CBS News Online, 2006, para 6). The U.S. inflation rate went from 3.6% to 10% in thirteen months, and remained at double digits until mid-1975 (U. S. Inflation Calculator , 2018, para 3). America in the early 1970s was in a stark political and economic crisis. Then in May 1974, the House of Representative began formal hearings into impeaching the President.

In this atmosphere, on June 20, 1974, *Chinatown* was released. Set in the 1930's, many of the political and emotional themes of the 1960s and early 1970s were echoed in this film written by a Californian and directed by a Polish émigré. Jack Nicholson starred as private investigator Jake Gittes,

Faye Dunaway as the elusive Evelyn Mulwray, and John Huston as her father and businessman, Noah Cross.

The movie falls into the genre that has been labeled neo-noir, a reference to an updated version of the classic film noir American films of the 1940s and 1950s. The genre of film noir emerged out of the 1920s and 1930s hard-boiled American fiction school with its initial masters of Dashiell Hammett, Raymond Chandler, and James Cain, followed soon after by Ross MacDonald. These works often featured male detectives uncovering the perpetrators of murder in dark city corners, where men's motives were disguised, women could be femme fatales, and distrust and being tough were needed to survive and prevail.

Film noir, according to Alain Silver and Elizabeth Ward, often features alienated protagonists, who may be haunted by traumatic pasts. There is a struggle to control the internal and external causes of distress (Silver & Ward, 1979, p.4). Foster Hirsch says film noir private detectives, victims, and criminals can become entangled in a menacing, unsettling web of illegal activity (Hirsch, 1981, pp. 10, 12). The stories are usually about individuals and social milieus rather than politics and government. The private eye noir films show the detective unraveling the circle of individual base motives. He resides among those who appear to be one kind of person, but are hiding sordid aspects of their character. The detective may uncover the truth and solve the crime, but the unruly world prevails even when in individual cases there has been justice and resolution. When noir was revived in the 1970s, it kept true to many of the genre's traditions, but altered others, in what has been called neo-noir. *Chinatown* is often considered the pinnacle of the neo-noir phenomenon (Ross, 2016). The idea and script for the movie came from Robert Towne. A Californian, he had been a well-known screen doctor, including working on *Bonnie and Clyde* and *The Godfather*. Towne had also written the script for *The Last Detail*, starring Jack Nicholson. Robert and Jack were buddies, had been roommates, and *Chinatown* was written for Nicholson to play the male lead (Simon, 2013, para 5).

Towne says there were two inspirations for the story, one was seeing a pictorial account of Raymond Chandler's 1930s Los Angeles, after which Towne began immersing himself in Chandler's writings. The other source was a 1946 book on Southern California that described a water scam in

CHAPTER 6: ROMAN POLANSKI'S *CHINATOWN*

1908. As Towne says, there is a chapter "about the despoliation of the Owens Valley by big investors buying out the San Fernando Valley, stealing water from the north, bringing it to the south and doing so by claiming the city was suffering from a terrible drought" (Luck, 2016). The book was written by Carey McWilliams, a lawyer and political activist who later became long-time editor of *The Nation*. His son was the late political scientist, Wilson Carey McWilliams, and Wilson's wife was psychoanalyst Nancy McWilliams.

After formulating the idea for *Chinatown*, it took Towne about 10 months and 20 drafts to complete the script, which had been purchased by Paramount pictures head, Robert Evans (Hamill, 1999, para 10). Roman Polanski, who had great success with *Rosemary's Baby*, was recruited to be Director. Filming started in late September, 1973, and as the writing had begun long before that, Watergate itself was not a source for the story. The script is ranked third best screenplay of all time by the Writers Guild of America (Writers Guild of America West, no date, para 4). Towne artfully reveals the complexities of the plot one step at a time, until the amazing conclusion. He had written one ending for the film, but Director Polanski insisted on what we now see on the screen.

The film centers on the adventures of private detective, Jake Gittes. As he says, his métier is investigating adultery, unlike other hard-boiled detectives for whom murder is their business. Gittes is about to become embroiled in an investigation beyond his usual expertise. A middle-aged woman identifying herself as Mrs. Evelyn Mulwray asks him to find out if her husband, Hollis Mulwray, the chief engineer of the LA water and power department, is cheating on her. Jake and his operatives get pictures of Mr. Mulwray spending time with a young, innocent looking blonde. Next thing Jake knows a tabloid has these pictures splashed in their pages, and identifies Gittes as the investigator. He is stunned, and then becomes more surprised when the actual Evelyn Mulwray, an elegant, classy woman, appears in his office with her lawyer and papers suing Gittes. Someone has set him up. Later, he says, "I', not the one who's supposed to be caught with my pants down" (Towne, 1974/1997, p. 35). The detective has been played for a fool. This is the first indication of a major theme in the film: the supposedly worldly-wise Jake Gittes is actually an innocent in a world of conspiracy and skullduggery beyond his understanding. *Chinatown* takes conventions of the hard-boiled noir films, and turns them on their head.

In the course of the initial investigation, Jake's detectives had seen Hollis Mulwray getting into an argument with an older man on the street. Later it turns out that this is Mulwray's father-in-law, Noah Cross, and also his one-time partner in a private water company. Next thing we know Mulwray has been washed up dead in one of the city's reservoirs. At the coroner's office, Gittes encounters the now widowed Evelyn Mulwray. She concocts a story that Jake goes along with. Later, she thanks him and says she will send him a check so that she is officially his client.

Still stunned by his being played for a fool, Jake seeks more information. From a coroner he finds out that Mulwray is not the only one "drowned" during the current LA drought. Curious, he returns to where Mulwray was found, runs into some rough characters, and has his nose sliced with a knife. For the rest of the movie, Gittes has a big bandage on his nostrils. Not only has he been humiliated, now he is visibly scarred. This only increases his desire to know what happened. In Hollis Mulwray's death, the police do not initially pick up that his demise is suspicious, as well Gittes suspects Mulwray's widow is concealing things. It is with crimes and cover-ups, public and personal that *Chinatown* echoes themes prominent in the Watergate era. In this later scandal, the Senate Watergate Committee, *Washington Post* reporters Woodward and Bernstein, and various federal special prosecutors sought to uncover what the President knew and when he knew it. In this movie, it is a private detective working alone who wants to solve the mysteries.

Jake confronts Evelyn Mulwray with his belief that she is hiding some things. After she concocts a story, Gittes again tells her that she is not being honest, and reveals her husband was murdered. He resumes investigating her deceased spouse, and finds out that Mulwray was partners with Noah Cross in privately owning the water company, until Mulwray decided that the water supply should belong to the city. Through a tip Gittes finds out that Cross has been secretly buying up and diverting the water supply for his own financial gain and political power. As Watergate eventually led to the oval office, here we see corruption in the city of Angels, a system where a wealthy businessman manipulates the public, creates a drought, uses the water to irrigate the land he bought. He

CHAPTER 6: ROMAN POLANSKI'S *CHINATOWN*

triumphs while devastating others. He has figuratively raped the citizens. One side of the mystery is coming into view.

Jake and Evelyn then collaborate in uncovering the means by which Cross could own so much land where water would become valuable and yet hide that he was the owner. But they run into trouble, and Evelyn helps him escape. Back at her home, he tells her the last time things got this hairy was when he worked for the D. A. in Chinatown. He says you cannot figure out what transpires there, and adds, "I thought I was keeping someone from being hurt, and actually I ended up making sure they were hurt" (Towne, 1997, p.105). Soon after this, Jake and Evelyn become lovers. Afterwards, the subject of her father arises, and she tells him Noah Cross is dangerous, and adds "You may think you know what's going on, but you don't" (Towne, 1974/1997, 108). Once again, the subject of Gittes believing he is knowledgeable but is not arises. The detective, who knows about individual crime, is out of his depth.

After Evelyn tells Jake she has to go somewhere, Gittes trails her, and waits outside a house where he sees the young woman in the photos with her husband. He confronts Evelyn who tells Jake she is her sister. Then soon after, he is inadvertently told by a policeman that Mulwray had saltwater in his lungs, and so could not have met his death in the reservoir where he was discovered. The police now suspect that Mrs. Mulwray actually killed her spouse, and is paying Jake off to hide her crime. Gittes goes to her house, she is absent, then he drifts out to the garden, where he has previously been. The Asian gardener looking at the pond repeats what he told Gittes before, "bad for glass." The first time Jake heard it he thought the gardener was saying bad for the grass, but this time the gardener adds "Salt water bad for glass" (Towne, 1974/1997, p. 123). A light bulb goes off; in the pond they find a pair of bifocals. Jake now believes Evelyn killed her husband, that her sister knows and Mrs. Mulwray is paying the young woman off. He confronts Evelyn, and asks for her name. She says, Katherine. He says Katherine who? Evelyn says, "She's my daughter." Jake slaps her face, and says "I said the truth." The answer is "she's my sister." He hits her again, "She's my daughter." Another slap. Evelyn blurts out, "My daughter, my sister." Again, he hits her. She then says, "she's my sister *and* my daughter... my father and I, understand, or is it too tough for you" (Towne, 1974/1997, pp. 128-129).

The hard-boiled detective, slow to understand what his lover is saying, is once again out of his depth. The film's plot has gone deep into the mire.

Evelyn then tells Jake, Hollis did not wear bifocals, and so those glasses were not his. Because the police and Noah Cross are after Evelyn, Jake tells her to go stay with her hired servant, who lives in Chinatown, and then persuades Cross to meet him at the Mulwray residence. He foolishly lets Cross know he is aware that Katherine is Evelyn's daughter, that as Cross is wearing bifocals that he also murdered Hollis, and about the water deal. Confronted about all that he has done including incest with his older daughter, Cross replies, "most people never face the fact that at the right time and right place, they're capable of anything" (Towne, 1974/1997, p. 141). Noah almost celebrates his misdeeds. He then orders his man to force Gittes to give up the glasses. Noah Cross consistently acts as if he is capable of anything malevolent.

Humiliated and out-foxed Jake then heads to Chinatown where Evelyn and Katherine are trying to escape in a car. Evelyn is shot and killed by a policeman. Once again Jake's efforts to help someone insured they were harmed. Gittes tries to tell the police that Cross is responsible for everything. The officer says "you're very disturbed. You're crazy, that's her father." This policeman is as ignorant and innocent as the private eye. In the carnage, Gittes' operatives take the distraught Jake away. One of them says, "Forget it, Jake, -it's Chinatown" (Towne, 1974/1997, p. 146). The film ends.

LA's Chinatown stands as a metaphor for an endless pit, where the dire prevails and all roads lead into the mire. It is not surprising that in Chinatown Noah Cross emerges unscathed. Towne in 1983, calls what Cross did to the land a rape. He writes, "The truly murderous act in the movie was [Noah Cross's] laying waste to land and to fragile communities… It was rape worse than Cross could visit on his own daughter" (Towne, 1994, para 8). Towne links the personal and the political. Cross's character is present in what he does to his own child and to the public. His villainy goes beyond that of the usual film noir murderer, he corrupts the land, government, and his elder daughter. Crime is not restricted to individual illegal acts; it can be pervasive in the body politic. It is extending the scope of the noir parameters that *Chinatown* gains much of its significance. The film is a mirror to a time when it seems as if a U.

CHAPTER 6: ROMAN POLANSKI'S *CHINATOWN*

S. President is doing to the political system what the fictional Cross did to Los Angeles and its environs.

Yet beyond Nixon's high crimes and misdemeanors, Noah Cross embodies the heart of darkness, the extremes some humans go to fulfill their perverted sexual desires, hunger for power, lust for violence, and enjoyment of betraying, exploiting, and soiling others. As for Jake, the other side of his innocence is that he makes his living exposing sexual betrayals of unfaithful spouses. Illicit and incestuous sex as part of the anything people will do under the right circumstances is a sub-text in this movie.

A number of critics connect the incest in the film to the Oedipus tale and complex and to Greek tragedy. In Sophocles' play, the son unknowingly murders his father and marries his widowed mother. Freud, of course, says it is the son's desire for the mother that leads him to wish to eliminate the father. In *Chinatown,* it is the father as rapist and not the child who is the offender. Freud and Sophocles both omit the initial criminal act in the Oedipal myth. Laius, Oedipus's father, forcibly raped the son of the King of Pisa. The curse laid upon Laius for his sexual violation was that his own son would kill him (Devereux, 1953/1988, p. 100).

In *Chinatown,* the father is not punished for his incest, it is his victim who is slaughtered. Yet Towne's original script echoed the full Oedipus myth with the rapist father being murdered by his daughter Evelyn. That ending would have been consistent with much Hollywood film noirs, where the killer is slain. As Robert Towne says, the film's Director, Roman Polanski, "hated that ending. He wanted Evelyn to die and Cross to live. His argument was: that's life. Beautiful blondes die in LA" (Lyttleton, 2012, para 5).

Polanski had a number of reasons for wanting a tragic ending. Living in Poland when World War II broke out, the young Jewish Roman saw his father taken away by the Germans and later transported to a concentration camp, while his mother died in Auschwitz. Roman survived by being sheltered by Catholics. As an adult, in 1969, Polanski's beautiful blonde wife, actress Sharon Tate, was brutally slaughtered by Charles Manson and his followers in Beverly Hills. Violent death was central to Polanski's life experience. Ironically, three years after *Chinatown* Polanski himself was arrested for raping an under-age girl. While he pleaded guilty to a lesser charge, as with Noah Cross he has escaped extensive jail time. Still, in choosing a tragic ending to the movie, Polanski brought the elements of the script together in a way that reinforced the central theme of violation triumphing over virtue and the worldly-wise private detective being out of his depth.

One part of Jake's innocence is his inability to recognize how deep and dominant malevolent forces may be. Another aspect of his innocence is that again in Chinatown his wish to help another leads to destruction. Some Freudians and others might say that benevolence disguises mixed motives, and that we may hide from ourselves our desire to harm those we love. Evelyn Mulwray's dilemmas have similarities to Jake's, except she doesn't have the luxury of innocence. She is not the typical film noir femme fatale. Central to her life is to protect her daughter/sister from their dangerous father. For years, she is successful. But then after forming a romantic and sexual alliance with Gittes, and trusting that he might protect her and Katherine, Evelyn and Jake's collaboration lead to her meeting a bloody end. While she lies dead besides her daughter/sister in the car, her father holds and cuddles the daughter he has produced through incest. Katherine is delivered to her father. If Evelyn is a femme fatale, her fatality ends up being towards herself. With the characters of Jake Gittes and Evelyn Mulwray we see how Towne's script both continues and modifies the film noir tradition. The private eye and a haunted female lead character are standard noir motifs. But here larger social forces help these characters fall into an ominous fate, Also, Towne alters the noir tradition in the character of Noah Cross who reveals an immorality that knows no bounds,

Chinatown is a masterful and bleak film. The mire prevails. Like much of tragedy, it has a one-sided depth. While innocence may disguise malevolence and self-deception, good intentions can include mixed motives, caring, and empathy. While human love may entail hostility and hate, it may also flow with a bountiful caring that brings joy, deep bonds, and fulfillment. Human intentions remain double-sided; tragedy and benevolence often are side by side.

Hardly anyone comments on the similarities between *Chinatown* and Robert Penn Warren's 1946 political and personal novel, *All the King's Men*. Loosely based on depression era Louisiana Governor and Senator

CHAPTER 6: ROMAN POLANSKI'S *CHINATOWN*

Huey Long. It contains the story of a corrupt southern Governor, Willie Stark, who through much of the book has a low estimate of humans: "Man is conceived in sin and born in corruption and he passeth from the stink of the didie to the stench of the shroud" (Warren, 1946, p. 54). Towards the end he tries to mend his ways, but is assassinated. As he is dying, he says it all could have been different. He repents and holds out hope for a better world amidst the dirt and mud of political endeavors and personal romances. No such repentance and light are evident in *Chinatown*. In the years since 1974, the mire of corruption has not faded away. The barons of the economy and the pardoned Richard Nixon were not punished for their violations. Almost all those who committed crimes leading to the Great Recession, like Noah Cross, not only escaped prosecution, but many have become more rich and powerful.

Then there are those, like Jake Gittes and the various generations of American radicals and reformers who have often been out of their depth. Too many liberals and radicals reveal their moral innocence in the belief that they stand for virtue while portraying undemocratic aristocrats as representing what is dreadful in the world. This assessment of our autocrats has much merit. Yet can be self-deceptive while proclaiming to stand for what is good, while not recognizing their own destructive tendencies and hostile intents. Their declarations of innocence too frequently hides illusion. These movements have been indispensable in bringing necessary reform and increasing social justice, but have been politically assaulted, internally divided, often turned against their own, and are deficient in self-knowledge.

For all the aspirations and achievements of Martin Luther King Jr. and other 1960s activists, some of the sons and daughters of slaves are still entrapped, many Americans have fallen victim to lethal forces, while simultaneously many of us are in amazing affluence, technological wonders, and self-actualization. Still, dark times have not faded away, and much of humanity is both free and yet not free at last.

REFERENCES

Brecht, B. (2003). *Poetry and prose.* Continuum.

CBS News (2006). The price of oil – In context. https://web.archive.org/web/20070609145246/http://www.cbc.ca/news/background/oil/.

Devereux, G. (1988). Why Oedipus killed Laius: A note on the complementarity Oedipus Complex in Greek drama. In G. Pollock & J. M. Ross, Eds., *The Oedipus papers* (pp. 97-116). International Universities Press. (Original work published 1953)

Hamill, D. (1999). Chinatown and the Spirit of '74. *New York Daily News,* http://www.nydailynews.com/chinatown-spirit-74-screenwriter-robert-towne-producer-robert-evans-recall-genesis-conspiracy-classic-article-1.832691.

Hirsch, F. (1981). *Film noir: The dark side of the screen.* Da Capo Press.

Lyttleton, O. (2012). 5 Things you might not know about Roman Polanski's 'Chinatown.' *Indie Wire.* Retrieved from https://www.indiewire.com/2012/06/5-things-you-might-not-know-about-roman-polanskis-chinatown-251663/.

Ross, G. (2016). The ten greatest neo-noir films. *Independent, http://www.independent.co.uk/arts-entertainment/films/the-ten-greatest-neo-noir-films-a7340126.html.*

Silver, A., & Ward, W. (Eds.) (1979). Introduction. In F. Hirsch (Ed.), *Film noir: An encyclopedic reference to the American style* (pp. 1-6). The Overlook Press.

Simon, A. (2013). Robert Towne: The Hollywood interview. http://thehollywoodinterview.blogspot.com/2009/10/robert-towne-hollywood-interview.html.

Towne, R. (1994, May 29). It's only LA Jake. *Los Angeles Times.* http://articles.latimes.com/1994-05-29/books/bk-63320_1_raymond-chandler-s-la-chinatown-oil-derrick.

Towne, R. (1997). *Chinatown and the last detail: Two screenplays.* Grove/Atlantic Inc. (Original work published 1974)

U. S. Inflation Calculator (2018). *Historical inflation rates 1914-2018.* http://www.usinflationcalculator.com/inflation/historical-inflation-rates/.

Warren, R. P. (1946). *All the King's men.* The Modern Library.

CHAPTER 6: ROMAN POLANSKI'S *CHINATOWN*

Writers Guild of America West (n.d.). 101 greatest screenplays. http://www.wga.org/writers-room/101-best-lists/101-greatest-screenplays.

CHAPTER 7

STEVEN SPIELBERG: THE QUEST TO BE A MORAL MALE

Steven Spielberg is a phenomenon. He is the only director with five movies on the American Film Institute's list of 100 best motion pictures and he has directed four of the 20 most highly watched films of all time (AFI, 1998; IMDb, 2020). His movies are the highest grossing of any director in the history of cinema (Lynch, 2017, para 1). Not surprisingly, as of 2018, Forbes ranked Spielberg as the second richest celebrity (Mallenbaum, 2018, para 5). In 2019, he was 225th on the Forbes list of 400 wealthiest Americans (Tognini, 2019, para 12). Of the twenty-nine films he directed through 2016, ten of them have historical subject matters. His astounding creativity, popularity, and concern with the past make him a good candidate for psychohistorical examination.

Understanding Spielberg's trajectory entails how he emerged from a certain family milieu, and with specific psychological issues. As he says, "Hardly a single one of my films isn't based on something that happened in my childhood" (Schickel, 2012, p. 1). Steven was born on December 18, 1946 in Cincinnati, the eldest child of Arnold Spielberg and Leah Posner Spielberg, an Orthodox Jewish couple. Three of Steven's grandparents were part of the great immigration wave before World War I. Arnold's life mirrored the recent phenomenon in American life. As with so many depression era young men, he was in the Army during World War II. Again, like so many of his generation, the GI Bill financed his bachelor's degree. His was in electrical engineering. Once his career started, instead of being rooted in one place, this workaholic moved his family for work reasons. First, he worked in his hometown of Cincinnati, and later in New Jersey, Arizona, and California. All this time, Arnold was making a number of advances in the computer field. Still, living in different places with an often absent father did not sit well with Steven. He says that after finally getting friends and being acclimated, the family would move. "This happened to me four major times in my life. And the older I got the harder it got. *E. T.* reflects a lot of that" (McBride, 2010, p. 47).

The moves unsettled Steven's mother. Leah had been a talented classical pianist, but gave up her studies, if not piano playing, when she became a full-time mother, eventually having four children. In Phoenix, she felt out of place. Arnold's workaholic tendencies meant she bore most of the child care responsibilities. In Arizona in their bedroom, Arnold and Leah would argue most nights. The children could hear them. Somewhere during this time, Leah began an affair with a family friend, and Leah and Arnold divorced in 1966. Steven resented his father. A number of Spielberg's movies show unhappy or disrupted suburban families. Though his father encouraged Steven, he was also critical of his only son. Steven reciprocated. As he told Lesley Stahl, the son blamed his father for the divorce, even after he found out that Leah left Arnold for another man. He put his mother "on a pedestal… it was easier for me to blame him." Steven admits to being angry at his father for "many, many, many wasted years." As Stahl notes, an absent father busy with his job is a character type recurring in many of his films (Stahl, 2013, para 32).

Out of all this disruption, other strands in his movies include a concern with how a man can be moral amidst challenges, and a focus on childhood and youth. According to Nigel Morris, in the 1980s Spielberg had a reputation "as a director of adolescent fantasy," and was "saddled with a Peter Pan image" (Morris, 2007, p.178). Another recurring motif is an adult male in dangerous or threatening situations. The protagonist may have had moral lapses or committed unethical actions, but somehow comes back to doing the right thing, or pays consequences for questionable conduct. Spielberg values men becoming moral after trials and tribulations.

In *Jaws,* there are four main male characters: police chief, mayor, oceanographer, and shark hunter. The mayor is an opportunistic official. The police chief, Martin Brody, is a family man with a wife and two children. There is an unattached oceanographer, Matt Hooper, and the renegade Quint is a navy veteran haunted by killer sharks in the war. In this Watergate era film, the mayor suppresses that a killer shark is preying on the town. Brody defers to his superior and goes along with the cover up. After another victim is killed, the parents confront the chief. Brody admits his fault. With his guilty conscience, he collaborates with Hooper and Quint to get rid of the shark. Quint is eaten by the shark, Hooper proves ineffective, while the chief ingeniously is able to blow the killer fish up. In doing so does he successfully makes reparations for going along with corrupt officialdom. Instead of an absent father pursuing his own career goals, in *Jaws*, we have a parent dedicated to family and community, admitting his own failures and making amends. Brody, the imperfect, honorable official, contrasts with the corruption of the mayor, and on a larger canvas, President Nixon and his crew (Spielberg, 1975).

In contrast, the swashbuckling Indiana Jones is a traditional male action film hero. He has dangerous enemies, perilous circumstances, and repeatedly takes heroic actions. This fantasy of a superman masquerading as an archeologist has had enduring appeal to the public in four different movies. Since 1993, there have been a series of Spielberg historical films connected to morally complex situations, with male characters becoming honorable and heroic. They were all made after Spielberg's second marriage in 1991 to Kate Capshaw. He found himself with a large family of his, mine, ours, and adopted children. At around the age Spielberg's parents divorced, he was finally settling into a comfortable domesticity. Soon some Spielberg films focused on historically significant events.

The first of these is 1993's *Schindler's List*. Oskar Schindler seems to be an unlikely hero, a Nazi and a spy. Yet in his own way he fits in with other male figures in Spielberg's films. Despite his morally compromised past, he risks his life to do right. In this case, Schindler is a factory owner who bribes fellow Nazi officials to protect the Jews who work in his factories. There were over 1,200 Jews whose lives were saved because of Schindler's actions. As with Chief Brody, Schindler eventually upholds principles; and shows heroism existing in immoral, terrifying and life-endangering situations. It is in character for Spielberg to make a Holocaust related movie showing how being ethical can emerge in evil circumstances (Spielberg, 1993).

In 1997, Spielberg returns to World War II in *Saving Private Ryan*. Amidst the carnage of D-Day and after, there is again moral action in the most brutal and compromising of circumstances. The U. S. government intervenes to preserve the life of the last son of a family whose other sons have all died for their country. The company commander in charge of this rescue is Captain Miller, portrayed by Tom Hanks. The solder being protected is Private Ryan, played by Matt Damon. During the course of the film, many of Miller's soldiers other than Ryan lose their lives. They have died to save one man; without this mission they might have survived. The last to succumb is Captain Miller. As Miller is dying, he says to private

Ryan, "earn this... earn it." The film then shifts: Ryan is an old man at the cemetery where Captain Miller is buried. Ryan turns to his wife and says, "Tell me I've led a good life, tell me I'm a good man" (Spielberg, 1997). Ryan knows many have died to save him. How could the course of his life undo these deaths? The barbarity of war leaves a stain on many, some lose faith in a moral order and their own virtue. Amidst the evils of war, Spielberg shows how no one remains unscathed, yet Miller, Ryan, and Spielberg search for the morality, the goodness amidst the moral violations inherent in modern war. How to be a good man in perilous circumstances is a recurring motif for Spielberg.

Munich from 2005 is the most morally complex of his historical movies. At the 1972 Olympics in Munich, Palestine terrorists kill eleven Israeli athletes. Israel's government plans to murder all those who took the lives of their young men. The film is the story of how these terrorists were hunted down and killed; it is based on George Jonas's book, *Vengeance*. There is an old testament eye for an eye element in this Israeli operation. To many, this retaliation is highly moral; to others it raises questions. The Israeli government authorizes Avner Kaufman to organize an independent team of assassins. They target and kill most of the original terrorists. Some of the Israeli's were also slain, and Avner's group also murdered a woman who killed one of their own. It also appears that the CIA is protecting the mastermind of the Munich attack. The line between justified revenge and other motivations gets blurred. Avner begins to doubt that all the Arabs targeted for elimination were actually Munich killers. He feels used, becomes disillusioned, and tired of all the betrayals and brutality.

Avner left his position with the Israeli government in 1974. He settled in Brooklyn with his wife and children, but suffered from post-traumatic stress. As Spielberg says of Avner, "there is something about killing people at close range... that is going to test a man's soul... I don't think he will ever find peace" (Schickel, 2012, p. 235). Some of what torments Avner is whether all this slaughter made any difference. With a view of the Empire State building, he meets his Israeli boss in Brooklyn and asks him, "Did we accomplish anything at all? Every man we killed has been replaced by worse. Did we kill to replace the terrorist leadership or the Palestinian leadership?" He is not given an adequate answer, and he refuses his superior's request to return to Israel. As the two men part and walk their separate ways, the movie ends as in the background, the World

CHAPTER 7: STEVEN SPIELBERG

Trade Center becomes visible. The clear message is that the age of terrorism continues. Spielberg says, "This movie is a prayer for peace" (Schikel, 2012, p. 232). He also says that it is about Avner's "struggles to keep his soul intact" (Schickel, 2012, p. 235). The concern with being moral in an immoral world recurs here as in other Spielberg films. If asked Ryan's questions about leading a good life and being a good man, it is hard to imagine Avner unequivocally answering yes (Spielberg, 2005).

In 2012's *Lincoln* and 2015's *Bridge of Spies,* Spielberg retreats from the complexities of character in some previous films. *Lincoln* centers on the period from January to April, 1865, when the President is assassinated. The focus is in Lincoln's political skill in getting the amendment abolishing slavery through Congress. The President is also shown on the battlefield, with his wife, and children, and with various political officials. His calm leadership and level headedness are featured. He appears as a model human and President. Lincoln's frequent melancholy, spiritual struggles, and his many racist statements about blacks are left out.

The movie ends with a shot of Lincoln delivering his extraordinary second inaugural address on March 4th 1865, but omits the rigorous religious self-examination he went through to write this speech. Lincoln says the terrible "scourge of war" was God's response to the persistent offense of slavery. The nation was punished and suffers because of this peculiar institution (Lincoln, 1865, pp.106-109). Yet though the inaugural was written during the time covered by the film, its composition is not part of the narrative. *Lincoln* is a portrayal of a heroic leader, without the moral torment integral to this melancholy man (Spielberg, 2012).

Bridge of Spies from 2015 is the story of the negotiations for the release of Gary Powers, captured after his spy plane was shot down in 1960 over Soviet air space. James Donovan, an attorney in private practice, who had been a prosecutor during the Nuremberg trials, and on request defended a Soviet spy, was chosen to negotiate a prisoner exchange to bring Powers home. There have been many movies about the shadowy world of espionage, and the subject matter of *Bridge of Spies* falls into this genre and also resembles film noir. In these genres, characters often exist in a morally cloudy universe. As most everyone is not who they appear to be, heroes are hard to find. If someone appears to have noble aims, there is usually reason to distrust them. As the lead protagonist, James Donovan is seen as a straight forward man of moral integrity, determination, and resourcefulness. He pulls off not only the return of Powers, but a Yale student imprisoned by the East Germans. He is a Spielberg hero navigating through perilous situations dealing with devious men. Any mixed motives Donovan might have are hidden (Spielberg, 2015). In both *Lincoln* and *Bridge of Spies* the admirable morality of the lead characters is stressed, their moral struggles are omitted.

Spielberg is only one of a few prominent contemporary film directors who will address questions of male morality in perilous situations. As Spielberg acknowledges, many of his films are rooted in his childhood. He has transformed these preoccupations into fully adult concerns, how can men act morally when there is immorality all around? He expresses psychological and ethical questions amidst covering significant events from the past. Spielberg sometimes illuminates and, at other times, evades the complex legacy of history and human character.

REFERENCES

American Film Institute. (1998). AFI's 100 Years…100 Movies.
   https://www.afi.com/afis-100-years-100-movies-10th-anniversary-edition/
IMDb (2015, November 14). Most watched films of all time .
   https://www.imdb.com/list/ls053826112/
Lincoln, A. (1991). *Great speeches.* Dover. (Original work published 1865)
Lynch, J. (2017). The 15 top earning movie directors of all-time at the U.S. box office. *Business Insider.*
   https://www.businessinsider.com/highest-earning-movie-directors-of-all-time-us-box-office-2017-8
Mallenbaum, C. (2018). Forbes names 2018 richest celebrities. *USA Today.* Retrieved from
   https://www.usatoday.com/story/life/people/2018/12/18/forbes-richest-celebrities-george-lucas-oprah-kylie-jenner-list/2358232002/
McBride, J. (2010). *Steven Spielberg: A biography.* University of Mississippi Press.
Morris, N. (2007). *The cinema of* Steven *Spielberg: Empire of light.* Wallflower Press.

CHAPTER 7: STEVEN SPIELBERG

Schickel, R. (2012). *Steven Spielberg: A retrospective.* Sterling.
Stahl, L. (2013). Spielberg: A director's life reflected in film. *60 Minutes.* https://www.cbsnews.com/news/spielberg-a-directors-life-reflected-in-film/4/.
Spielberg, S. (1975). *Jaws.* Universal Pictures.
Spielberg, S. (1993). *Schindler's List.* Universal Pictures.
Spielberg, S. (1997). *Saving Private Ryan.* DreamWorks.
Spielberg, S. (2005). *Munich.* DreamWorks.
Spielberg, S. (2012). *Lincoln.* DreamWorks.
Spielberg, S. (2015). *Bridge of spies.* DreamWorks.
Tognini, G. (2019, October 2). Early beginnings: How the 400 richest Americans got their entrepreneurial start. *Forbes.* https://www.forbes.com/sites/giacomotognini/2019/10/02/early-beginnings-how-the-forbes-400-richest-americans-got-their-entrepreneurial-start/#15da0762670d.

CHAPTER 8

STEVEN SPIELBERG'S *THE POST*: A REVIEW AND PSYCHOHISTORICAL COMMENTARY

In the words of Yogi Berra: it's like déjà vu all over again. There are many echoes of Nixon in the Trump era. Donald Trump in January 2018 tried to stop the publication of a book about his Presidency just as in 1971 Nixon enjoined further publication by the *New York Times* of a highly secret Defense Department report on the Vietnam war, *The Pentagon Papers*. Soon after Trump tried prior restraint comes the nationwide release of Steven Spielberg's *The Post* about that newspaper and the Pentagon report. The origins of this film are that Liz Hannah, a former production assistant for actress Charlize Theron, read *Washington Post* owner Katharine Graham's memoirs and drafted a screenplay. Sony Picture head Amy Pascal purchased it, hired Oscar winning screenwriter Josh Singer as a co-writer. Steven Spielberg was soon on board, then Meryl Streep and Tom Hanks signed on as the leads. The director told Josh Singer "Look, the reason I'm gonna get this up this year is because I haven't said anything about Trump. This is my way to respond to what's going on" (Lynch, 2017, para 5).

The Post has a number of different strands, underlying them all is the importance of a free press to check government deception and abuse of power. The film opens in 1966 in South Vietnam in the midst of jungle combat, with civilian government employee, Daniel Ellsberg as an observer. Soon after on an airplane flight he talks to Secretary of Defense Robert McNamara who expresses his skepticism about the war, which Ellsberg shares. When the plane lands, an untruthful McNamara tells the press how optimistic he is about the war's progress.

Government lying preoccupies Ellsberg. Later as an employee of the Rand Corporation, he makes copies of a secret Pentagon report that McNamara had commissioned. This document delineates how Presidents from Truman through Lyndon Johnson deceived Americans about our purposes and prospects in Vietnam. Ellsberg quotes someone who said that 70% of the reasons America was in Vietnam was to save face for ourselves in the Cold War. That our sons and daughters died for a cause Presidents knew to be unwinnable deeply troubles Ellsberg. He gets the papers to the *New*

York Times, which publishes excerpts on June 13, 1971. The Nixon administration then gets a court order stopping further publication. It was the first time in American history that the federal government obtained prior restraint of a news story.

The rest of the movie focuses on the efforts by *Post* executive editor Ben Bradlee to publish the *Pentagon Papers,* the paper's owner, Katharine Graham's struggles balancing business interests and her commitment to an unfettered press, and the centrality of newspapers as a check on government abuses. *The Post* in its own way is reminiscent of the 1939 populist Frank Capra movie *Mr. Smith Goes to Washington,* starring Jimmy Stewart and Jean Arthur. Both films present courageous individuals fighting on behalf of democracy against powerful interests. Stewart plays a naïve man who is inexplicably picked to be a U. S. Senator after the death of his predecessor. He comes to the nation's capital as an ignorant idealist, and observes government abuses. He is schooled by one of his staff, played by a savvy Jean Arthur. Mr. Smith eventually comes to expose corruption on behalf of democratic principles.

Katharine Graham, portrayed by Streep, is neither naive nor inexperienced. The movie portrays her as at first lacking confidence in her role as owner and publisher. Tom Hanks's Bradlee collaborates with and educates Graham as Arthur does Stewart. While the characters in the earlier film are middle-class, in real life both Katharine Graham and Ben Bradlee were children of wealth and privilege. Graham's financier father, Eugene Meyer, bought the *Washington Post,* and later handed the paper over to his son-in-law, Philip Graham. After her husband's suicide in 1963, Katharine became owner then publisher in 1967. Bradlee too had been born to affluence in a New England family going back to the 1630s. He graduated Harvard, became a journalist, then executive editor of the *Post* in 1968. Both Graham and Bradlee were personally friends with members of the nation's power elite.

The central dramatic scenes in the film occur after the newspaper acquires the *Pentagon Papers* just as the *Post* is for the first-time selling stock in the company on Wall Street. There is a clause with the bank underwriting the stock offering that if within a week there is a catastrophe the deal can be cancelled. Publishing a report that has already been enjoined could be considered such a dire event. The paper's lawyers are then brought in to

CHAPTER 8: STEVEN SPIELBERG'S *THE POST*

ascertain what jeopardy the *Post* would be in if they printed the Pentagon document. The business advisers and the lawyers advising caution are in a tug of war with the journalists. Katharine Graham has the final authority, and she is torn in different directions. With the presses ready to roll, tension mounts as the climactic decision approaches.

During the stand-off, Bradlee tells his wife that he is courageous in fighting for publication of the report. His wife reminds him that Katharine Graham would be much more courageous than he because she is a woman in a man's world. He appears to absorb this lesson. Graham herself confronts her good friend former Defense Secretary Robert McNamara about how duplicitous his actions were in the Vietnam War. The publisher and executive editor also have a heart to heart about the changing ways of Washington. As mentioned, both had been close friends with the wielders of power, including Graham going to LBJ's Texas ranch, and Bradlee being close friends with President Kennedy. Each had held information in confidence that was certainly newsworthy. In seeking to convince Graham to publish, Ben tells Katharine that now these relationships can no longer proceed, and that we are in a different time in the nation's history.

Later as the deadline to publish is almost at the zero hour, with the financial and legal advisers in the same room with her, Graham no longer can delay a decision. The camera closes in on her while she contemplates her action. After hesitating, she says "Let's go, Let's publish." The die was cast.

Nixon's Attorney General sues to prevent further publication by Graham's paper. The Supreme Court holds a hearing with the defendants being the *New York Times* and the *Washington Post*. The Court rules for a free press; the Nixon administration is defeated. Then later, the camera looks into the White House, where with his back to the camera, the actual voice of Richard Nixon is heard. On the phone, he says that the *Post* is to be forbidden access to the White House. After his intemperate rant, the next shot is of a security guard finding tape on the door of the offices of the Democratic National Committee. The guard calls the police. This of course is the infamous Watergate break-in. The movie ends. In Watergate, we had a vengeful, angry, paranoid President who was out of control. If Spielberg made this movie to give his opinion about President Trump,

Nixon's actions and anger at the opposition is clearly a prelude to the twitter President.

There is a missing link between the publication of the Pentagon report and the Watergate break-in. Nixon established a White House group known as the Plumbers, led by Howard Hunt and Gordon Liddy. The Plumbers were formed to conduct surreptitious actions to get dirt about Daniel Ellsberg and to further that goal burglarized Ellsberg's psychiatrist's office. Later, it was Hunt and Liddy who masterminded the Watergate break-in. Of course, it was the reporting of the *Post's* Woodward and Bernstein under Bradlee and Graham's direction that uncovered the activities of Nixon and his associates that eventually led to Nixon's resignation as President. Forty-five years later, the *Washington Post* under the ownership of Amazon's Jeff Bezos is among those in the forefront of reporting the hidden secrets of Donald Trump. Journalism is much altered since the 1970s. With new technologies, journalism is no longer as dominated by the then three television networks, a few national newspapers, and three news weeklies. The proliferation of news organizations in print, on-air, and on the internet make for a radically different journalistic condition. As the Watergate era was a pinnacle of journalism, we are once again in the midst of a golden era of reporting. The free press was under siege with President Nixon, and Trump views the press as enemies of the people. That the U. S. has a constitutional protection for free speech and a free press is one of the treasures of our often-dysfunctional political system. Spielberg was right to single out this issue in his film centering on Katharine Graham and the top-secret Pentagon report.

Yet there are important issues Spielberg leaves in the background. During the first world war, radical American journalist, Randolph Bourne, declared "war is essentially the health of the State" (Bourne, 1918/1977, p. 359). During World War I and World War II, the power of the American Presidency along with the increase in the military and intelligence enterprises helped alter the nature of the federal government.

After the Cold War became institutionalized, various terms came into public discourse to describe this state of American affairs. Eisenhower warned against the military-industrial complex, historian Arthur Schlesinger had a 1970s best-seller documenting *The Imperial Presidency* (1973), others speak of the warfare state. In the twentieth and twenty-first

CHAPTER 8: STEVEN SPIELBERG'S *THE POST*

centuries America is a global power with commercial, intelligence, and military interests throughout the planet. Outside of a few incursions into Latin America, all of America's actual wars since 1945 have been far away in Asia. I served in the army in DaNang, South Vietnam in 1969, 8,373 miles from my home in Albany, New York. Between 2001 and 2014 in the Iraq and Afghanistan wars the United States has spent $1.4 trillion (Qiu, 2016, para 7). This is big, big business.

With global power comes many secret endeavors of the Presidency, the intelligence services, and the military. People in power often want to keep what they do secret, and the press often wishes to make what is hidden public. An informed citizenry is seen as integral to a free society. Beyond this, in the background of Spielberg's film, Nixon and his cronies are portrayed as a diabolical force threatening American institutions. Spielberg's stated intentions call for us to compare the personalities and actions of Nixon and Trump. Richard Nixon was a loner with paranoid tendencies, but it would be a stretch to say he had an antisocial personality disorder. Harvard psychiatrist Lance Dodes claims Trump is sociopathic (Dodes, 2017, p. 83). Following psychoanalyst Otto Kernberg's findings, another psychiatrist, John D. Gartner shows the ways he thinks Trump's actions correspond to malignant narcissism (Gartner, 2017, p. 94-95). Eminent novelist Philp Roth, whose 2004 novel *The Plot Against America* is seen as foretelling much of the present, says Trump is a "massive fraud, the evil sum of his deficiencies, devoid of everything but the hollow ideology of a megalomaniac" (McGrath, 2018, para 14). Princeton historian Sean Wilentz (2018) sees Nixon as having a "mixture of arrogance and paranoia" (para 11), but says that Trump's "first year has been an unremitting parade of disgraces that have demeaned him as well as the dignity of his office... he is the first president to fail to defend the nation from an attack on our democracy by a hostile foreign power – and to resist the investigation of that attack. He is the first to enrich his private interests, and those of his family, directly and openly" (Wilentz, 2018, para 19).

The Post champions a female in power, a free press and implicitly warns against Presidential abuse. As much similarity as there is between these two Presidents, Trump brings unprecedented attributes to the Presidency. He is not carrying out the constitutional mandate to take care that the laws are faithfully executed as he is willfully ignorant of the constitution and the nations' statutes. Trump is ill-informed as he does not read reports submitted to him. In addition, Trump made over 2,000 false and misleading statements in his first 355 days in office (Kessler & Kelly, 2018, para 1). Trump frequently alters his positions. How can he make America great again when he cannot make up his own mind? Senator Schumer said negotiating with President Trump is like dealing with Jell-O (Bolton, 2018, para 1).

Then there is our President's ineptitude in foreign affairs. Trump is unpopular in Britain, our closest ally for over a century. He was condescending to Germany's Angela Merkel, argumentative with Australia's Prime Minister, plays school boy verbal confrontation with North Korea, has offended most of Africa, and ignores Russia's violations. In less than a year he has done more to reverse America's prior policies and commitments in the world than any President since 1900.

Nixon had an enemies list, used the IRS to go after his political enemies, while Trump has a viciousness and mendacity for anyone who crosses him that certainly equals Nixon's. Our Commander in Chief is both incompetent and malevolent. Spielberg's movie may have been his indirect way of commenting on our current President, but as he well knows his allusions between Nixon and Trump barely scratches the surface of the extraordinary Trump Presidency. The difference between Nixon and Trump is that under a Democratic Congress, Nixon resigned rather than face the likelihood of being impeached and convicted, while Trump with a Republican Senate was impeached for parallel crimes, but not convicted.

REFERENCES

Bolton, A. (2018, January 20). Schumer: Negotiating with Trump like negotiating with Jell O. *The Hill*.
https://thehill.com/homenews/senate/369929-schumer-working-with-trump-like-negotiating-with-jello

Bourne, R. (1977). *The radical will: Selected writings 1911-1918*. Urizen Books. (Original work published 1917)

Dodes, L. (2017). Sociopathy. In B. Lee, *The dangerous case of Donald Trump* (pp. 83-92). St. Martin's Press.

CHAPTER 8: STEVEN SPIELBERG'S *THE POST*

Gartner, J. (2017). Donald Trump Is: (A) Bad, (B) Mad, (C) All of the Above. In B. Lee, *The dangerous case of Donald Trump* (pp. 93-109). St. Martin's Press.

Kessler, G., & Kelly, M. (2018, January 10). Trump has made over 2,000 false or misleading claims over 355 days. *Washington Post.* https://www.washingtonpost.com/news/fact-checker/wp/2018/01/10/president-trump-has-made-more-than-2000-false-or-misleading-claims-over-355-days/?utm_term=.cfe67a740ba1

Lynch, M. (2017, December 8). How *The Post* became the hottest screenplay in Hollywood. *Vanity Fair.* https://www.vanityfair.com/hollywood/2017/12/how-the-post-became-the-hottest-screenplay-in-hollywood

McGrath, C. (2018, January 16). No longer writing, Philip Roth still has plenty to say. *New York Times.* https://www.nytimes.com/2018/01/16/books/review/philip-roth-interview.html

Qiu, L. (2016, October 27). Did the U.S. spend $6 trillion in Middle East wars? *Politifact,* http://www.politifact.com/truth-o-meter/statements/2016/oct/27/donald-trump/did-us-spend-6-trillion-middle-east-wars/

Schlesinger, A. (1973). *The imperial presidency.* Houghton, Mifflin.

Wilentz, S. (2018, January 20). They were bad. He may be worse. *New York Times.* https://www.nytimes.com/2018/01/20/opinion/sunday/trump-bad-presidents-history.html

CHAPTER 9

ARTHUR MILLER'S SELF-UNDERSTANDING IN *THE CRUCIBLE*

Prelude

The paper that follows was written as a response to James William Anderson's symposium piece "The Psychology of Artistic Creativity: With Reference to Arthur Miller and *The Crucible*" in the December 2011 issue of the psychohistory journal, *Clio's Psyche*, founded and edited by Dr. Paul Elovitz. In this piece, Anderson defends a thesis that authentic art reflects the struggles within the writer's soul, and must touch an inner core of that person's being. Anderson also asserts that these soul issues are personal more than political. He uses Arthur Miller's 1953 play *The Crucible* to make his point. As Anderson points out this drama was written during the height of the McCarthy era, when the Wisconsin Senator held hearings designed to uncover how Communists were undermining the American government. What McCarthy did in the Senate, the hysteria and conspiracy theories that he was promoting had a parallel in the activities of the House Un-American Activities Committee. In setting his play during the Salem Witch trials of the 1690s, Miller found a historical parallel to the rampant McCarthyism of the time he was composing his drama.

Anderson focuses on the parts of *The Crucible* that deal not with the injustice of the witch trials but with the personal and moral crisis of Massachusetts landowner John Proctor. Proctor had an adulterous encounter with his house servant Abigail and betrayed his wife in the process. Abigail, the forsaken lover, has now become a chief accuser during the witch trials. Miller and Anderson focus on the moral self-questioning and justification Proctor goes through in the play. Anderson stresses what he sees as Miller's admirable self-knowledge. Anderson also draws the parallel in the play with Miller's adulterous desires towards the sexual icon, actress Marilyn Monroe, that had not been consummated. At the time the drama was written, the married playwright had two children. Miller later left this family and married Monroe. In the play, Proctor ultimately proclaimed his own honesty, refused to accuse others of being witches and was executed as a witch, Arthur Miller when later testifying before Congress refused to name names. Miller then openly answered about his own activities but did not attack the injustice of this congressional enterprise. As well, *The Crucible* is less focused on the horrors of the trials than Proctor's crisis of conscience. In the response I wrote to Jim Anderson's piece, I show how Miller did not exhibit the self-knowledge in the play that Anderson attributes to him. I also question the assertion that the political themes are not as inspiring for the artist as more intimate relations. If I were to add to this essay now almost a decade later, I would stress that Miller in both his play and Congressional testimony focused less on the outrages in the public show trials than the personal issues it raised. In some later plays Miller exhibited greater self-knowledge than he did in this 1953 celebrated drama. Arthur Miller lived in the same Connecticut county where I reside, and I had occasion to briefly talk to him at two public events and twice on the phone. To me, his under-appreciated autobiography, *Timebends*, is one of Miller's greatest achievements, despite that Google (on January 31, 2020) it has 122,000 hits, while *The Crucible* has almost 37 million, and *Death of A Salesman* over 50 million hits.

Arthur Miller's Self-Understanding In The Crucible

While the psychoanalysis of art has often focused on the internal conflicts in the creator's life, psychobiographical sources are integral to understanding the process of artistic creativity but are not its equivalent. It is how the writer shapes and presents the personal that creates great works. In his essay on Arthur Miller's *The Crucible*, James William Anderson quotes from Tolstoy and Miller on how the "soul" of the artist should be revealed in the creations. Many have the depth of soul that Tolstoy and Miller say are needed, but few have the talent and capacity to make their inner experience sear the souls of readers, listeners, or viewers. Discussions of creativity then should encompass the full process from the recesses of the creator's soul to the art, craft, and authenticity that are present within the work. With these caveats, I turn to Anderson's essay on Arthur Miller and *The Crucible*.

Anderson asserts that it is the sexual liaison Miller wanted to have with Marilyn Monroe and the guilt the dramatist felt about it that was the creative well for this 1953 historical drama on the Salem Witch Trials. While the play appears to have sources in the contemporary Red Scare,

CHAPTER 9: ARTHUR MILLER'S SELF-UNDERSTANDING IN *THE CRUCIBLE*

Anderson declares, "Miller's feeling about McCarthyism is not the kind of personal concern, rooted deeply within inner conflicts and obsessions, that I am claiming is at the heart of artistic creativity" (Anderson, 2011, p. 254). Why not? Are not the feelings of betrayal, of corruption, and of disillusionment with authority prominent themes in Miller's earlier popular plays *All My Sons* (1947) and *Death of a Salesman* (1949) as well as in *The Crucible*? Cannot these themes awaken deep personal conflicts and become preoccupations?

By favoring sexual preoccupations over conflict between generations, Anderson risks his study's being psychologically incomplete. Commentators on the biographical sources of a writer need to look at the whole life, the creative work preceding the particular one in question, and the multiple themes within the work being examined. In focusing on the inner turmoil Miller experienced in his desire for the glamorous and tortured movie star, Anderson does not place Miller's agony within the full context of Miller's psyche, including his preoccupation with the sins of those with power and position. These themes are present in the corruption of the manufacturer in *All My Sons* and in *Death of a Salesman*'s Willy Loman's adultery and the disillusioning impact it had on his son, Biff. The sins of fathers are at the heart of one side of Millers inner conflicts and artistic creativity.

Anderson thinks highly of Miller. He writes that the playwright had "an exceptional and penetrating understanding of himself" (Anderson, 2011, p. 250). He uses as his example of Miller's insight how John Proctor in *The Crucible* mirrors the conflicts that preoccupied Miller while writing the play. When Miller first became enamored with Marilyn Monroe, he was married with two children. Miller found that "a radiating force" entered him and he could "lose" himself in "sensuality" (Miller, 1987, p. 307). Miller's guilt over his illicit desires is enacted in the play by the conflicts John Proctor feels between his sexual encounter with his former servant, Abigail, and his desire to preserve his marriage with Elizabeth.

When we first meet John Proctor, he rebuffs the advances of Abigail though he acknowledges he still is drawn to her. Later with his wife, he fears her judgment of him because of his affair with Abigail. Elizabeth tells John that she is not his judge and that the "magistrate sits in your heart that judges you" (Miller, 1953/1981, p. 258). The guilt-ridden Proctor seeks reconciliation with his wife. Elizabeth provides him with the opportunity to redeem himself and for a restored alliance with her. When the couple finds out that the accusations of witchcraft in Salem have resulted in trials and that the charges are based on false statements from Abigail and others, Elizabeth beseeches John to tell the authorities the knowledge he has that these are false allegations. Proctor then becomes a reformed man who will act virtuously amidst the hysteria in Salem. He confronts the accusers and the court, and is sentenced to death. On the day scheduled for his execution, to be with his wife he confesses to consorting with the Devil but refuses to name names. Before his false confession, he talks about the need for honesty and to let "them that never lied die to keep their souls" (Miller, 1953/1981, p. 326). When pressured to name names, he tears up his signed confession. This act of defiance lifts him up, despite the death sentence imposed upon him. The character says of himself, "I see some shred of goodness in John Proctor" (Miller, 1953/1981, p. 332). Miller portrays Proctor as ultimately an upright, moral man despite the fact that he has sinned sexually and lied to the court. If Proctor is a stand-in for Miller, the author is presenting himself as honorable, if flawed.

Contrast this with how Miller portrays Abigail, Proctor's partner in sexual crimes. She uses her sexuality to seduce and betray and seeks vengeance on Elizabeth Proctor. Abigail is the leader of those who make false accusations of witchcraft against Salem residents. The woman who represents what Miller called "the sensuousness of a female blessing" is here presented as a lying temptress (Miller, 1987, p. 327). It could even be said that Miller views Abigail as acting evilly. The questionable motives in this drama are projected more onto Abigail than anyone else. She becomes the embodiment of sin, while a reinvigorated John Proctor fights for truth and justice. This division between the moral conscience of Proctor and the malevolence of Abigail is an easy way out for the Arthur Miller who wishes to abandon himself to the luxurious life of fulfilled sensuality with Marilyn Monroe. *The Crucible*, then, seems less an example of Miller's penetrating self-understanding than a rationalization for his need to retain a self-image of having a degree of moral integrity. Proctor's courage is contrasted with Abigail's uncontrolled sexuality and deceptions. This dichotomy gives the play a melodramatic element, which may be a reason for its appeal, but means it is less authentic. In this play, Miller is keeping some of the secrets of his soul from himself, while projecting them onto a female temptress. His art suffers for it. Psycho-analysis, when confronting creative works, can use its understanding to show both the manifold ways

CHAPTER 9: ARTHUR MILLER'S SELF-UNDERSTANDING IN *THE CRUCIBLE*

we humans have of being self-deceptive and illuminate when an artist has reached the depths of insight that create enduring works of the highest quality. In Miller's life, after he had divorced his first wife, married and then divorced Monroe, he did come to greater self-understanding that was evident in *After the Fall* (1964) and *The Price* (1968) and in his remarkable 1987 autobiography, *Timebends: A Life*. But in *The Crucible*, Miller does not reach the level of self-honesty that is his ideal.

In considering *The Crucible*, the political dimensions of the play also must be confronted. Toward the end of his article, Anderson recognizes the political intent of the drama and asserts how political stances can come from personal concerns. He then goes on to recount what Miller writes about how familial rivalries motivated his personal and political ambitions. Oddly enough, Anderson then does not relate these psychological motivations to his earlier statement that the playwright's feelings about McCarthyism could not be a source for artistic creativity. Nevertheless, Miller does himself acknowledge that current politics and their resemblance to the Salem Witch Trials that motivated him to compose this work with a moral message. What can "safeguard" humanity against "human delusion," he writes, are the sacrifices of the "courageous few." He wants to show the centrality of "conscience" in these dire circumstances (Gottfried, 2003, p.198). In *The Crucible*, authority becomes abusive when a mentality of hysteria overtakes a political community and destroys innocent lives. What is needed when the community goes so far astray is for righteous voices to speak truth to power. In *The Crucible*, we have another Miller play that addresses the malfeasance of authority and how standing up to abuse can free the soul, even if it means sacrificing one's life. For Miller himself, the figure of John Proctor enacted the guilt that haunted him, and yet for both a sense of virtue was restored in defying unjust authority. What makes this drama less authentic is Miller's creation of a scapegoat in the female character of Abigail that embodied the sins he could not quite face in himself.

REFERENCES

Anderson, J. W. (2011). The psychology of artistic creativity: With reference to Arthur Miller and *The Crucible. Clio's Psyche*, *18*(3), 249-260.

Gottfried, M. (2003). *Arthur Miller: His life and work.* Plenum Publishing Company.
Miller, A. (1981). *The crucible.* In *Eight plays.* Nelson Doubleday (original work published 1953)
Miller, A. (1987). *Timebends: A life.* Harper & Row.

CHAPTER 10

FOREVER YOUNG: 1960'S-1970'S COUNTERCULTURE ROCK

Rock and roll, like love, is a many-splendored thing. The counterculture rock of the sixties and seventies is one of those splendors. Folk, folk-rock, and rock songs of this period championed the younger generation. Through the music's lyrics, this chapter is an account of the journey of how these cultural radicals evolved from alienation, aspiration, communion, and peaks to disappointments, disillusionment, reversals, and resilience.

The 1960 counterculture manifested itself in local community enclaves, as in San Francisco's Haight-Ashbury district, alternative community newspapers like the Berkeley Barb and East Village Other, rural and urban communes, alternative FM rock radio stations, and nationwide magazines such as Rolling Stone. Recorded popular music of the 1960s and 1970s reached a national and international audience. This music connected cultural radicals in America and Europe, and was one means of establishing and promulgating the generational identity.

The story of this counterculture generation can in part be told through lyrics. I cover mostly the period from the mid-sixties to the mid-seventies, as after then the counterculture movement fragmented. In some ways, it evolved and in other ways dissipated.

Of course, the appeal of counterculture rock was in both the music and the lyrics. As I omit the music, I am telling only half the story. Still, the love generation in and of itself was quite a happening. From the Greenwich village folk clubs to Woodstock, from the Summer of Love to murder at the Altamont music festival, as the Grateful Dead (1970) sang about their generation, "What a long, strange trip it's been."

The 60s counterculture was not the first generation of aspiring rebels to have a long, twisting, and phenomenal journey. The roots of cultural radicalism reached a first peak in the American transcendentalism of Emerson, Thoreau, and crew, then reappeared in the progressive era, the 1930s depression, and the beat movement of the 1950s. The parallels between earlier eras and the 1960s and 1970s are inescapable.

The tradition of cultural radicalism, contains political elements, but primarily seeks transformation of a culture through promoting youth, vitality, and peak experiences of various kinds. It contains a rebellion against what is perceived as the staid, deadening culture of elders, and goes from promise to doubt, from strength to disillusion. The recurring cyclical pattern in American cultural and political radical movements is evident in the music of the sixties and seventies. I came upon this repeated pattern in the 1970s while researching my doctoral thesis on the progressive era anti-war radical and champion of youth, Randolph Bourne. Echoes of his celebration of being young are fully present in the music of the counter-culture generation.

My Generation – Celebration of Youth

If being young is a unifying force, then clearly Bob Dylan appointed himself as a spokesman for youth. Sounding like an old testament prophet in 1964, he lectured parents that "your sons and daughters are beyond your command," so "you better get out of the way if you can't lend a hand" for "the times they are a-changing" (Dylan, 1964). Dylan's message is that the young will overturn the old order. Youth is better than age. In 1964s "My Back Pages," he sings: "I was so much older then, I'm younger than that now" (Dylan, 1964).

The Who in 1965 celebrate "my generation" over their elders who do things that "look awfully cold." Jefferson Airplane in 1969 proclaim: one generation got old, "our generation has soul." In San Francisco, Scott McKenzie (1967) sings of "a whole generation with a new explanation." And "Never trust anyone over thirty" was a slogan first heard in 1964's Berkeley Free Speech movement.

As time waits for no one, those who survive youth pass into adulthood. This makes some in the 1960s counterculture uneasy. The Who declare: "I hope I die before I get old" (The Who, 1965). In 1967, the Rolling Stones' "Ruby Tuesday" says, "lose your dreams and youth, you lose your mind" (Rolling Stones, 1967). When the Jefferson Airplane's "Lather" turned thirty, "they took away all his toys" and he became disoriented (Jefferson Airplane, 1968). Some in the 1960s generation were afraid they were living on borrowed time, while others wished to extend youth into eternity.

CHAPTER 10: FOREVER YOUNG

Critique of Mainstream Culture

If youth was salvation, what was wrong with their parents' generation? They were conformist, oppressive, repressive, neurotic and war-loving. Malvina Reynolds wrote and Pete Seeger recorded that they live in "little boxes" that "are made out of ticky-tacky" and all look "just the same" (Seeger, 1963). In "Plastic People," the Mothers of Invention caricature America as a brave new world filled with plastic people and run by Nazis (Mothers of Invention, 1966).

In 1966, the Kinks had Top 40 hits with "Well Respected Man" and "Dedicated Follower of Fashion" (Kinks, 1966). Both songs were critical of the conformism, punctuality, conservatism and lifelessness in the upwardly mobile middle class. In the Rolling Stones' (1966) "Mother's Little Helper," stay-at-home mothers needed sedatives to get through their "dying day." Employment outside the home was no better. Dylan portrayed working on "Maggie's Farm" as arbitrary, restrictive and punitive. He thought the system made most everyone into conformist proletariat (Dylan, 1965). "Twenty years of schooling and they put you on the day shift," he sang in "Subterranean Homesick Blues." The American dream is a fraud; the power elite have stolen it. As Dylan sings, "The pump don't work" for "the vandals took the handles" (Dylan, 1965). In commenting on the life style of upper middle-class of "Mrs. Robinson," Simon and Garfunkel declare: "Every way you look at it – you lose" (Simon and Garfunkel, 1968).

Not only is society corrupt, its leaders make sacred the massacre of war; the sending of youth into battle to die or suffer trauma. Some of the cultural radicals' indictment of society has a political element. In 1962, the Kingston Trio made the singles charts with Pete Seeger's "Where Have All the Flowers Gone?" Young men have gone off to war as soldiers and have "gone to graveyards everyone . . . when will they ever learn?" (Kingston Trio, 1962). Country Joe and the Fish advise parents in the Vietnam era to "be the first ones on your block to have your boy come home in a box" (Country Joe and the Fish, 1967). Dylan indicts the masters of war for justifying the slaughter of war as being blessed by God (Dylan, 1963). Buffy Saint-Marie's "Universal Solider" talks about the soldier who knows he shouldn't kill and without whom we cannot put an end to the tragedy of war (St. Marie, 1966).

In a lesser known folk song from 1966, "My Son John," Tom Paxton tells the tale of a loyal, dutiful son who was always there when his father needed him, and who patriotically goes off to war. His buddies are dying all around him. When he returns home, he is no longer the obedient son. He will not answer his father's questions about combat, and instead locks himself in his room (Paxton, 1966). The evils of war cause Phil Ochs to defiantly declare: "I ain't marching anymore" (Ochs, 1965). We praise freedom, but to Ochs (1966), we are really the imperialistic "cops of the world." At the end of the decade, John Lennon beseeches leaders to move away from destruction, and to "give peace a chance" (Lennon, 1969).

Rebellious youth identify with victims of the rulers, whether it is those traumatized by war or political discrimination at home. The civil rights of American blacks captured the imagination of urban fold troubadours in the early 1960s. Dylan wrote a number of songs about the plight of African-Americans. In "Blowin' in the wind," he asked, "how long must it take for some people to be free" (Dylan, 1963). Phil Ochs railed against Mississippi's war against blacks. Buffy Saint-Marie documented the white man's persecution of Native Americans in a number of songs. American racism was a symptom of what was wrong with the country. Phil Ochs (1966) reminded his listeners that "there but for fortune go you or I." "Eleanor Rigby" is a portrait of the lost and lonely, where no one is saved (Beatles, 1966).

Alienation and Identity in 1960s Counterculture

A reason that many 1960s' cultural and political radicals can sympathize with the less fortunate is the sense of both: living in a dangerous, destructive, desolate and surreal setting and/or of being self-doubting. In Dylan's "Ballad of a Thin Man," routine expectations are confounded within the surreal carnival world (Dylan, 1965). A similar topsy-turvy world is prevalent in Donovan's "Season of the Witch," where "beatniks are out to make it rich." "It's strange, so strange," he keeps uttering, it "must be the season of the witch" (Donovan, 1966).

Apocalyptic fears recur in counterculture rock. "The future's uncertain and the end is always near," The Doors sing in "Roadhouse Blues" (Doors, 1970). "The End" is The Doors' account of the termination of all that is safe (The Doors, 1967). The most popular of the counterculture jeremiads

CHAPTER 10: FOREVER YOUNG

is Barry McGuire's "The Eve of Destruction," which fears the imminence of a nuclear holocaust (McGuire, 1965). "Please don't drop that H bomb on me," is the plea of Country Joe and the Fish (1967).

Alienation and isolation are present in much counterculture rock. "Desolation Row" is home to Dylan. His "Tom Thumb's Blues" find him in despair over being abandoned. "Everybody said they'd stand behind me/ When the game got rough/ But the joke was on me/ There was nobody even there to bluff/ ... I do believe I've had enough" (Dylan, 1965).

As well as being discouraged by the world and what others may do, there is a dark internal side to the self. "I look inside myself and see my heart is black..., it's not easy facing up when your whole world is black," Mick Jagger sings (Rolling Stones, 1966). John Lennon declares it's getting hard to be someone in "Strawberry Fields Forever" (Beatles, 1967). He sings "I'm crying" in "I Am the Walrus" (Beatles, 1967). People laugh at him so he advises others to hide their love away. Jimi Hendrix suffers from "Manic Depression," which he declares "is a frustrating mess." "I Don't Live Today" is another admission Hendrix makes, and then adds "there ain't no life nowhere" (Hendrix, 1967). A world bereft of redemption and vitality is present in the salad days of the counterculture. This is the underside of the whole generation with a new explanation. There is a desperate desire to transcend the infections of a fallen and estranged world.

This alienation for some, but not others, leads to uncertainty about their identity and self-doubt. Bob Dylan, despite the many stages he passed through, often exhibited a self-certainty. His severe super ego was often directed outward at criticizing others, be it the masters of war, the woman who wanted his soul in "Don't Think Twice" or his target in "Positively Fourth Street."

In "Fixing A Hole," Paul McCartney affirms himself by singing, "it really doesn't matter if I'm wrong, I'm right Where I belong" (Beatles, 1967). John Lennon, on the other hand, needs someone's help as he is "not so self-assured" (Beatles, 1965). He confesses: "I'm not what I appear to be," and describes himself as a loser (Beatles, 1965). Lennon advises others to hide their love away and says it is getting hard to be someone (Beatles, 1965). Paul Simon admits that he is "fakin' it/ I'm not really makin' it." He is "empty and aching" and does not know why. He bemoans what has become of himself while "I looked around for my possibilities" (Simon and Garfunkel, 1967). Paul McCartney, in "Eleanor Rigby," wonders where all the lonely people come from (Beatles, 1966). This song captured a certain prevalent feeling, and three different versions of it made the Top 40 in the 1960s. The theme of loneliness was present in the Beatles' "She's Leaving Home," where a young woman is departing after living alone for so many years (Beatles, 1967). Some claim loneliness is the theme of the concept album *Sergeant Pepper's Lonely Hearts Club Band*. The self-awareness, the emotional stresses and identity concerns of youth and adolescence lead Country Joe and the Fish (1967) to ask "Who Am I?" In the early 1970s, Alice Cooper sings about being eighteen both a child and a man, and not knowing what he wants (Cooper, 1971).

Community and Freeing the Mind

In 1955, political scientist Louis Hartz wrote that a "manic depressive mentality...has always characterized the American Democratic movement (p. 75). And clearly, the counterculture is characterized by lows and highs. The other side of the darkness of desolation row is the brightness of Penny Lane. The flip side of alienation, depression and self-doubt in counterculture rock is the desire for freedom, self-expression, harmony and communal love. For mystical drug experiences, the wonders of nature and self-actualization lead to peak experiences that transform despair into hope and glory, that help realize the generational dream of love, freedom and togetherness.

This sense of communality appears in a variety of songs in the decade. In 1962, Peter, Paul and Mary popularized Pete Seeger's "If I Had a Hammer." The folk trio harmonizes about "freedom" and "love between my brothers and sisters all over this land" (Peter, Paul, and Mary, 1962). The Youngbloods in 1966 implore listeners to "smile on your brother... Everybody get together try to love one another right now" (Youngbloods, 1966). For as John Lennon wrote, "I am he as you are he as you are me and we are all together" (Beatles, 1967). His fellow Beatle, George Harrison found a core commonality among humans, as "we're all one, and life flows on within you and without you" (Beatles, 1967). In 1969, Sly and the Family Stone echoed these sentiments: "I am no better and neither are you. We are the same whatever we do... We got to live together" (Sly

CHAPTER 10: FOREVER YOUNG

and the Family Stone, 1969). Jefferson Airplane implores: "Everybody together. We should be together" (Jefferson Airplane, 1969). The spread of communes in the late 1960s was a reflection of the hope for human unity and love.

Another path out of despair and oppression was the celebration of freedom, that very typical Anglo-American ideal. In 1969, The Who proclaimed: "I'm free" and "freedom tastes of reality" (The Who, 1969). Three years earlier, Cream exclaimed: "I Feel Free" (Cream, 1966). This freedom was manifested in moving like the sea with a lover and being oneself even when surrounded by a big crowd. Freedom was both bodily and spiritual. The Rascals' 1968 top 10 hit exhorted that "All the world over people got to be free." At Woodstock in 1969, Richie Havens chanted "freedom" over and over to the cheering multitudes (Havens, 1969). The next year at the Isle of Wight festival, Jimi Hendrix wanted "freedom," so "I can live, so I can give" (Hendrix, 1971). Freedom was not a solo act but part of human interconnection and a hope for a transformed world. Graham Nash sang out: "We can change the world, rearrange the world" (Nash, 1971).

To some rock icons in the 1960s, this rearrangement was one of consciousness and not of radical politics. The Beatles were critical of Chinese Communist Chairman Mao, institutional and constitutional revolution. Their alternative was "to free your mind instead" (Beatles, 1968). As the Rolling Stones sang: "Think the time is right for Palace Revolution. But where I live the game to play is Compromise Solution! Well then what can a poor boy do except to sing for a Rock 'N' Roll Band" (Rolling Stones, 1968). This is better than sleeping on the ground. Dylan had led the way in moving from radical politics to cultural radicalism. In "My Back Pages," referring to his political songs he wrote "I'd become my enemy. In the instant that I preach." The refrain in this composition is "I was so much older then, I'm younger than that now" (Dylan, 1964). Revolution in consciousness, celebrating youth, and a freeing of the mind are the choices of some culture radicals over political revolution.

Paths to Liberation I: Nature, Leisure and Love

How does one get from being stultified to being liberated? There were three main paths to this new freedom present in counterculture rock: a leisurely communion with nature often joined by a romantic partner, the use of mind-expanding drugs, and the culmination of it all is the romantic experience of love, physical and spiritual.

The beauties of the natural world lead to an immersion in extended moments and an experience of love. The rock musical "Hair"(1967) promised that this was going to be the dawning of the Age of Aquarius and everyone is supposed to let the sunshine in. The Beatles (1966) sing "Good Day, Sunshine." In "Good Vibrations," The Beach Boys sing of the "way the sunlight plays upon her hair," and that the woman with the "colorful clothes" and the singer go to "a blossom world," where they experience "good vibrations . . . excitations" and elations" (Beach Boys, 1966). There is airiness and high spiritedness in many 1960s songs that contrast with the blackness and desolation of other recordings.

In "Groovin," a sunny Sunday stroll by two lovers is accompanied by birds chirping leads to the exclamation: "Life can be ecstasy. You and me endlessly." (Rascals, 1967). Similarly, a city walk free from worldly responsibility lead Simon and Garfunkel (1966) to sing: "Life, I love you. All is groovy." On a beautiful day, John Sebastian escapes from work, takes a walk outside in the sun, dreams of his bundle of joy and has a marvelous time. Daydreams, he sings, can last into the night and maybe a thousand years (Lovin' Spoonful, 1966).

Johnny Rivers 1967 hit, "Summer Rain," is filled with imagery of nature. The setting for glory is within the generous bounties of the natural world and with a precious lover. She stepped out of a rainbow and is as warm as the sunshine. Johnny and his love will let tomorrow be (Rivers, 1967). In Canned Heat's (1968) "Going Up the Country," the fussing and fighting in the city stand in the way of the enjoyment of life. Up country, the water tastes like wine, and happiness can be found. Singer-songwriter David Ackles says of his children in "Subway to the Country," that living in New York City, "there's so much dirt, that they think snow is grey" and "their childhoods waste away." He is searching for a "subway to the country" to carry his children "through clean, green meadow smelling rain." They better go quick for we're "getting older" (Ackles, 1969). Joni Mitchell's "Woodstock" exemplifies this redemptive vision of nature. She feels like a cog in the machine, and needs to escape the smog. On the land, the soul

CHAPTER 10: FOREVER YOUNG

can become free. She sings: "We are stardust. We are golden. And we've got to get ourselves back to the garden" (Mitchell, 1970).

In these songs, happiness and the world of work and responsibility do not mix. Nature, leisure and love awaken the ecstatic spirit. Transcendence through love and an expanding self is the way to the garden of earthly delights.

Path to Liberation II: Mind Expanding Drugs

Another path to rejuvenation is through mind expanding drugs. "Smoking marijuana is more fun than drinking beer," Phil Ochs sings in "Outside A Small Circle of Friends" (Ochs, 1967). The counterculture chose smoking dope and acid trips over alcohol, not only for the fun but for the spiritual experience. There are references to marijuana in songs such as Fraternity of Man's "Don't Bogart Me," featured in the 1969 film "Easy Rider," David Peel's "Have a Marijuana," "Marijuana" by Country Joe and the Fish, "Dope Again" by Serpent Power, The Association's "Along Comes Mary," Tom Paxton's "Talking Vietnam Pot Luck Blues," Spanky and Our Gang's "Commercial," and, of course, Dylan's goof "Rainy Day Women 12X35." Dylan (1966) sings: "Everybody Must Get Stoned." Just as later, the Beatles gently declare "I'd Love to Turn You on" in "A Day in the Life," where Paul smokes and then immediately goes into a dream (Beatles, 1967). In "Commercial," a garbage man is given a funny looking little weed to smoke, then is riding high and everything's cool as he floats along, the song's refrain is "pot's too good to be just for the young" (Spanky and Our Gang, 1967). Marijuana is seen as a consciousness altering substance that gets the smoker "high," slows down the perception of time and leads to a spaced out, floating along. Marijuana is an alternative to the anxious life in the fast lane of upwardly mobile corporate America.

It is LSD that is seen as the drug that opens up a spiritual experience. In the United States the best-known proselytizers of this chemical substance in the 1960s were Timothy Leary and Ken Kesey. Leary, a Harvard psychologist, coined the slogan turn on, tune in, drop out about the LSD experience. The Moody Blues, in 1968, released "Legend of A Mind" about Leary, who flew an "astral plane" and took you on a "trip" with highs and lows (Moody Blues, 1968). Donovan's 1966 "The Trip," according to Matthew Greenwald, is a "virtual travelogue" of an LSD experience that Donovan had in May of 1966 in Los Angeles. The songwriter sings about how his mind was almost blown and he was "caught in a coloured shower" (Greenwald, no date, para 1). Jefferson Airplane's drug infected top 10 hit from the summer of 1967, "White Rabbit," begins with "one pill makes you larger and one pill makes you small." In the song, Alice becomes ten feet tall, "logic and proportion" fall "sloppy dead" and the mind is "moving low." It ends with the injunction to "feed your head" (Jefferson Airplane, 1967). The song's composer, Grace Slick, confessed that she wrote the song after taking "acid" (Myers, 2016). Jimi Hendrix's 1967 "Purple Haze," according to Sheila Whiteley (1992), is "named after a particular brand of acid" (p.17). Hendrix admits that the haze in his brain and eyes, now things don't seem the same and he does not know if it is day or night. He wants to be excused "while I kiss the sky" (Hendrix, 1967).

A song that captures the experience of LSD musically is Country Joe and the Fish's 1967 recording "Bass Strings." At the end of the song, the letters LSD. are whispered. In this moody masterpiece, the narrator confesses: "My world is spinnin', yeah, just got to slow it down." He thinks about acid and says: "one more trip now, you know I'll stay high, All the time, all the time." He will go down to the seashore where he will let the "waves wash my mind, open up my head now just to see what I can find." Country Joe is not only on an acid trip but a journey of self-understanding. Yet he cannot quite get what he wants. "Truth lives all around me, but it's just beyond my grasp." The singer says that the stars, the sand and the wind carry him back. He is torn between the wish to stay high all the time and using his trips to uncover his past and discover his real self. It is a spiritual journey with his head opening up, but no final revelations (Country Joe and the Fish, 1967).

Paths to Liberation III: Spiritual Journeys

Some other 1960s classic counterculture songs, which may or may not be explicitly about drugs, have the same emphasis on opening up one's head and embarking on a spiritual journey as do the drug songs. In 1965's "Mr. Tambourine Man," Dylan sings about his "weariness" amazing him, how his "senses have been stripped," and his "ancient empty street's too dead

CHAPTER 10: FOREVER YOUNG

for dreaming." He wants to awaken from his torpor, and asks the tambourine man to:

> Take me on a trip upon your magic swirlin' ship...
> I'm ready to go anywhere...
> Then take me disappearin' through the smoke rings of my mind,
> Down the foggy ruins of time...
> ... Out to the windy beach,
> Far from the twisted reach of crazy sorrow.
> Yes, to dance beneath the diamond sky with one hand waving free,
> Silhouetted by the sea, circled by the circus sands,
> With all memory and fate driven deep between the waves,
> Let me forget about today until tomorrow... (Dylan, 1965)

Dylan seeks to transcend his dead world and live for the intense moment of peak experience. This entails being fully in the now, or living for today, as the Grass Roots would later sing. The past will be driven down to the depths of the sea, and there will be the liberty of dancing with one hand waving free while getting into the mind's depths. Johnny Rivers would later sing about letting tomorrow be. Here Dylan is doing that for today, the essential spiritual journey begins when a person can open up to the secrets of their own psyche, and this receptivity to inner experience is connected to a spiritual life force. The Amboy Dukes 1968 top 40 hit, "Journey to the Center of the Mind," advises the listener to:

> Leave your cares behind
> Come with us and find
>
> The pleasures of a journey to the center of the mind...
> Beyond the seas of thought
> Beyond the realm of what...
> For it's the land unknown to man
> Where fantasy is fact...
> How happy life could be
> If all of mankind
> Would take the time to journey to the center of the mind...
> (Amboy Dukes, 1968).

The same year, Steppenwolf had a hit single with "Magic Carpet Ride." John Kay sings: "I like to dream" on "a cloud of sound." Any "place it goes is right." It goes to "the stars away from here." He invites a "little girl" to tell her dreams to him. "You don't know what we can see.../ Fantasy will set you free" (Steppenwolf, 1968). Spiritual self-exploration, fantasy, is the road to freedom and fulfillment.

Jimi Hendrix also recommends going to this inner world. He revives the centrality of being "experienced." Being experienced is not "necessarily stoned, but beautiful." You can get "your mind together," and we can watch the sun rise from the bottom of the sea. In order to get the most out of this, you need to be experienced (Hendrix, 1967). An inner awareness, an opening up is required to get to the center of the mind and spirituality.

Two closely related songs recorded in the spring of 1966 center around these spiritual wanderings. One is by the Beatles and the other by the Byrds. "Tomorrow Never Knows" was recorded in early April of 1966. John Lennon wrote the composition after reading the classic religious tract "Tibetan Book of the Dead." Receptivity to spiritual forces, letting things be is necessary so as to be open to spiritual matters. Lennon advises:

> Turn off your mind, relax and float downstream...
> Surrender to the void...
> ... you may see the meaning of within
> It is being, it is being...

The meaning of being, Lennon declares, is love. He sings: "Love is all and love is everyone. It is knowing." This lesson can be learned if you "listen to the color of your dreams." Then play the game of existence to the end of the beginning (Beatles, 1966). Opening up to inner meaning we can come to know the universality of love and the circularity of time.

Recorded a month later, in The Byrds' *Fifth Dimension*, Roger McGuinn is "floatin." He is "relaxed and paying attention," but his two-dimensional boundaries have disappeared. He is shown "that joy innocently is" and he needs to "be quiet and feel it around you." Then, "And I opened my heart to the whole universe,/ And I found it was loving,/ And I saw the great blunder my teachers had made,/ Scientific delirium madness." As in the Beatles song, McGuinn "will remember the place that is now. That has ended before the beginning" (Byrds, 1966). Both songs perceive a loving universe and circular time. As in "White Rabbit," scientific logic is not a representation of what really matters, but is a form of delirium. It is not through proportion and logic, but through seeing the inner meaning that the higher, loving reality is recognized. As Procol Harum (1967) declared, "There is no reason, And the truth is plain to see." The songs of ecstasy and experience lead away from the mundane world of everyday experience and towards a joyous, expanded self within a loving universe.

Not all counterculture rock artists held to the vision of the universe as loving as expressed in these songs. Where Lennon and McGuinn had a revelation that the universe is loving; to Country Joe, the truth is just beyond his grasp. The counterculture had different strands that diverged in direction and emphasis. There are some who live for the intensity and peak experiences of the extended moment, but know the moment will end. There are others who wish for life to be ecstasy and to go on endlessly. The highest ideals of the 1960s counterculture that love is all and the universe is loving are expressed in "Tomorrow Never Knows" and "5D (Fifth Dimension)." Along with communalism, freedom and the celebration of youth, these are 1960s cultural radicals' vision of the good life.

Is Love Liberation or Complication?

Love, that romanticized ideal, that conventional sentiment, is the counterculture's prescription for curing what is wrong with existing human arrangements. Not without reason are the hippies called the love generation. Underneath these proclamations of love's redemptive power is a great deal of uncertainty as to whether the course of true love can be as utopian as is proclaimed. There are evident divisions in the counterculture between glorious expectations of paradise now and fearful visions of alienation and despair.

When these two aspects of counterculture rock are brought together, a contradictory and complex understanding of love is present, one that is far removed from the loving universe The Beatles and The Byrds envision. While the songs about the redeeming power of love are one facet of counterculture rock songs about love, and the other is the variety of feelings and outcomes in dyadic romantic relationships. The divisions present in the songs are also seen within the communalism and fate of the youth culture in the late 1960s and early 1970s.

The most popular and influential rock band of the 1969s were, of course, the Beatles. They were among those that celebrated love as knowing. Their songs of romance can be divided into two types: one, about the course of love in human relationships, and the other on the nature and philosophy of love. "The Word," from 1965's Rubber Soul is an instance of the latter kind of love song. The word in the song is, of course, love, which is described as sunshine and so fine. Say or spread the word and "you'll be free," for the "word is just the way." There is definitely a proselytizing element to this song. The singer proclaims: "I'm here to show everybody the light." Love is a bright, redeeming goodness (Beatles, 1965). "The Word" is a prelude to the later declaration that love is all and love is everyone. The heart of being human, the way to the light and freedom is through spreading the word about, giving and receiving love. In a multi-layered, multi-meaning hit single from 1967, an overt message is "All You Need Is Love." If you want to be productive, feeling, helpful, knowledgeable, "It is easy. All you need is love" (Beatles, 1967). Love is balanced, a world of give and take. For "in the end," The Beatles sing on Abbey Road, "The love you take. Is equal to the love you make" (Beatles, 1969). This reciprocal world of giving and receiving is the way to be free and to bask in the light.

The Beatles songs about individual romantic relationships are not as full of redemption as are the love as redemption infused records. Some of the songs are about symbiosis and some show fear of conflict. A song about all enveloping intimacy appeared on "Revolver." "To lead a better life I need my love to be here," Paul sings in "Here, There and Everywhere." She can change his life with just a "wave of her hand." He sings:

> I want her everywhere and if she's beside me
> I know I need never care
> But to love her is to need her everywhere
> Knowing that love is to share...
> Each one believing that love never dies. (Beatles, 1966)

CHAPTER 10: FOREVER YOUNG

In these lyrics, love is eternal and about continual togetherness. Love removes care, sharing leads to happiness and the elimination of anxiety and worry.

Yet sometimes in Beatles songs love dies; there are break-ups, loss and sorrow. In "Yesterday," Paul's lover has suddenly abandoned him. When she was nearby, all his troubles seemed so far away. All of a sudden, a shadow is hanging over him. "Suddenly, I'm not half the man I used to be... I need a place to hide away" (Beatles, 1965). Without a loving relationship, the singer feels incomplete and lost. If we are all together and love is all, romantic disintegration is deeply painful. "If she's gone, I can't go on," John sings. Then he withdraws and sings: "Hey, you've got to hide your love away" (Beatles, 1965).

If break-ups are devastating, the presence of conflict and contrariness in relationships are not welcomed in Beatles songs. In "It's Only Love," the lovers fight every night, and yet the sight of his love makes the night time bright. Still, John sings: "It's so hard loving you" (Beatles, 1965). Another example of a trying romance is "Girl." This woman puts John down when friends are near, and he feels like a fool. When he tries to break up with her, she cries; then promises the world to him. He believes her, though after "all this time I don't know why" (Beatles, 1965). In "Hello, Goodbye," contraries counter each other. Whatever one says, the other says the opposite. The couple remains trapped in a battle of wills; and yet there is puzzlement over this perpetual conflict. "Oh no, I don't know why you say goodbye. I say, hello" (Beatles, 1967). Arguing goes against what the Beatles want in human relationships. In "Fixing a Hole," Paul sings about "the people who . . . disagree and never win" and don't get in his door (Beatles, 1967). John sings in "We Can Work It Out," that:

> Life is very short, and there's no time
> For fussing and fighting, my friend
> I have always thought that it's a crime
> So I will ask you once again
>
> Try to see it my way
> Only time will tell if I am right or I am wrong.
> Why do you see it your way

> There's a chance that we might fall apart before too long.
> (Beatles, 1965)

John beseeches the other to try to work it out. Resolving conflict is an imperative, for fussing and fighting can lead to things breaking in two. Concealment can be as negative as conflict. "I never give you my number. I only give you my situation... in the middle of investigation. I break down" (Beatles, 1969). Falling apart and breaking down brings dread, sorrow and the feeling of not being able to go on. Conflict can be destructive. In the single version of "Revolution," Lennon sings "when you talk about destruction. Don't you know you can count me out." He does not have much use for "people with minds that hate." His remedy, as stated before, is to "free your mind instead" (Beatles, 1968). Does he mean that a free mind does not hate? It's not as if John is unfamiliar with jealousy and anger in romance. He would rather see his girl dead than to see her with another man in "Run For Your Life" (Beatles, 1965). In "You Can't Do That," he declares that if he catches his partner talking to that boy again, he is going to leave her flat (Beatles, 1964). He considers flirting a sin, and he will not tolerate it. The ideal in Beatles love songs remains faithfulness, togetherness and harmony.

Conflict in relationships is problematic in Beatles' love songs. They would like to retain the faith, expressed in "Revolution," that it's "gonna be all right" (Beatles, 1968). Their remedy for being in times of trouble is passive. "There will be answer. Let it be" (Beatles, 1970). The hope is that through openness and receptivity, minds can be freed and a positive answer will emerge. Incorporating conflict, loss and destruction into their conception of love is difficult for them. Yet in their recordings, love engenders conflicts and difficulties as well as serenity and togetherness. If love is a mixture of goods and evils, it is not the way to the harmonious light of a better world as the Beatles preached. Love does not always bring redemption.

Not all counterculture rock artists in the 1960s were as sold on the virtues of romance and the universality of love as were the Beatles. Bob Dylan can have an occasional song such as "Visions of Johanna," where the absence of the lover leaves a real void (Dylan, 1966). Most characteristically he uses romantic relationships as a foil to show the failings of his partner. In "Don't Think Twice, It's All Right," there is woman to whom

CHAPTER 10: FOREVER YOUNG

he gave his life, but that wasn't enough for she wanted "his soul" (Dylan, 1963). He looks askance on romantic ideals of togetherness and sacrifice in "It Aint't Me, Babe." The "babe" tells him she wants someone "who will promise never to part... Someone who will die for you an' more." Dylan replies that he will only let her down, and that he is not the man for her (Dylan, 1965).

The Rolling Stones focus on the dark side of romance. Mick Jagger sings about his "Heart of Stone" and declares "I ain't got no love. I ain't the kind to meet" (Rolling Stones, 1965). He often looks at women as disposable and stupid, he admits to being a user. Who wants yesterday's papers, who wants yesterday's girls is a question posed in one song. The answer is nobody in the world (Rolling Stones, 1967). Jagger talks about stupid girls, one-night stands and backstreet girls. In "Lady Jane," the singer marries the noble woman because of her position not because of love (Rolling Stones, 1966). For all his put downs of women and love, he is occasionally amazed at benevolent emotions that women possess. In "She Smiled Sweetly," he describes himself as forever anxious and his hair is turning gray as a result. His partner has peace inside her most every day. She smiles sweetly and says don't worry. He admits: "I understood for once in my life" and now he is feeling good almost every day (Rolling Stones, 1967).

This song, not surprisingly is an exception. Much more common is his accusation about some of "the sick things a girl does to a man" and his admission that since he was "young I've been very hard to please." His friends who got married "mortgaged up their lives" (Rolling Stones, 1967). He remains unresolved, and would rather sit on the fence than make up his mind. In Rolling Stones' songs of the 1960s, love is more a battlefield than a harmonious symbiosis.

Other rock songs of the counterculture era shared the Beatles elevated version of love, as well as some of the recognition of its imperfections. In their top 10 hit from 1968, the Troggs sing:

> I feel it in my fingers I feel it in my toes.
> Well love is all around me, and so the feeling grows.
> It's written on the wind, it's everywhere I go. (Troggs, 1968)

In this song is sense of love as pervading every nook and cranny of being. It is sensual and tactile. In "Tommy," the title character repeatedly beseeches: "See me, feel me/ Touch me, heal me" (The Who, 1969).

Recognition of the redemptive power of love is present in Lesley Duncan's 1969 recording of her "Love Song," which was later covered by Elton John. The lyrics are:

> Love is the opening door
> Love is what we came here for...
> Love is the key we must turn...
> Freedom the lesson we must learn. (Duncan, 1971)

The millennial romantic, Donovan, had a top 40 hit in 1967 with "Wear Your Love Like Heaven." In his otherworldly fashion, he sings:

> Wear my love like heaven... Lord kiss me once more
> Fill me with song...
> Cannot believe what I see
> All I have wished for will be
> All our race proud and free. (Donovan, 1967)

Love can liberate. A little more complicated championing of love is present in "The Girl With No Eyes" by It's A Beautiful Day (1969):

> Doesn't everybody know, everybody know
> love takes a lifetime.
> And doesn't everybody know, everybody know
> love is the eye sight
> it's the eye sight of a lifetime.

Some other assorted sixties counterculture love songs celebrated romance while others dealt with loss and pain. In "Darling Be Home Soon," John Sebastian sings that the time he spent confused was the time he spent without his love. He asks her to be home soon (Lovin' Spoonful, 1967). The Rascals wonder how in a world that is constantly changing they can be certain. The answer is that with this lover "I'm sure with you." Neil Young declares that he could spend the rest of his life with a cinnamon girl and he is searching for a heart of gold (Neil Young, 1970; 1972). In

CHAPTER 10: FOREVER YOUNG

"Up On Cripple Creek," the Band sing about "little Bessie." She takes care of everything for him:

> If I spring a leak she mends me.
> I don't have to speak she defends me
> A drunkard's dream if I ever did see one. (The Band, 1969)

In other songs, love is not so certain or everlasting. In 1968's "Like to Get To Know You," Spanky and Our Gang (1968) sing:

> Now I can't promise that I'll spend a day with you.
> Can't promise that I'll find a way with you...
> I can't promise that I'll love you.

Tim Hardin (1965), in "Misty Roses," sings:

> You look to me like love forever
> Too good to last but too lovely not to try...

Another Tim Hardin's (1966 song is entitled "It's Hard to Believe in Love for Long." Without questioning romance, some singers recognize that they will hurt their loved ones or be hurt by them. Janis Joplin (Big Brother and the Holding Company, 1968) sings:

> Ah, I'm a mean, mean woman
> And I don't mean no one man, no good...
> I ain't the kind of woman
> Who'd make your life a bed of ease...

In 1971's "River" from the album "Blue," Joni Mitchell (1971) admits:

> I'm so hard to handle
> I'm selfish and I'm sad...

The last two songs on that remarkable album give two sides to love. In "A Case of You," which is one of the most remarkable love songs ever written, Joni is told to go to this man and stay with him, but "be prepared to bleed." Despite his devils and deeds and that he tastes so bitter and so sweet, she still affirms: "I could drink a case of you... And I would still be on my feet." She says "'Love is touching souls,' Well, surely you touched mine... you're in my blood like holy wine" (Mitchell, 1971). In this song, romance in its double-sidedness is celebrated.

In the concluding song on the album, "The Last Time I saw Richard," the title character tells the narrator:

> ...all romantics meet the same fate someday
> Cynical and drunk and boring someone in some dark cafe...
> You like . . . pretty men to tell you
> All those pretty lies . . . just pretty lies... (Mitchell, 1971)

The narrator acknowledges she is a "good dreamer" hiding behind bottles in dark cafes. Through her sadness, she tells herself that it is "Only a phase, these dark cafe days" (Mitchell, 1971). Romance can hurt, especially for those who are hard to handle, selfish and sad. Romance itself involves pretty lies. Self-deception is built into the very structure of two people coming together.

A singer songwriter who knows about Joni's dark cafes, the intricacies of romantic entanglements, and Joni Mitchell herself is Leonard Cohen. The two of them were lovers for a while, and "A Case of You" is at least in part based on their relationship (Chiasson, 10/2/2017, para 21). Leonard's accounts of intimacy diverges from The Beatles, Dylan, and The Stones.

Where Mick Jagger sings of having no love to give, in "Suzanne," Cohen (1967) sings:

> ...just when you mean to tell her
> that you had no love to give her
> she gets me on her wavelength
> and she lets the river answer
> that you've always been her lover...

Sexual/romantic relationships can be transformative. In a later song, Leonard sings how after an intimate encounter the trouble that had long been in the woman's eyes had been taken away (Cohen, 1971). Yet as in "A Case of You," for Cohen romantic partnerships are double-edged. He declares that "the duty of lovers is to tarnish the golden rule" (Cohen,

CHAPTER 10: FOREVER YOUNG

1967). Leonard also admits that he "has torn everyone who has reached out to me" (Cohen, 1969).

He will not be surprised to be both tarnished and entranced by partners in romantic adventures. He sings of a longer-term romance when a couple nurtures a baby, yet emotional fluctuations characterize the relationship. On one hand he says, "I tried to leave you...at least a hundred times." Then he acknowledges that he wakes "every morning by your side" and "my arms are open wide." He is "a man working for your smile" (Cohen, 1974).

From another angle, he says that there is "a war between the man and woman." This war is essential to being, if you can endure the battles, "*You can still get married*" (Cohen, 1974). He elaborates more on the meaning of these conflicts in "Field Commander Cohen." To a lover, he sings that after she is her "sweetest self a while", he will "ask for more." Cohen wants "the other selves to be rung" until "love is pierced and love is hung, and every kind of freedom done" (Cohen, 1974). To Leonard Cohen, the severe, rigorous, adventures of love can open us up to being free to the fullness of being, in its beauty, suffering, inner and outer terrors, to the revelation of the rawness, and sweetness of our deeper selves, that our arms are open wide and that we tear apart those we love.

In counterculture songs, love may be the eye sight of a lifetime, but it can also bring despair and disillusionment. The love generation has faith in romance, but it is a battered faith that sometimes lives up to and sometimes does not live up to its ideals.

Drugs: Liberation or Hallucination Horrors?

As the sixties advanced into the seventies, the counterculture's belief in the wonders of the drug culture becomes tarnished. LSD led to bad trips. As early as 1965, the Fugs in referring to acid and mescaline talked about getting the "Hallucination Horrors" (Fugs, 1965). Some prominent rockers, such as Brian Jones of the Rolling Stones, became debilitated by drugs. Canned Heat warned in "Amphetamine Annie" that speed kills (Canned Heat, 1968). Paul Revere and the Raiders" "Kicks" discussed a girl who goes on magic carpet rides but kind kicks harder to find. She is advised to get herself straight before it is too late (Paul Revere and the Raiders, 1966). In "Sister Morphine," Mick Jagger sings about a morphine user who is trying to score. He knows that in the morning he will be dead (Rolling Stones, 1971). There are perils in substance abuse. Steppenwolf, who had advocated magic carpet rides, began to talk about burned out drug users with tombstone in their eyes (Steppenwolf, 1968). In "The Needle and the Damage Done," Neil Young (1972) bemoans:

> I hit the city and I lost my band
> Watched the needle take another man
> Gone, gone, the damage done....
> Sing the song because I love the man
> Know that some of you don't understand....
> I've seen the needle and the damage done.

Another song about heroin use is Love's (1966) "Signed D.C.," where the narrator says:

> I've pierced my skin again, Lord....
> My soul belongs to the dealer
> He keeps my mind as well....
> I've got one foot in the graveyard
> No one cares, cares
> For me, cares for me.

The Velvet Underground (1966), in Lou Reed's "Heroin," details the highs and lows of heroin. Chemically opening the doors of perception may lead to heaven but can lead to the abyss as well. Neither love nor mind altering drugs are sure paths to the promised land of the counterculture.

Assassination, Police Riots, Woodstock, Altamont, Beatles Break-Up, Deaths, Kent State

The dream of a generational identity ran into some rough paths, some external obstacles and some internal divisions. The radical left began to divide over black power. Many radical women began to feel that even within the movement they were treated as unequal. Feminism reappeared and divided radical groups. In the spring of 1968, Martin Luther King and Robert Kennedy were assassinated. At the Democratic National Convention in August, 1968, there was a police riot against the radical youth gathered to oppose the war. The next year, the politically radical group,

CHAPTER 10: FOREVER YOUNG

SDS split into three groups. The Haight-Ashbury district of San Francisco, which had given birth to 1967s well-publicized Summer of Love, was falling on harder times. Bob Dylan, after a motorcycle accident in 1966, had withdrawn from the scene and when he reappeared was much chastened. When the Beatles White Album appeared in the fall of 1968, it was evident that Paul and John were not composing songs together any more. Tension was appearing within the fab four. When the Rolling Stones released their album, Beggars Banquet, founding member Brian Jones barely participated in the sessions due to his instability.

Nineteen Sixty-Nine saw two major peace rallies; and the aforementioned splintering of SDS. On July 3, 1969, Brian Jones was found dead in his swimming pool. The Woodstock Festival in August 1969 became legendary when multitudes of youth listened to rock music and partied without many disruptive incidents over a three-day period. In December 1969, the Rolling Stones organized a free music festival in Altamont, California. Unfortunately, a black youth, Meredith Hunter, was murdered by the Hells Angels motorcycle gang, while the Rolling Stones performed on stage. The Angels had been hired by the festival's organizers to keep order. Destruction and violence had found its way into the counterculture.

As the seventies began, anti-war leaders at the 1968 Democratic Convention were put on trial instead of the police. The Nixon administration had begun a publicity campaign against radical youth. Then on April 10, 1970, Paul McCartney announced he was leaving the Beatles. The group had fallen apart. The symbol of generational unity was gone. Things went from bad to worse. On April 30, 1970, President Nixon announced he was invading Cambodia. Demonstrations broke out on college campuses throughout the country. On May 4, 1970 at Kent State University, armed National Guardsman shot and killed four demonstrators, later in the month black college students were gunned down at Jackson State in Mississippi. The war had come home.

Jimi Hendrix died on September 18, 1970 from drug related causes. Less than three weeks later, on October 4, 1970, a heroin overdose took the life of Janis Joplin. Beloved Pearl was dead; another counterculture star had succumbed to drugs. Jim Morrison of the Doors died on July 3, 1971, two years to the day after Brian Jones. Hendrix, Joplin, Jones and Morrison were all twenty-seven years old. In the prophetic words of Pete Townsend, they all had died before they got old, before they had reached the untrustworthy age of thirty. The counterculture was falling apart at the seams.

Disillusionment had been creeping into the music for a while, but intensified after the break-up of the Beatles, the deaths of star performers and other catastrophes. There were two songs written about Kent State. The first, by Neil Young, called "Ohio" was a top twenty single in the summer of 1970. Young writes about tin soldiers and Nixon coming. "This summer I hear the drumming. Four dead in Ohio... Soldiers are gunning us down." Young repeats that we are finally on our own; there is no one to protect us (Crosby, Stills, Nash, and Young, 1970). Actually, those sworn to uphold order are doing the killing. The Beach Boys' "Student Demonstration Time' from 1971, reviews the history of the student movement from Berkeley Free Speech to the Kent State massacre. Writing about the killing at Jackson State, Mike Love sings: "The pen is mightier than the sword, but no match for a gun." On Kent State: "Four martyrs earned the new degree. The Bachelor of Bullets... we are all fed up with useless wars and racial strife... next time there's a riot, well, you best stay out of sight" (Beach Boys, 1971). The Beach Boys' Mike Love recognizes that excessive force is being used, but advises people to stay away for their own safety. Fear and intimidation win. As the seventies begin, there is no longer as much confidence that love, drugs and generational unity will bring millennial social change. Disenchantment, disillusionment and division begin to be pervasive in counterculture rock.

The Dream is Over

Urban folk artists, including Phil Ochs and Bob Dylan, went through negative recognitions about the social prospects earlier than did mainstream counterculture rockers. In 1967, Phil Ochs (1967), in his song "Cross My Heart," sings: "It seems that every single dream... tumbles in despair. And it starts to bend. Till by the end it's a nightmare." In the same year, his "Outside of A Small Circle of Friends," notices that neither murder, racial strife, denial of free speech, or jailing drug users awaken many people to these outrages. Only a select few pay attention. Most keep up their consumer culture activity while the country goes to ruin (Ochs, 1967). The people are more interested in their own leisure than in social justice. So much for freedom leading to democracy.

CHAPTER 10: FOREVER YOUNG

Just after Christmas 1967, Bob Dylan released the album, John Wesley Harding. On it, in "I Dreamed I Saw St. Augustine," Dylan has the Catholic theologian proclaim: "No martyr is among ye now, Whom you can call your own." Dylan dreams of the saint that "I was amongst the ones, That put him out to death." He awakes in anger, alone and terrified. "I put my fingers against the glass, And bowed my head and cried" (Dylan, 1967). This is a humbled, remorseful Bob Dylan. He dreams he has persecuted the holy and virtuous. Mike Marqusee (2003) comments on this song: "The movement's reassuring dream of redemption through history has been replaced by a nightmare of unqualified bleakness and failure" (p.235). In a similar vein, in "All Along the Watchtower," the thief beseeches the joker: "let us not talk falsely now, the hour is getting late" (Dylan, 1967). Dylan does not believe we are entering any Age of Aquarius.

In late 1967, the Lovin' Spoonful released an album with John Sebastian's song "Younger Generation." The composer in 1969 sang it at Woodstock. He begins by asking "Why must every generation think their folks are square." It becomes clear this is a song about a counterculture advocate who as a parent must deal with how his children are surpassing him. The last stanza goes like this:

> Hey, Pop, my girlfriend's only three
> She's got her own videophone and she's taking LSD.
> And now that we're best friends she wants to give a bit to me
> But what's the matter Daddy? how come you're turning green?
> Can it be that you can't live up to your dreams?
> (Lovin' Spoonful, 1967)

The status of the high hopes of the love generation became a growing concern. Almost three years after the Lovin' Spoonful song, and eight months after the demise of the Beatles came a John Lennon solo album. He had been through primal scream therapy with Arthur Janov. Like, Dylan, Lennon had a lot to process through including his mother's early death and the break-up of the Beatles. Disillusionment is one prominent theme in the album. In the song "God," Lennon sings: "God is a concept/ By which we measure/ Our pain." He then lists fourteen things in which he does not believe; the fifteenth is:

> I don't believe in Beatles
> I just believe in me
> Yoko and me...
> The dream is over
> What can I say?..
> And so dear friends
> You just have to carry on
> The dream is over... (Lennon, 1970)

Lennon sheds his former identity as the Walrus, he says, and is reborn as John, a less mythical figure. As he now only believes in himself and Yoko, love is no longer everyone. After shedding so many beliefs, Lennon is filled with doubts. Some of these uncertainties about love, in particular, are expressed in 1971's "How?":

> How can I give love when
> I don't know what it is I'm giving?
> How can I give love when
> I just don't know how to give?
> How can I give love when love is something
> I ain't never had?....
> You know life can be long....
> And the world she is tough
> Sometimes feel I've had enough... (Lennon, 1971)

His despair is about love and self. The dream indeed is over, at least for a while. The area of sacredness has been reduced to the conventional domestic pair seeking haven from a heartless world.

In December 1970, George Harrison's "Isn't It A Pity," as the flip side of "My Sweet Lord," hits the singles charts. This is another song about the failure to love:

> Isn't it a pity?
> Isn't it a shame?
> How we break each other's hearts, and cause each other pain
> How we take each other's love, without thinking anymore
> Forgetting to give back
> Isn't it a pity? (Harrison, 1970)

CHAPTER 10: FOREVER YOUNG

Earlier Beatles songs expressed confidence that things could be worked out, that everything will be all right; in times of trouble, just let it be. For Lennon and Harrison, there are strains in their songs that reflect pity and despair, the loss of belief, the end of a dream.

1971-1975: Further Disillusionment

In the following year, 1971, significant songs of counterculture disillusionment become top 40 hits. As in earlier songs of estrangement and alienation, these songs on one hand look at the external environment and on the other turn inwards towards a darker self-assessment. In August, 1971, The Who's "Won't Get Fooled Again" entered the Billboard top 40. It is a song about the "new revolution" and the "new constitution." The only problem is that after the revolution, "the world looks just the same/ And history ain't changed.../ Meet the new boss, Same as the old boss." The revolution is a farce; it is just shifting who rules, not implementing ideals. As the old saying goes fool me once shame on you; fool me twice, shame on me. Echoing this, the Who sing: "I'll get on my knees and pray, We won't get fooled again" (The Who, 1971). If history and politics are not the answer, what about the counterculture dream of love and freedom? The Who answers: "My love is vengeance. That's never free." Townsend sees himself as a sad and bad man. He is no exuberant flower child. At one time, he thought the older generation was awfully cold. In "Behind Blue Eyes," he sees his "conscience" as "empty" (The Who, 1971). The new boss and the old boss may be the same, and there may be more similarities between Townsend's and the older generation than is comfortable to admit.

Ten Years After's "I'd Love to Change the World" first entered the charts in November 1971. After listing a variety of social problems, the singer confesses: "I'd love to change the world. But I don't know what to do. So I'll leave it up to you." They are bewildered and resigned (Ten Years After, 1971). The next month Don McLean's "American Pie" began its seventeen-week run on the top 40, with four weeks as number one. This song chronicled the rise and fall of the rock and roll generation. To McLean, the end of the rock era is the 1969 murder of Meredith Hunter at the Altamont concert. Echoing Lennon in "God," McLean (1971) writes:

> There we were all in one place
> A generation lost in space.

With no time left to start again.

The death of the music and the hopes of the rock generation impacts on the personal as well as the political. In "Dreidel" from 1972, another top 40 single, McLean (1972) admits that:

> My world is a constant confusion
> My mind is prepared to attack
> My past, a persuasive illusion
> I'm watchin' the future it's black. ....
> What can you show? Nothing of
> What you believe....
> as you sell your soul and you sow your seeds
> and you wound yourself and your
> loved one bleeds
> and your habits grow, and your conscience feeds
> on all you thought you should be
> I never thought this could happen to Meeeeeeeeee.

This same sense of disintegration is present in Paul Simon's 1971 composition "Everything Put Together Falls Apart" (Simon, 1971). In "American Tune," Paul Simon captures the end of an era, where the personal and the political intertwine. After admitting that he has been mistaken, forsaken, confused, misused and is weary to his bones, he extends his own condition to a larger sphere:

> And I don't know a soul who's not been battered
> I don't have a friend who feels at ease
> I don't know a dream that's not been shattered
> Or driven to its knees....
> Still, when I think of the road
> We're traveling on
> I wonder what went wrong... (Simon, 1973)

In 1975, Traffic's Jim Capaldi in "Living on A Marble," gave his assessment of what went wrong. It was believing in love is all and love is everyone. Capaldi (1975) sings:

CHAPTER 10: FOREVER YOUNG

> Universal love would be a good thing
> If everybody stays on their own soil
> It's when everybody tries to get together
> That's when the blood begins to boil.

The disillusionment and shattering of dreams brought a variety of reactions. For some side by side with their despair was a renewal of hope, a beginning of a new dream or a reframing of the old. For some disillusionment was connected to other forms of instability. Themes of madness, which had been in the background in mid- 60's rock came more to the fore at the end of the 1960s and the early 1970s. The Guess Who in 1969 sing about a woman who has come "undun" (Guess Who, 1969). A year earlier, Procol Harum (1968) sung about their "befuddled brain is shining brightly, quite insane." James Taylor writes about his incarceration in a mental hospital in 1968's "Knocking Around the Zoo" (Taylor, 1968). Wendy Waldman's "Mad, Mad Me," from 1974, is about a couple each of whom thinks the other is crazy. In 1975, Paul Simon admits to being still "crazy after all these years." He fears he may do damage one day, but it doesn't matter. "I would not be convicted by a jury of my peers... Still crazy after all these years (Simon, 1975). Madness has infected his generation.

Pink Floyd is intimately familiar with madness. Their initial leader, Syd Barrett, began a mental decline in 1967, sometimes going catatonic on stage. He was replaced, but his illness made a significant impact on the band. A recurring theme in subsequent Pink Floyd recordings is insanity. Their 1973 seminal album, Dark Side of the Moon, was on the Billboard Top 200 albums for 917 weeks, more than any other album ever (Billboard, 2020). Sheila Whiteley places the album in historical perspective. To her, the visionary "experience and self-discovery" of earlier rock music "had failed to confront the dominant culture, and progressive rock...had, to some extent stagnated." Dark Side of the Moon seems "to close the book" on "the counter-culture's belief, 'change the mode of consciousness and you change the world.'" In this album, work, "money, growing old, growing mad are expressed through a song cycle which begins and ends with a fading heartbeat" (Whiteley, 1992, p. 104). Consciousness was changed all right, but in Syd Barrett's and other cases, the change was not to positive revelation but to mental debilitation. This experience seems an echo of Allen Ginsberg's 1956 poem, "Howl," which begins: "I saw the best minds of my generation destroyed by madness." (Ginsberg, 1956, p.9).

As the first track of this Pink Floyd classic begins, a voice in the background mutters "I've been mad for... years, absolutely years, over the edge." In "Brain Damage," the lunatic is on the grass, in the hall, in my head. "There's someone in my head but it's not me." There may be a kinship of those whose sanity is threatened. For "if your head explodes with dark foreboding too. I'll see you on the dark side of the moon." There is also a statement in the song about the band you're in starts playing different tunes. While Barrett was with the band, he would sometimes play different compositions than the rest of the group. 1975's "Shine On You Crazy Diamond" is Roger Waters and Pink Floyd's explicit tribute to their wayward former member. It chronicles how Barrett went from a visionary to being incapacitated. When Barrett was young, he "shone like the sun." Now the look in his eyes is "like black holes in the sky." He was caught in the "crossfire of childhood and stardom," as he "reached for the secret too soon" and "cried for the moon." The narrator wants Barrett to "shine" again as a "raver" a visionary, a "painter... piper and prisoner." This is a cautionary tale, the underside of the counterculture dream of a stairway to heaven induced by drug enhanced peak experiences (Pink Floyd, 1973).

Beyond madness, in 1975's "Wish You Were Here," Pink Floyd's (1975) dark skepticism is expressed in these lyrics:

> So, so you think you can tell
> Heaven from hell
> Blue skies from pain....
> Did they get you to trade
> Your heroes for ghosts?....
> Did you exchange
> A walk on part in the war
> For a leading role in a cage?

Vacillation

And yet for all the losses, shattered lives, and disillusionment, there was a certain resilience among those in the counterculture who had seen the dark path. This continuity of faith vacillates with darker feelings; the moving

CHAPTER 10: FOREVER YOUNG

from one pole to another continues. Not long after proclaiming the death of the dream, John Lennon becomes explicitly political and calls for "Power to the People" (Lennon, 1971).

In 1971, he imagines "all the people living for today... living life in peace... sharing all the world." People may accuse him of being a "dreamer," but if people join him "the world will be as one" (Lennon, 1971). This is a reversion to his faith in "I Am the Walrus" of humans being "all together" and in "Tomorrow Never Knows" contending that "love is all and love is everyone." But later despair threatens, and he sings that whatever get you through the night is all right (Lennon, 1974). The dark night of the soul is not far away. Lennon is perplexed by the division between millennial expectations and black forebodings, between peace and dread.

Dylan follows a different path to rejuvenation than does Lennon. As the seventies begin domesticity becomes an ideal. His "New Morning" celebrates marriage and parenting (Dylan, 1970). Sometimes he will write a political song about deceased prisoner George Jackson, and other times he will sit on the bank of sand and watch the river flow. "People disagreeing...about everything...Makes you stop and wonder why" (Dylan, 1971). For Dylan, domestic bliss does not endure. His 1975 album, Blood on the Tracks chronicles the disintegration of his marriage with a return to disillusionment and harsh self-judgment. In "Shelter from the Storm," he sings, "I bargained for salvation and she gave me a lethal dose," and also "nothing really matters much, it's doom alone that counts" (Dylan, 1975). A dire lethality pervades this song of promise and loss. Later in the decade though, Dylan turns to fundamentalist Christianity, one of his many relatively short-lived enthusiasms.

Paul Simon's 1970s journey also led in contradictory directions. In the late sixties he had been critical of the middle-class affluence of Mrs. Robinson. In the 1970s, he both chronicled the disintegration of the dream, and asked God to bless and maintain America's high standard of living (Simon, 1975).

The Who in 1971, shortly after declaring the new boss is the old boss and that their love is unfree and full of vengeance, called for action and freedom in their top 40 song, "Let's See Action." "Let's be free, let's see who cares," The Who declare. Yet despite their clarion calls, there is still uncertainty: "I'm so tired of running from my own heat… I don't know where I'm going, I don't know what I need" (The Who, 1971). In "Love Reign O'er Me," The Who seek love to escape from darkness and uncertainty. He spends nights apart and alone, these evenings "are hot and black as ink" and he "can't sleep." The remedy for this restless insomnia is love. For only love can "bring the rain" that "makes you yearn to the sky" and "falls like tears from on high" (The Who, 1973). The Who's faith in love then bounces back some from the self-doubt of 1971. It still has some healing powers, but now it is also seen as alternating with the restless dark nights, and the not knowing what is needed or where things should be headed.

Summation

The inner divisions in the counterculture present at the inception remain when the millennial hopes have faded. Expectations of generational identity and a transformed world dissipated, and yet the vacillation between despair and grand hopes were characteristic of some of the more prominent counterculture musicians in the 1970s. Yet before the 1960s hippies became 1980s yuppies, in the 1970s the communal ideals turned into the spiritual self-improvement movements of the 1970s, as well as a concern to be pure and natural that were part of the New Age sensibility of the "me decade." The 1970s, then, were a strange mixture of retreat, continuity and reversal. The counterculture generation neither sustained their transcendent vision nor resolved their contradictory loyalties. It brought with it millennial expectations, peak experiences, disillusionment, renewed hopes, and going back and forth between them.

Cultural radical movements envision a transformed world where communality and liberation co-exist, while they dread immersion in corruption and an empty materialism. Yet they have loyalties to the affluence they appear to disregard; few rock stars reject the wealth they accumulate. Success and status were embraced by many former youthful rebels who once rejected materialistic values.

The 1960s-1970s counterculture were not the first generation of youthful American and British rebels. They actually repeated a U.S. cycle that has been going on since the days of the American revolution. Every generation

CHAPTER 10: FOREVER YOUNG

of American cultural and political radicals have over time often embraced contradictory actions. In 1776, the American revolutionaries were against the autocracy of the English King in the name of the inalienable rights of liberty and the pursuit of happiness. Less than a dozen years later, a Constitution was drafted that institutionalized slavery and created a potentially powerful presidency. This governmental document both gave this Commander in Chief extensive powers and sought to limit them. They found themselves somewhat moving away from the principles that justified their war for independence. Subsequent generations of radicals have had equally contradictory impulses and over time have gone from millennial hopes to disillusionment and sometimes embracing what they once rejected. These movements periodically reappear and go through a parallel cycle of idealistic, even transcendent rebellion, retreat, resilience, vacillation, and self-contradiction.

Many former 60's cultural radicals lived out their middle and later years upholding values against which they protested as youths. Some went from being yippies to yuppies. The journeys of two non-musicians and one-time allies, Jerry Rubin and Abby Hoffman are illustrative. On August 24, 1967 to protest the Vietnam War and capitalism, pranksters Hoffman, Rubin and friends threw money down at the traders on the floor of the New York Stock Exchange. In March, 1968, they announced the formation of the Youth International Party, or yippies, an attempt to unite cultural and political radicals. As the seventies wore on Hoffman kept the political and revolutionary faith, but was diagnosed as bipolar, and as his hopes faded, took his own life in 1989. Jerry Rubin in a clear reversal of prior beliefs, became a capitalist, one of the earliest investors in Apple. Rubin declared, "wealth creation is the real American revolution. Money is power," He goes on, that he can be "more effective" in a suit and "working on Wall Street" than "dancing outside the walls of power" (Moretta, 2017, p. 354). Then there is the journey of Jane Fonda. She is the daughter of legendary screen actor Henry Fonda, a movie star herself at a young age, then in the 1970's she was labeled Hanoi Jane for her anti-Vietnam war activities, in the 1980s she sold millions of copies of an exercise video. In 2019, at the age of 81, she protested weekly in DC in front of the Capitol about climate change. She was arrested on multiple successive Friday's.

As the Grateful Dead said way back when, it has been a long, strange trip. Many of the once cultural radicals of the 1960s continued to vacillate, reverse themselves, reject themselves, affirm values they once rejected, achieve elf-realization, and/or find creative alternatives for themselves. The recurring dilemma for the various generations of cultural radicals is learning how to face the ways in which redemption and destruction are too often interconnected. The vitality identified with youth needs to recognize its relationship with hate and darkness. No generation of cultural radicals has fully confronted this dilemma, has integrated the dark and the light. The legacy of the 60s and various other generations of youthful cultural radicals are also lessons in life. In modern existence, while resolving conflicts, solving what appears to be insolvable, self-actualization, and progress happen all the time, yet not all self-deceptions are recognized, nor are all paradoxes and contradictions resolved. Movements and individuals have traits that often move in opposite directions at the same time.

REFERENCES

Ackles, D. (1969). Subway to the country. On *Subway to the country.* Elektra.

Amboy Dukes. (1968). Journey to the center of the mind. On *Journey to the center of the mind.* Mainstream.

Band, The. (1969). Up on Cripple Creek. On *The Band.* Capitol: 132.

Beach Boys. (1966). Good vibrations. Capitol. 5676.

Beach Boys, (1971). Student Demonstration Time, On *Surf's Up.* Reprise: RS 6453.

Beatles. (1964). You can't do that. On *A Hard Day's Night.* Parlophone: CDP 7464372.

Beatles. (1965). Help! On *Help!* Parlophone: CDP 7464392.

Beatles. (1965). It's Only Love, On *Help!* Parlophone: CDP 7464392.

Beatles. (1965). Yesterday. On *Help!* Parlophone: CDP 7464392.

Beatles. (1965). You've got to hide your love away. On *Help!* Parlophone: CDP 7464392.

Beatles. (1988). We can work it out. On *Past masters, Vol. 2.* Parlophone: CDP 7900442. (Original work released 1965)

Beatles. (1965). Girl. On *Rubber Soul.* Capitol: 2442.

Beatles. (1965). Run for your life. On *Rubber soul.* Capitol: 2442.

Beatles. (1965). The word. On *Rubber soul.* Capitol: 2442.

Beatles. (1966). Eleanor Rigby. On *Revolver.* Capitol: ST 2576.

Beatles. (1966). Good day sunshine. On *Revolver.* Capitol: ST 2576.

CHAPTER 10: FOREVER YOUNG

Beatles. (1966). Here, there, and everywhere. On *Revolver*. Capitol: ST 2576.
Beatles. (1966). Tomorrow never knows. On *Revolver*. Capitol: ST 2576.
Beatles. (1967). A day in the life. On *Sgt. Pepper's Lonely Hearts Club Band*. Capitol: 2653.
Beatles. (1967). Fixing a hole. On *Sgt. Pepper's Lonely Hearts Club Band*. Capitol: 2653.
Beatles. (1967). She's leaving home. On *Sgt. Pepper's Lonely Hearts Club Band*. Capitol: 2653.
Beatles. (1967). Within you, without you. On *Sgt. Pepper's Lonely Hearts Club Band*. Capitol: 2653.
Beatles. (1967). Hello, goodbye. On *Magical Mystery Tour*. Capitol: SMAL-2835.
Beatles. (1967). I am the walrus. On *Magical Mystery Tour*. Capitol: SMAL-2835.
Beatles. (1967). Penny Lane. On *Magical Mystery Tour*. Capitol: SMAL-2835.
Beatles. (1967). Strawberry fields forever. On *Magical Mystery Tour*. Capitol: SMAL-2835.
Beatles. (1968). Revolution. On *White Album*. Apple: CDP 7 46443 2.
Beatles. (1969). The end. On *Abbey Road*. Apple: 383.
Beatles. (1969). You never give me your money. On *Abbey Road*. Apple: 383.
Beatles. (1970). Let it be. On *Let It Be*. Apple: AR 34001.
Big Brother and the Holding Company (1968). Turtle blues. On *Cheap Thrills*. Columbia KCS 9700.
Billboard. (2020). Dark side of the moon. https://www.billboard.com/articles/events/greatest-of-all-time/6760799/pink-floyd-dark-side-of-the-moon-most-weeks-billboard-200-title
Canned Heat. (1970). Amphetamine Annie. On *Cookbook*. Liberty. LST 11000.
Canned Heat. (1970). Goin' up the country. On *Cookbook*. Liberty: LST 11000.
Capaldi, J. (1975). Living on a marble. On *Short Cut Draw Blood*. Island: ILPS 9336.
Chiasson, D. (2017, October 2). Joni Mitchell's openhearted heroism, *The New Yorker*.

https://www.newyorker.com/magazine/2017/10/09/joni-mitchells-openhearted-heroism

Cohen, L. (1967). One of us cannot be wrong. On *Songs of Leonard Cohen.* Columbia: CS 9533.

Cohen. L. (1967). Suzanne. On *Songs of Leonard Cohen.* Columbia: CS 9533.

Cohen. L. (1969). Bird on a wire. On *Songs From A Room.* Columbia: CS 9767.

Cohen, L. (1971). Famous blue raincoat. On *Songs of Love and Hate.* Columbia: 88697047412.

Cohen, L. (1974). Field commander Cohen. On *New Skin for the Old Ceremony.* Columbia: C 33167.

Cohen, L. (1974). I tried to leave you. On *New Skin for the Old Ceremony.* Columbia: C 33167.

Cohen, L. (1974). There is a war. On *New Skin for the Old Ceremony.* Columbia: C 33167.

Cooper, A. (1971). Eighteen. On *Love It to Death.* Straight: WS 1883.

Country Joe and the Fish (1967). Bass Strings. On *Electric Music for the Mind and Body.* Vanguard: VSD 79244.

Country Joe & the Fish (1967). The bomb song. On *I Feel Like I'm Fixing' To Die.* Vanguard: VSD-79266.

Country Joe & the Fish (1967). I-feel-like-I'm-fixing'-to-die rag. On *I Feel Like I'm Fixing' To Die.* Vanguard: VSD-79266.

Country Joe & the Fish (1967). Who am I. On *I Feel Like I'm Fixing' To Die.* Vanguard: VSD-79266.

Cream. (1966). I feel free. On *Fresh Cream.* Atco: SD-33-206.

Crosby, Stills, Nash and Young (1970). Ohio. On *So Far.* Atlantic: SD 19119-2.

Donovan. (1966). Season of the witch. On *Sunshine Superman.* Epic: BN 26217.

Donovan. (2004). Wear your love like heaven. On *The Essential Donovan.* Epic: EK 90625. (Original work released 1967)

Doors. (1967). The end. On *The Doors.* Elektra: EKS 74007.

Doors. (1970). Roadhouse blues. On *Morrison Hotel.* Elektra: EKS-75007.

Duncan, L. (1971). Love song. On *Sing Children Sing.* Columbia: C 30663.

Dylan, B. (1963). Blowin' in the wind. On *The Freewheelin' Bob Dylan.* Columbia: CL 1986.

CHAPTER 10: FOREVER YOUNG

Dylan, B. (1963). Don't think twice it's all right. On *The Freewheelin' Bob Dylan*. Columbia: CL 1986.
Dylan, B. (1963). Masters of war. On *The Freewheelin' Bob Dylan*. Columbia: CL 1986.
Dylan. B. (1964) The times they are a-changin.' On *The Times They Are A-Changin.'* Columbia: CS 8905.
Dylan, B. (1964). My back pages. On *Another Side of Bob Dylan*. Columbia: CS 8993.
Dylan, B. (1965). It ain't me babe. On *Bringing It All Back Home*. Columbia: CS 9128.
Dylan, B. (1965). Maggie's farm. On *Bringing It All Back Home*. Columbia: CS 9128.
Dylan, B. (1965). Mr. Tambourine man. On *Bringing It All Back Home*. Columbia: CS 9128.
Dylan, B. (1965). Subterranean homesick blues. On *Bringing It All Back Home*. Columbia: CS 9128.
Dylan, B. (1965). Ballad of a thin man. On *Highway 61 Revisited*. Columbia: CL 2389.
Dylan, B. (1965). Desolation row. On *Highway 61 Revisited*. Columbia: CL 2389.
Dylan, B. (1965). Just like Tom Thumb's blues. On *Highway 61 Revisited*. Columbia: CL 2389.
Dylan, B. (1965). Like A rolling stone. On *Highway 61 Revisited*. Columbia: CL 2389.
Dylan, B. (2000). Positively fourth street. On *Essential Bob Dylan*. Columbia: C2K 85168. (Original song released 1965)
Dylan. (1966). Rainy day women 12x35. On *Blonde on Blonde*. Columbia: C2S 841.
Dylan, B. (1966). Visions of Johanna. On *Blonde on Blonde*. Columbia: C2S 841.
Dylan, B. (1967). All along the watchtower. On John *Wesley Harding*. Columbia: CS 9604.
Dylan, B. (1967). I dreamed I saw St. Augustine. On *John Wesley Harding*. Columbia: CS 9604.
Dylan, B. (1970). *New morning*. Columbia: 30290.
Dylan, B. (1971). Watching the river flow. On *Greatest Hits, Volume II*. Columbia: C2K 65976.
Dylan, B. (1975). Shelter from the storm. On *Blood On the Tracks*. Columbia: CK 92398.

Fugs (1965). Hallucination horrors. On *Virgin Fugs*. ESP: 1038.
Ginsburg, A. (1956). *Howl*. City Lights Books.
Grateful Dead (1970). Truckin.' On *American Beauty*. Warner Brothers: WS 12893.
Greenwald, M. (n.d.). The trip. Allmusic. https://www.allmusic.com/song/the-trip-mt0027175328.
Guess Who (1971). Undun. On *Best of the Guess Who*. RCA: 1004 (original work released 1969).
Hardin, T. (1994). Misty roses. On *Hang on to a Dream: The Verve Recordings*. Polydor: D 202549. (Original work released 1965)
Hardin, T. (1994). It's hard to believe in love for long. On *Hang on to a Dream: The Verve Recordings*. Polydor: D 202549. (Original work released 1966)
Harrison, G. (1970). Isn't it a pity. On *All Things Must Pass*. Apple: STCH 639.
Hartz, L. (1955). *The liberal tradition in America*. Harcourt, Brace & Co.
Havens, R. (1970). Freedom. On *Woodstock*. Cotillion: SD 3-500.
Hendrix, J. (1967). Are you experienced? On *Are You Experienced*. Reprise: RS-6261
Hendrix, J. (1967). I Don't Live Today. On *Are You Experienced*. Reprise: RS-6261.
Hendrix, J. (1967). Manic depression. On *Are You Experienced* Reprise: RS-6261.
Hendrix., J. (1967). Purple haze. On *Are You Experienced* Reprise: RS-6261.
Hendrix, J. (1971). Freedom. On *The Cry o Love*. Reprise: MS2034.
It's A Beautiful Day (1969). Girl with no eyes. On *It's A Beautiful Day*. Columbia: CS 9768.
Jefferson Airplane (1967). White rabbit. On *Surrealistic Pillow*. RCA Victor: LPM-3766.
Jefferson Airplane. (1968). Lather. On *Crown of Creation*. RCA Victor: LSP-4058.
Jefferson Airplane. (1969). Volunteers. On *Volunteers*. RCA Victor: LSP4238.
Jefferson Airplane. (1969). We can be together. On *Volunteers*. RCA Victor: LSP4238.
Kingston Trio. (1990). Where Have All the Flowers Gone. On *Capitol Collector's Series*. Capitol: CDP-592710. (Original work released 1961)

CHAPTER 10: FOREVER YOUNG

Kinks. (1966). A Well-Respected Man. On *Greatest Hits.* Reprise: RS-6217.
Kinks. (1966), Dedicated Follower of Fashion. On *Greatest Hits.* Reprise: RS-6217.
Lennon, J. (1997). Give Peace a Chance. On *Lennon Legend.* Parlophone: 724382195429 (original work released 1969).
Lennon, J. (1970). God. On *Plastic Ono Band.* Apple: SW 3372.
Lennon, J. (1971). How. On *Imagine.* Apple: SW 3379.
Lennon, J. (1971). Imagine. On *Imagine.* Apple: SW 3379.
Lennon, J. (1971). Power to the people. On *Lennon Legend.* Parlophone: 724382195429.
Lennon, J. (1997). Whatever Gets You Thru the Night. On *Lennon Legend.* Parlophone: 724382195429. (Original work released 1974)
Love. (1966). Signed D.C. On *Love.* Elektra: EKS-74001
Lovin' Spoonful. (1966). Daydream. On *Daydream.* Kama Sutra: KLPS-8051.
Lovin' Spoonful. (1990). Darling Be Home Soon. On *Anthology.* Rhino: R2 70944. (Original work released 1967)
Lovin' Spoonful. (1990). Younger generation. On *Anthology.* Rhino: R2 70944. (original work released 1967).
Marqusee, M. (2003) *Chimes of freedom: The politics of Bob Dylan's art* , 2003, New Press.
McGuire, B. (1965). Eve of Destruction. On *Eve of Destruction.* Dunhill: 50003.
McKenzie, S. (1967). San Francisco. On *The Voice of.* Ode: Z12 44002.
McLean, D. (1971). American Pie. On *American Pie.* United Artists: UAS 5535.
McLean, D. (1972). Dreidel. On *Don McLean.* United Artists: UAS 5651.
Mitchell, J. (1970). Woodstock. On *Ladies of the Canyon.* Reprise: 6376.
Mitchell, J. (1971). A case of you. On *Blue.* Reprise: 2038-2.
Mitchell, J. (1971). River. On *Blue.* Reprise: 2038-2.
Mitchell, J. (1971). The last time I saw Richard. On *Blue.* Reprise: 2038-2.
Moody Blues (1968). Legend of a mind. On *In Search of the Lost Chord.* Deram: 18017.
Moretta, J. (2017), *The hippies: A 1960s history.* McFarland & Company.

Mothers of Invention. (1967). Plastic People. On *Absolutely Free.* Verve: V6-5013.

Myers, M.. 2016. How Jefferson Airplane's Grace Slick wrote 'White Rabbit.' *Wall Street Journal.* https://www.wsj.com/articles/how-jefferson-airplanes-grace-slick-wrote-white-rabbit-1464712102.

Nash, G. (1971). Chicago/We can change the world. On *Songs for Beginners.* Atlantic: SD 7204.

Ochs, P. (1965). Here's to the State of Mississippi. On *I Ain't Marching Anymore.* Elektra: EKS-7287.

Ochs, P.., (1965). I Ain't Marching Anymore. On *I Ain't Marching Anymore.* Elektra: EKS-7287.

Ochs, P. (1966). There but for fortune. On *In Concert.* Elektra: EKS-7310.

Ochs, P. (1967). Cross my heart. On *Pleasures of the Harbor.* A & M: 133.

Ochs, P. (1967). Outside of A Small Circle of Friends. On *Pleasures of the Harbor.* A & M: 133.

Paul Revere and the Raiders. (1966). Kicks. On *Midnight Ride.* Columbia: CS 9308.

Paxton, T. (1999). My son, John. On *The Best of Tom Paxton.* Elektra: R2 73515. (Original work released 1966)

Peter, Paul, and Mary. (1962). If I had a hammer. On *Peter, Paul and Mary.* Warner Brothers: WS 1449.

Pink Floyd. (1973). *Dark side of the moon.* Capitol: CDP 7 46001-2.

Pink Floyd. (1975). Shine on you crazy diamond. On *Wish You Were Here.* Columbia: PC 33453.

Pink Floyd. (1975). Wish you were here. On *Wish You Were Here.* Columbia: PC 33453.

Procol Harum. (1967). Whiter shade of pale. On *Procol Harum.* Deram: DES-18008.

Procol Harum. (1968). Shine on brightly. On *Shine on Brightly.* A & M: SP-4151.

Rascals. (1967). Groovin'. On *Groovin'.* Atlantic: SD 8148.

Rascals. (1968). People got to be free. On *Freedom Suite.* Atlantic: SD-2-901.

Rivers, J. (1968). Summer rain. On *Realization.* Imperial: LP12372. (Original work released 1967)

Rolling Stones. (1965). Heart of stone. On *The Rolling Stones, Now!* London: 420.

CHAPTER 10: FOREVER YOUNG

Rolling Stones. (1966). Lady Jane. On *Aftermath*. London: PS 476.
Rolling Stones. (1966). Mother's little helper. On *Aftermath*. London: PS 476.
Rolling Stones. (1966). Paint it black. On *Aftermath*. London: PS 476.
Rolling Stones. (1967). Ruby Tuesday. On *Between the Buttons*. London: PS 499.
Rolling Stones. (1967). She smiled sweetly. On *Between the Buttons*. London: PS 499.
Rolling Stones. (1967). Yesterday's papers. On *Between the Buttons*. London: PS 499.
Rolling Stones. (1967). Sittin' on a fence. On *Flowers*. London: PS 509.
Rolling Stones. (1968). Street fighting man. On *Beggars Banquet*. London: PS 539.
Rolling Stones. (1971). Sister morphine. On *Sticky Fingers*. Rolling Stone Records: COC 59100.
Seeger, P. (2002). Little boxes. On *Greatest Hits*. Columbia: CK 65711. (Original work released 1963)
Simon, P. (1971). Everything put together falls apart. On *Paul Simon*. Columbia: KC 30750.
Simon, P. (1973). American tune. On *There Goes Rhymin' Simon*. Columbia: KC 32280.
Simon, P. (1975). Still crazy after all these years. On *Still Crazy After All These Years*. Columbia: PC 33540.
Simon and Garfunkel. (1966). 59th street bridge song. On *Parsley, Sage, Rosemary and Thyme*. Columbia: CL 2653.
Simon and Garfunkel. (1968). Fakin' it. On *Bookends*. Columbia: KCS 9529.
Simon and Garfunkel. (1968). Mrs. Robinson. On *Bookends*. Columbia: KCS 9529.
Sly and the Family Stone (1969). Everyday people. On *Stand*. Epic: 26456.
Sly & the Family Stone (1970). Everyday people. On *Greatest Hits*. Epic: KE 30325
Spanky and Our Gang. (1967). Commercial. On *Spanky and Our Gang*. Mercury: SR 61124.
Spanky and Our Gang. (1968). Like to get to know you. On *Like to Get to Know You*. Mercury: SR 61161.
Steppenwolf. (1968). Magic carpet ride. On *The Second*. Dunhill: 5007.
Steppenwolf. (1968). The pusher. On *Steppenwolf*. Dunhill: DS-50029.

St. Marie, B. (1966). The universal soldier. On *It's My Way*. Vanguard: VSD-79142.
Taylor, J. (1968). Knocking around the zoo. On *James Taylor*. Apple: SKAO-3352.
Ten Years After. (1971). I'd love to change the world. On *A Space in Time*. Chrysalis: ZCHR 1001.
The Byrds. (1966). 5D. On *Fifth Dimension*. Columbia: CS 9349.
Troggs. (1968). Love is all around. On *Best of*. Fontana: TL 640.
Velvet Underground. (2005). Heroin. On *Gold*. Polydor: B0004373-02. (Original work released 1966)
Waldman, W. (1974). Mad, mad me. On *Gypsy Symphony*. Warner Brothers: BS 2792.
Whitely, S. (1992). *The space between the notes: Rock and the counter-culture*. Routledge.
Who. (1965). My generation. On *My Generation*. Decca: DL 4664.
Who. (1969). I'm free. On *Tommy*. Decca: DXSW 7205.
Who, (1969). We're not gonna take it. On *Tommy*. Decca: DXSW 7205.
Who. (1971). Behind blue eyes. On *Who's Next*. Decca: DL 79182.
Who. (1971). We won't get fooled again. On *Who's Next*. Decca: DL 79182.
Who. (2002). Let's see action. On *The Ultimate Collection*. MCA: 088112877-2. (Original work released 1971)
Who. (2002). Love reign o'er me. On *The Ultimate Collection*. MCA: 088112877-2. (Original work released 1973)
Young, N. (1970). Cinnamon girl. On *Everybody Knows This is Nowhere*. Reprise: 6349.
Young, N. (1972). Heart of gold. On *Harvest*. Reprise: MS 2032.
Young, N. (1972). The needle and the damage done. On *Harvest*. Reprise: MS 2032.
Youngbloods. (1967). Get together. On *The Youngbloods*. RCA Victor: LPM-3724.

CHAPTER 11

THE AGE OF MIRACLE AND WONDERS: PAUL SIMON AND THE CHANGING AMERICAN DREAM

When the Soviets launched the Sputnik satellite in October 1957, it burst the bubble of American technological supremacy and ushered in an era of self-questioning. Since the end of World War II, the U. S. had been transforming the way it lived. Affluence was spreading, families were moving to suburbs in droves; their homes became their castles. These dwellings became stocked with washers, televisions, high fidelity systems, and all sorts of mechanical marvels. More cars were being purchased than ever before, individuals were getting married younger, the country was in the midst of a baby boom, and a national celebration of itself. Yet all was not heavenly in the split-level paradise. A restlessness and unease were also part of these new wonders. That the Soviets could be ahead of us in direct competition was a narcissistic blow. Historian William Leuchtenburg captured something when he titled his history of post- World War II America, *A Troubled Feast*.

A few months after Sputnik, two teenage boys from Queens had a hit record entitled "Hey Schoolgirl." Fifty-eight years later, one of them, Paul Simon, remains a cultural icon. He garners attention whether in 2015 he is the closing act on the 40th Anniversary broadcast of Saturday Night Live or he and his bride of two decades get arrested in 2014 for disturbing the peace in their suburban Connecticut home. Through it all, Simon has been chronicling the joys and angst of American life, amidst our nation's changing ideals.

In the nineteenth century, as work became separated from home and immigrants flooded the country, the American dream had a distinctly male cast. It was centered around economic opportunity and career success for men. Women and families fit into this dream with wives taking care of home, hearth, and children. Males and females were usually seen as occupying separate spheres, and having different interests and natures. With the rise of the consumer culture in the twentieth century, affluence spread into the home in new ways, and the scope of the American dream was expanding. An ideal of companionate marriage appeared. Husbands and wives were supposed to find fulfillment material, spiritual, and sexual with their marriage partners. The pursuit of happiness spread from the boardroom to the bedroom. The popularity of movies, magazines, radio, television and records brought new horizons to many. The American dream for many now consisted of career success, family happiness, relational fulfillment, and romantic union. In the 1960s, a generational consciousness emerged among an influential segment of the baby boomers. The songs and singing of Paul Simon were a central part of this movement. This presentation will examine the dimensions Simon brings to our understanding of how the American dream has altered.

Paul Simon was born on October 13, 1941 in Newark, New Jersey to Jewish parents who were both educators. His father was also a jazz musician. Paul's brother, Eddie, is four years his junior. The family moved to the Forest Hills section of Queens, where he met Art Garfunkel when they were eleven. After their initial success with "Hey Schoolgirl," there were no more hits for the duo before they graduated high school. Simon went on to major in English at Queens College, briefly attended law school, left to pursue a career in music, and reunited with Garfunkel. The duo recorded an acoustic folk album in 1964 for Columbia records that commercially went nowhere. Later, the album's producer added electric guitars and a rock backbeat to one of the tracks, "The Sounds of Silence." Released as a single in late 1965, the song made it to number one on the Billboard charts. Simon has been a prominent singer-songwriter from then until now. He is a member of the Songwriters Hall of Fame, has been elected twice to the Rock n' Roll Hall of Fame, and has won twelve Grammy's, three of which were for album of the year.

An unstated undertone in Paul Simon's compositions connects the personal with the collective. He chronicles the ups and downs of the pursuit of happiness, including the ways our emotional beings intertwine with the state of the union. Simon sometimes adds a religious or spiritual dimension to this mix of concerns.

Simon and Garfunkel's first hit, "The Sound of Silence" from late 1965, contains an early hint of the connection between our emotional and collective states. Initially the singer is talking to his old friend, darkness, then he is recounting a dream. It seems we are infected by silence, by a distance between ourselves and others. The dreamer sees ten thousand people maybe more. This crowd talks and hears, but does not listen. The

CHAPTER 11: THE AGE OF MIRACLE AND WONDERS

singer tells the multitude that silence grows like a cancer, but he is not heard as they are praying to a neon God. There are messages to be heard, as prophets write them on subway walls and tenement halls. There is then an underground alternative to the growing malady of silence (The Sound of Silence 1965).

Three years later, "Mrs. Robinson" made it to number one on the Billboard singles chart. The singer asks Joe DiMaggio, the retired Yankee centerfielder, where he has gone, then says, "A nation turns its lonely eyes to you." This song is about those in the U.S. who have lost their way. The singer tells Mrs. Robinson that he would like to help her learn to help herself and that Jesus loves her more than she knows. But help herself from what? The answer is from secrets and hiding places that, among other things, are kept from the children. The lonely malaise is not only about a life of disguise. In choosing between political candidates, among other things, "Every way you look at it you lose." Neither politics nor affluent domesticity have brought satisfaction. It is not surprising then that the song concludes with the line "'Joltin' Joe' has left and gone away" (Mrs. Robinson, 1968). Our unease cannot be remedied when national heroes abandon the field of dreams. The pursuit of happiness has turned into lonely lives of deception. The American dream is not fulfilling its promise.

Also in 1968 is the song entitled "America." Here the personal and collective seem to be equated. Kathy and the singer board a bus in Pittsburgh. He tells her, "I've come to look for America." At first, they are playing and laughing together, then silence and distance appear. When she falls asleep, the singer says, "Kathy, I'm lost… I'm empty and aching and I don't know why." Looking for America he has found a hole in his soul. And he is not alone. While counting cars on the New Jersey Turnpike, he recognizes too that all of them have come to look for America. The implication is that as a nation we have not found our way (America, 1968).

The collective discontent is connected to the personal. In 1967, Simon sings about being hard to please, about seeing what's become of me while looking for "my possibilities." He is told to hang on to hope, but then sings "if your hopes should pass away, Simply pretend that you can build them again" (A Hazy Shade of Winter, 1966). It is not always easy to follow novelist William Dean Howells advice to look at the smiling aspects of life. Simon sings of being "a dubious soul" who gets worn down walking in the garden. He admits that "I've just been fakin' it / Not really makin' it" (Fakin' It, 1967). Being lost is not just individual, Simon sees our nation as lonely and aching.

On his first solo album in 1971, Simon notices "so many people slipping away." There are those who take downs to sleep and ups to get on their way. Some folks "are crazy" and others "walk that borderline" (Everything Put Together Falls Apart, 1971). There does not seem to be hope in politics. When Simon goes to Washington to see his Congressman, he is not received. Simon becomes weary, and says "I've about waited all I can" (Armistice Day, 1971). With all these problems, Simon recognizes, "Everything put together Sooner or later falls apart" (Everything Put Together Falls Apart, 1971).

Yet despite this fragmenting, on the other hand, even though there are those who oppress others by beating them with wires and chains, Simon says, "you can't outrun the history train" (Peace Like A River, 1971). It seems then that there is suffering and self-abuse, that things put together will fall apart, yet there is a movement that will bring freedom, if not happiness or personal hope.

In the United States in the late 1960s and early 1970s, many things were moving in opposite directions. There were the national traumas of the 1968 assassinations of Martin Luther King Jr. and Bobby Kennedy, and the continuing mire of the Vietnam War. The economy had been somewhat floundering since 1968, divorces were rising significantly, some in the youth generation were questioning dominant values, and feminism was reviving. At the same time the civil rights movement and radical left had splintered. After 1970, anti-war demonstrations attracted fewer people. Cultural radicals were becoming disillusioned. John Lennon sang of the dream being over, The Who did not want to get fooled again, and Ten Years After said they would love to change the world but they did not know what to do.

Into this mix, in 1973 Paul Simon released his second composition with America in the title, and again connects the personal with the collective. "American Tune" begins with Simon singing of his being confused, mistaken, misused, forsaken, and weary. He then extends this to others.

CHAPTER 11: THE AGE OF MIRACLE AND WONDERS

Simon does not know anyone who has not been battered, and none of his friends feel at ease. This malaise impacts the nation, "I don't know a dream that's not been shattered or driven to its knees." He cannot help wondering "what went wrong." As in "Sounds of Silence," the song's narrator starts to dream. In this state, he clearly sees the "Statue of Liberty Sailing Away to sea." As with Joe DiMaggio abandoning ship, here the grand statue that represents freedom and opportunity is leaving our shores. Those who placed faith in the American promise have been forsaken; our collective dreams have battered. Simon comes "in the age's most uncertain hour" to "sing an American tune." He recognizes that we did live well for a long time and we cannot be "forever blessed." Amidst this uncertainty and disillusionment, he still must go on. Tomorrow, he sings, is "another working day" and he wants to "get some rest" (American Tune, 1973). Simon was weary when his Congressman would not see him and now this returns amidst national confusion.

Simon revisits this mixture of the personal and the collective in 1975. He recounts meeting an old lover on the street, then sharing beer and reminiscing about old times. He concludes that they are still crazy after all these years. He includes himself in this madness, as he "ain't no fool for love songs That whisper in my ears." He knows he is "Longing my life away," but so what "It's all gonna fade." Still this personal dissatisfaction may take its toll. He worries about doing damage one day. But, if he commits crimes he will "not be convicted By a jury of my peers... Still crazy after all these years" (Still Crazy After All These Years, 1975). We live among those who are equally disordered and who will acquit peers who commit criminal acts. The age's hour remains uncertain.

The American dream includes political democracy and economic opportunity. With DiMaggio having left and the Statue of Liberty sailing out to sea, as the years pass Simon finds that those in power do not always face social misery. He sings of "all the suffering that mankind must endure" (Senorita with A Necklace of Tears, 2000). For "people are suffering All over the world" (Adios Hermanos, 1997). To him, "It's outrageous to line your pockets off the misery of the poor. Outrageous, the crimes some humans must endure" (Outrageous,2006). We pay a price "When evil walks the planet, And love is crushed like clay, The master races, the chosen peoples, the burning temples, the weeping cathedrals" (Love, 2000). These injustices show that exploitation and destruction rather than opportunity and communion may often prevail. Public officials may not respond to these threats or to their constituents. During the Vietnam War, Simon longed for an armistice and goes to Washington, then finds "my Congressman [is] avoiding me" (Armistice Day, 1971). Simon is aware of both the evasion of those who are elected to serve us, and the human costs of exploitation and armed conflict. He writes of how in war families are "scattered and broken," and how a mother draws her "babies closer" and to "drive away despair she says a wartime prayer" (Wartime Prayers, 2006). Simon laments how "many wars have come and gone." As well, "Genocide still goes on" (Old, 2000). These are all disturbing phenomenon. Sometime Simon worries that he may be "blind/ To the fate of mankind, /But what can be done?" (Have A Good Time, 1975). It is this sense that political action may be futile that concerns Simon. He declares, "Politics is ugly" (Love Is Eternal Sacred Light, 2011). It has not been unusual in American history for those aware of suffering and injustice to become weary and disillusioned with reform or revolution, and like Simon are not sure that the political side of the American dream holds promise. Some have maintained that the disenchantment with political action in the American dream has been replaced by ideals of affluence, consumerism, personal fulfillment, romance, and family happiness. While love songs have long been a staple of popular music, not that many songwriters address marriage and parenthood. Paul Simon has multiple songs about the side of the American dream.

I begin with Paul Simon's treatment of parenthood. In "Loves Me Like A Rock," a son sings, "My mama loves . . . me. She gets down on her knees and hugs me. She loves me like a rock…" (Loves Me Like A Rock, 1973). Not a bad legacy. In "St Judy's Comet," Paul's son's bedtime has long been past, and his "famous daddy" is trying to sing his youngster to sleep. Paul tells his boy he longs to see the "spray of diamonds" from "St Judy's Comet Sparkle in your eyes." Still though his son has "weary eyes," despite his father's serenade, he is not falling asleep (St. Judy's Comet, 1973). In his 1977 hit single, "Slip Slidin' Away," Simon knows of a father who travels a long way to see his son. The dad's intention is to explain to his child all the things he has done. He finds him, kisses the boy, then heads back. Clearly, this is a situation where the child and father do not reside together. We then have a different family reality.

CHAPTER 11: THE AGE OF MIRACLE AND WONDERS

In "Graceland," the singer is traveling with his nine-year-old son, the child of his first marriage. They are heading to Elvis's former home in Memphis, where he expects he and his child will be received (Graceland, 1986). On the same album, a different male narrator tells his son, "You are the burden of my generation. I sure do love you, But let's get that straight" (That Was Your Mother, 1986). But that last composition is an exception to Simon's sentiments about parenthood. More typical is "Father and Daughter," where he tells his youngster:

> I'm gonna stand guard like a postcard of a Golden Retriever.
> And never leave 'til I leave you with a sweet dream in your head.
> I'm gonna watch you shine,
> Gonna watch you grow...
> There could never be a father
> who loved his daughter more than I love you"
> (Father and Daughter, 2006)

Whatever the ups and downs of a marriage, Simon usually sings of the special bond a parent feels towards children, and the good wishes, the love parenthood awakens. It is not infrequent for there to be ambivalence in the songs of Paul Simon. This is much less so in his compositions about children and parents.

In writing about relationships, early on, Simon had written about inauthentic dangling conversations with "superficial sighs" (Dangling Conversation, 1966). Later, he changed. In 1975, he writes that "Once in a while from out of nowhere. When you don't expect it, and you're unprepared, Somebody will come and lift you higher And your burdens will be shared" (Gone At Last, 1975). In the most popular composition of his long career, Simon addresses someone who is weary, feeling small, crying, and alone. Then he writes, "If you need a friend, I'm sailing right behind, Like a bridge over troubled water, I will ease your mind" (Bridge Over Troubled Water, 1970). Humans can reach across the gap of silence and turn isolation into sharing and caring.

But what about love? We get a different slice of the exaltation of romantic and marital companionship of the American dream in what Simon writes. He says that "We crave [love] so badly. Makes you want to laugh out loud when you receive it. And Gobble it like candy." He adds, "Sometimes it's easy. But it's not easy. You're going to break down and cry." Despite the volatility of love, Simon thinks, "We should be grateful" (Love, 2000). He is preoccupied with both the fulfillments and frustrations of romance. For love can ease your demons. Simon writes, "I was in crazy motion/ 'Til you calmed me down.../ It took a little time/ To Get to me" (Something So Right, 1973). In another song, "You rescued me when I was blind. And you put me on your pillow/ When I was on the wall" (You're Kind, 1975).

But sustaining the magic of intimacy is the challenge. Simon writes of "the arc of a love affair" (Hearts and Bones, 1982). He sings, "I loved her the first time I saw her.../ The light of her beauty was warm as a summer day./ No hint of rain to come." But then, things altered: "when the rains came, the tears burned... It's easy to be generous when you're on a roll. It's hard to be grateful when you're out of control. And love is gone" (Love and Hard Times, 2011). Simon declares, "Negotiations and love songs, /Are often mistaken for one and the same" (Train in the Distance, 1981). One side of Simon is somewhat skeptical about these arcs in love affairs. On his first solo album, he writes, "Love is not a game. Love is not a toy. Love's no romance. Love will do you in. And love will wash you out" (Congratulations, 1971). Nearly thirty years later, a character in one of his songs proclaims, "Romance is a heartbreaker" (Darling Lorraine, 2000).

There are a variety of reason why love brings pain. Simon finds that sometimes kindness is not enough to sustain a relationship. He writes, "Why you don't treat me like the other humans do is just a mystery to me." He is delighted when he thinks "You're gonna love me now indefinitely." But then he does not stay. "I'm gonna leave you now. And here's the reason why. I like to sleep with the window open. And you keep the window closed. So goodbye" (You're Kind, 1975). Compatibility as well as tenderness are essential in keeping love going.

If romance without marriage is hard to sustain, what is marriage like? In "Hearts and Bones," "one-and-a-half wandering Jews" get married and travel. They are thrilled. "Love like lightning shaking till it moans." Things change. Later, the bride asks why don't you love me for who I am. The newlywed husband replies, "Cause that's not the way the world is baby. This is how I love you baby. This is how I love you baby." When they have returned from their journey, they "speculate who had been damaged the most," and wait to see if love is "restored." Then Simon says

CHAPTER 11: THE AGE OF MIRACLE AND WONDERS

something about what love is like, "You take two bodies and you twirl them into one. Their hearts and their bones. And they won't come undone" (Hearts and Bones, 1982). At least that is the hope. Simon writes about a couple who married and have a son. Yet even during pregnancy, "disagreements had begun. And in a while they fell apart. It wasn't hard to do." They stay in contact for the child and disagree about the meaning of the contract of marriage. Yet once in a while "He makes her laugh. She cooks a meal or two" (Train in the Distance, 1981). The ebb and flow of intimacy. In "Graceland," the singer recalls his first wife returning to tell him she is leaving. He says of course he knew what was happening in his own bed. She then says "losing love is like a window in your heart. Everybody sees you're blown apart" (Graceland, 1986).

In Simon's songs not all marriages collapse, not everything that is put together falls apart, yet turmoil and contradictions inevitably occur. One of his most remarkable compositions is from 1999 and is about the marriage of Frank and Lorraine. The first time he saw her, Frank knew she was what he was looking for. He thought she was hot and cool, and he was just "a fool in love with darling Lorraine." The couple married, but one day out of the blue she announces she is leaving. She says she is not a homemaker and she is tired of being darling Lorraine. Then the recriminations ensue. He says Lorraine is not the woman he married, you just stay in bed, I don't need you. But on a Christmas day, she wakes him up after making pancakes. They watch television, "All afternoon/ 'It's/ A Wonderful life.'" Later Lorraine is ill. Frank tells her "You're breathing is like an echo of our love." He gives Lorraine an extra blanket, and offers to go get her something sweet. Yet, "the moon in the meadow took darling Lorraine." Death finally separated this couple who loved and fought, who were bonded, yet she remained unsettled and unhealthy. In this song, no matter what as Frank says, "Darling Lorraine, Lorraine, I long for your love" (Darling Lorraine, 1999). Marriage has confrontations and recriminations . It may bring bliss or end in divorce. Simon knows that amidst the ebbs and flows, it is love that cements marriage. On his most recent studio album, in "Love and Hard Times" as in "Darling Lorraine," the man falls in love at first sight. He is generous when love flourishes, and out of control when it does not. And as in "Something So Right," the man is unsettled. He is not able to relax and has an uneasy heartbeat. "And then your hand takes mine. Thank God, I found you in time. Thank God I found you" (Love and Hard Times, 2011). "Love and blessings. Simple kindness.

Ours to hold but not to keep" (Love and Blessings, 2011). Love and marriage will always have arcs. Who knows in the twirl of romance and marriage what will keep the hearts and bones united and what will break them into pieces. Still, love and kindness bring blessings.

What Simon portrays about romantic coupling diverges from the ideal of the American dream of love everlasting with harmony and togetherness. As with his views on politics and America's uncertain hours, he often views the underside of the American promise. Yet even here, this is not the whole story of Paul Simon's complex relationship with his homeland and its dreams.

In 1975, he writes of his life being a mess, yet he insists, "I'm having a good time." He does wonder if he is "laughing [his] way to disaster." He then sees that his ability to enjoy himself is connected to American affluence. He declares: "God bless the goods we were given... [and] ... our standard of living./ Let's keep it that way, /And we'll all have a good time" (Have A Good Time, 1975). While we may not be able to bring order to our personal and collective fortunes, we can keep our country prosperous and enjoy ourselves, even if the world is falling apart. He is salvaging something from dreams being shattered. Simon is a champion of the affluence that American business brings. In 1976, he tells an interviewer, "practically speaking, I'm on the side of the capitalists" (Luftig, 1997, p. 113).

Simon desires to enjoy himself. In the "59th Street Bridge Song," he is "lookin' for fun" and wanting the morning time to drop all it petals on him. Reveling in the moment, he concludes, "Life, I love you, All is groovy" (59th Street Bridge Song, 1967). Nature brings pleasure on "a sunny day" with birds in the trees and "singing songs" on the radio. With nary a cloud in the sky, "Not a negative word was heard" (Was A Sunny Day, 1973). Similarly, the "cool, cool river Sweeps the wild, white ocean." Then Simon proclaims, "I believe in the future." His "radio" is "tuned to the voice of a star" (The Cool, Cool River, 1990). "Maybe love's an accident... But you and I were born beneath a star of Dazzling Blue" (Dazzling Blue, 2011). Our pleasure is enhanced by the universe in which we are embedded, and not only the cosmos, but the creations of humanity. The technology that is part of our standard of living brings both a good time and something beyond it. For "Kodachrome" gives us "nice bright

CHAPTER 11: THE AGE OF MIRACLE AND WONDERS

colors... the greens of summers." It makes "you think all the world's a sunny day" (Kodachorme, 1973). And there is more. To Simon, "These are the days of miracle and wonder." For not only does "the camera" follow "us in slo-mo" but we can gaze on a "distant constellation." We live where "medicine is magical and magical is art." We receive "signals of constant information" and miracle of miracles there may arise a "loose affiliation of millionaires And billionaires and baby." Yes, these are days of miracles and wonder. And one of these is that "every generation throws a hero up the pop charts" (The Boy in the Bubble, 1986).

As one who ascended to popularity, it is not surprising for Simon, that music too is a source of satisfaction, release, even redemption. He recalls that as a young man living in London in 1964, "the music was flowing. Amazing, And flowing my way" (The Late Great Johnny Ace, 1981). Then there is the "deep forbidden music" of Simon's adolescence, including the doo-wop groups the Penguins, Moonglows, Orioles and Five Satins. Simon sings that Rene and Georgette Magritte were longing for these sounds which brought forth an "easy stream of laughter" (Rene and Georgette Magritte With Their Dog After the War, 1982). At times, Simon can feel the weight of the world. His remedy is to have a good time, and music is often involved. To help himself he intends to take his burdens to Mardi Gras in New Orleans. There you can let "the music wash your soul" (Take Me to the Mardi Gras, 1973).

Sometimes Simon has to "Reach in the darkness... To overcome an obstacle or an enemy. He then turns to the rhythm of the saints and finds there "is smiling in heaven" (The Rhythm of the Saints, 1990). Music can have that quality of magic. Simon sings of one day being inspired by "a capella groups" then picking up his guitar, he went into a club, turned up his amp, and "blew that room away." Again, with "all the music seeping through" something wondrous happened (Late in the Evening, 1980).

Good times may start with looking for fun and feeling groovy but through music, miracle and wonder it can reach to the whole planet and then to the stars. There is also the magic of the invention of the telephone, the long-distance call, the lasers in the jungle, the recorded music sending heroes up the charts. While for Simon, politics may be a dead end, dreams may be shattered, romance may be a blessing or a trial, yet besides disappointment, we have the world of spectacular accomplishments around us and can reach inside the darkness and find the music and the beauty flowing our way. Despite all the troubles within and without, Simon holds out hope that we will all be received in Graceland. Somehow this mansion of the deceased King of Rock and Roll transformed into a tourist trap can have redemptive promise.

With Simon's songs, we are in the familiar world of human paradox, caught between despair and promise, between the Statue of Liberty sailing out to sea, the strange alliance of billionaires and babies, between being weary and loving life, being immersed in darkness and amazed by the miracles and wonders within and without. The American dream has both been shattered and through technology and affluence can open us up to pleasure, discovery, and intense meaning. Simon has celebrated our technological advances from cameras, to phones, from our observing distant constellations to the magic of medicine. It is, he says, the age of miracle and wonders. The invention of mechanical marvels is an area where the American dream flourishes beyond what could have been imagined when adolescent Paul Simon first entered a primitive recording studio in 1957.

If the American dream is connected to affluence and economic growth, the glory days for the United States were after World War II. The U.S. Gross National Product between 1950 and 1970 grew annually at 3.9 percent, which may be the highest in our history (Matusow, 1984, p. xiii). In 1970, in gross domestic product per capita, the U.S. was 3rd in the world; in 2013, we were 15th (Kushnir, 2014, para 4). Real hourly wages are about the same now as in 1979 (Desilver, 2014, para 2). In 1975, Paul Simon was advocating keeping our standard of living high. For the average American, we are not doing as well now as we were then.

Another part of the American dream concerns love, marriage, families and children. These are areas where much of Simon's work focuses. Whatever the fortunes of love might be these days, marriage is not as popular as it was in 1959 when Paul graduated high school. In 1960, 72 percent of adults over 18 were married, in 2010 it was 51 percent. While divorce skyrocketed from the late 1960s to the mid-1980s, it has stabilized since then. Simon himself has been twice divorced, and now has been married to Edie Brickell since 1992. He has one son from his first and three children from his current marriage. None of his offspring were born

CHAPTER 11: THE AGE OF MIRACLE AND WONDERS

outside of wedlock. Now for women under thirty years of age, more than half of all babies are born to unmarried women. In 1950, 7 percent of children lived in single parent families, in 2013, it was 32 percent (Sawhill, 2014, pp. 18 & 54). The dream of stable two parent families finding happiness and raising children jointly happens to a lower percentage of Americans. What Simon chronicles well is the emotional cost of failed marriages and the turmoil in relationships. Where love and marriage had been idealized when Simon was young, he is insightful as to the contradictory feelings awakened when intimacy rears its ecstatic and volatile head.

The consumer culture promotes desire and pleasure. Simon has bought into that part of the American dream. This is not surprising since he has been drawn to the joys of music since he was a boy, and has been a pop culture star for half a century. As well as seeing music as a way to commune with others and to feed the soul, Simon has extended the realm of pleasure beyond the consumer culture to find the universe a wondrous and dazzling place. While aware of exploitation and barbarism, he finds meaning in a broader consciousness. Simon has been instrumental in incorporating music from different cultures within and outside of his native land into his recordings. His involvement with the music of the globe and the magic of the cosmos is in some ways outside the American dream, and yet somehow is an extension of it. The pursuit of happiness can include the hunger for understanding.

Simon's intentions were certainly not to illuminate the fate of the American dream. Yet arriving during America's uncertain hours, he has delineated our glory and discontent. His work reminds us that the evils of war and genocide remain and that too often political leaders are not up to the challenges that face the nation and the planet. He shows the extra-ordinary magic of our technology and the wonders of living in a spectacular universe. His most poignant work concerns how the personal is entwined with the collective. In our intimate relationships, the deepest bonds are inextricably connected to conflicts and contradictions. The meaningfulness of our lives is inseparable from satisfaction and suffering. Our troubles may lead to things falling apart and yet a loved one can soothe us with a touch of the hand. The American dream in Paul Simon's songs remains in an uncertain time and yet may bring the enduring bonds that make life endlessly enriching. This enrichment includes how tribulations and the wondrous are joined.

PAUL SIMON SONGS:

A Hazy Shade of Winter (1966). On *Bookends.* Columbia: KCS 9529 (LP).
Adios Hermanos. (1997). On *Songs from the Capeman.* Warner Brothers: 9 46814-2 (CD).
America. (1968). On *Bookends.* Columbia: KCS 9529 (LP).
American Tune (1973). On *There Goes Rhymin' Simon.* Columbia: KC 32280 (LP)
Armistice Day. (1971). On *Paul Simon.* Columbia: KC 30750 (LP)
Boy in the Bubble. (1986). On *Graceland.* Warner Brothers: 946430-2 (CD)
Bridge Over Troubled Water (1970). On *Best of Simon & Garfunkel.* Columbia CK 66022 (CD)
Congratulations. (1971). On *Paul Simon.* Columbia: 30740 (LP)
Cool, Cool River (1990). On *The Rhythm of the Saints,* Warner Brothers 92609802 (CD)
Dangling Conversation (1966). On *The Essential Simon & Garfunkel.* Columbia: 5134702 (CD)
Darling Lorraine (1999). On *You're the One.* Warner Brothers: 947844-2 (CD)
Dazzling Blue (2011). On *So Beautiful or So What.* Concord HRD 32814-02 (CD)
Everything Put Together Falls Apart (1971). On *Paul Simon.* Columbia KC 30750 (LP)
Fakin' It (1967). On *Bookends,* Columbia KCS 9529 (LP)
Father and Daughter (2006). On *Surprise.* Warner Brothers: 49982-2 (CD)
Fifty Ninth Street Bridge Song (1966). On *Best of Simon & Garfunkel.* Columbia CK 66022 (CD)
Gone at Last (1975). On *Still Crazy After All These Years,* Columbia PC 33540 (LP)
Graceland (1986). On *Graceland.* Warner Brothers 946430-2 (CD)
Have A Good Time (1975). On *Still Crazy After All These Years.* Columbia PC 33540 (LP)

CHAPTER 11: THE AGE OF MIRACLE AND WONDERS

Hearts and Bones (1983). On *Hearts and Bones*. Warner Brothers 923942-1 (LP)
Kodachrome (1973). On *There Goes Rhymin' Simon*. Columbia KC 32280 (LP)
Late Great Johnny Ace (1981). On *Hearts and Bones*. Warner Brothers 923942-1 (LP)
Late in the Evening (1980). On *One Trick Pony*. Warner Brothers HS 3472 (LP)
Love (2000). On *You're the One*. Warner Brothers 947844-2 (CD)
Love and Blessings (2011). On *So Beautiful or So What*. Concord HRD 32814-02 (CD)
Love and Hard Times (2011). On *So Beautiful or So What*. Concord HRD 32814-02 (CD)
Love Is Eternal Sacred Light (2011). On *So Beautiful or So What,* Concord HRD 32814-02 (CD)
Loves Me Like A Rock (1973). On *There Goes Rhymin' Simon*. Columbia KC 32280 (LP)
Mrs. Robinson (1968). On *Bookends*. Columbia KCS 9529 (LP)
Old (1999). On *You're the One*. Warner Brothers 947844-2 (CD)
Outrageous (2006). On *Surprise*. Warner Brothers 49982-2 (CD)
Peace Like A River (1971). On *Paul Simon*. Columbia KC 30750 (LP)
Rene and Georgette Magritte With Their Dog After the War (1983). On *Hearts and Bones,* Warner Brothers 923942-1 (LP)
Rhythm of the Saints (1990). On *Rhythm of the Saints*. Warner Brothers 926098-2 (CD)
Senorita With A Necklace of Tears (2000). On *You're the One*. Warner Brothers 94784402 (CD)
Slip Slidin' Away (1977). On *Negotiations and Love Songs*. Warner Brothers W225789 (CD)
Something So Right (1973). On *There Goes Rhymin' Simon*. Columbia KC 32280 (LP)
Sounds of Silence (1965). On *Best of Simon & Garfunkel*. Columbia CK 66022 (CD)
St. Judy's Comet (1973). On *There Goes Rhymin' Simon*. Columbia KC 32280 (LP)
Still Crazy After All These Years (1975). On *Still Crazy After All These Years*. Columbia PC 33540 (LP)
Take Me To the Mardi Gras (1973). On *There Goes Rhymin' Simon*. Columbia KC 32280 (LP)

That Was Your Mother (1986). On *Graceland.* Warner Brothers 946430- (CD)

Train in the Distance (1983). On *Hearts and Bones.* Warner Brothers 923942-1 (LP)

Wartime Prayers (2006). On *Surprise.* Warner Brothers 49982-2 (CD)

Was A Sunny Day (1973). On *There Goes Rhymin' Simon,* Columbia KC 32280 (LP)

You're Kind (1975). On *Still Crazy After All These Years.* Columbia PC 33540 (LP)

REFERENCES

Desilver, D. (2014). For most workers, real wages have barely budged for decades. Pew Research Center. pewresearch.org/fact-tank/2014/10/09

Kushnir, I. (2014). Gross Domestic (GDP) in the world 1970-2013. http://kushnirs.org/macroeconomics/gdp/gdp_world.html

Luftig, S. (1997). *The Paul Simon companion.* Schirmer Books.

Matusow, A. (1984). *The unraveling of America.* Harper & Row.

Sawhill, I. (2014). *Generation unbound.* Brookings Institution Press.

CHAPTER 12

DELIVER ME FROM THE SAYS OF OLD: LYRICAL THEMES IN 1950'S ROCK & ROLL

In 1954, Peter Ford was a 9-year-old Californian, who like many youngsters would listen to records at home. One day after work his dad brought home a co-worker, and they over heard the songs Peter played. His father's 42-year-old colleague actually was movie director Richard Brooks and his father, actor Glenn Ford. They were making a film about a high school teacher and his "juvenile delinquent" students, called *Blackboard Jungle*. Peter's father borrowed some of his son's records. One of these singles had as its A side a song entitled "Thirteen Women," which in the spring of 1954 made it to number 23 on the charts, and then was forgotten. When the movie opened in May 1955, the film makers had chosen the B-side of "Thirteen Women" to be played as the film started (Ford, n.d., para 6,7,15)

Decca records wisely re-released the single, and there was a sensational response. The original B-side was "Rock Around the Clock" by Bill Haley and the Comets (Haley, 1954). It was number 1 for 8 weeks, and remained on the Billboard charts for 24 weeks (Whitburn, 2004, p. 270). Popular music historian Ed Ward writes, "If we had to pick a moment when rock & roll was born as a major movement in American popular music" a "good candidate" would be Bill Haley's top-charting single (Ward, 2016, p. 100).

While certainly "Rock Around the Clock" was not the first rock and roll recording, it began a trend that soon was prominent on the record charts. Rock and Roll when it first emerged as a popular phenomenon was an amalgam of different genres. An early description of this new music was in – of all places – on the liner notes to Elvis's second RCA Victor album. The anonymous writer says Elvis uniquely combines the four fields of "country, gospel, rhythm and pop" (Anonymous, 1956). Within rhythm and blues, there were various sub-genres, including risqué rhythm and blues and doo-wop. While the latter started as African-American, it later became biracial. Whatever the forms of rock and roll, it soon became controversial.

Many decried this newly popular music as being too sexual, too raucous, and arousing inappropriate emotions in the teenagers who bought the music in droves. When Elvis Presley became a star in early 1956, his hip shaking non-televised performances seemed to simulate sexual activity, the uproar increased. All of a sudden 1950s rock and roll became associated with rebellion, sex, wild dancing and disruptive behavior. When the music and lyrics about sex are listened to, there are complications present. In this paper, I will try to understand dominant themes in rock and roll. In 1950's popular white rock and roll, sex arouses as much anxiety as it does pleasure. A satisfaction is found in dancing that cannot be readily and consistently found in sexual intimacy. In 1950's rock and roll, the music and dancing are seen as the possession of adolescents and young adults. A youthful world of expression and release is contrasted against an adult world of work and subordination. Chuck Berry, a seminal rock and roll figure, appears to make a rock and roll ethic out of youthful rejection of adult restriction. But Berry's rebellion is filled with contradictory loyalties. He affirms the American dream of affluence and opportunity that other times he sees as life-denying. What remains is that rock and rollers seek pleasure and fulfillment. They find in dancing and music, this release from the deadening routines of work and school, ambivalence about sexual and romantic intimacy, and contradictory attitudes toward the adult world.

To develop my thesis, I will compare sexuality in selected rhythm and blues songs with sexual themes in the records of male white rock and rollers: Jerry Lee Lewis, Gene Vincent and Elvis Presley. Then I will look at what rock and roll means in the works of Bill Haley, Little Richard, Carl Perkins, Fats Domino, Johnny Cash, and Chuck Berry.

In one strand of 1950s sexual rhythm and blues songs, sexual intercourse is engaged in because it is pleasureful and fulfilling. These selected songs roughly fall into three categories: songs of sexual prowess, male pleasure, and sexual mutuality. The Dominoes' "Sixty Minute Man" from 1951 is a song of sexual prowess. The narrator, Dan, is a self-proclaimed sexual technician. He is more concerned with his endurance and technique than bringing the woman to climax (Dominoes, 1951). Joe Turner's "TV Mama" and "Honey Love" by the Drifters are songs of male sexual pleasure. Turner sings, "Every time she loves me, man, she makes me scream" (Turner, 1953). The Drifters' lead singer, Clyde McPhatter, brags

CHAPTER 12: DELIVER ME FROM THE SAYS OF OLD

about how his baby's honey love "thrills his spine" and makes him feel so fine (Drifters, 1954).

On the other hand, Hank Ballard and the Midnighters' Annie songs from 1954 are about male pleasure and sexual mutuality. In "Work With Me Annie," Hank not surprisingly cries "work with me, Annie," and "Let's get it while the getting is good" (Ballard, 1954). He not only wants his pleasure, but her arousal and their collaboration. In a later record, the needs of a child interrupt Annie and Hank's love making in "Annie Had a Baby." They get started but then stop while Annie walks the baby across the floor. Hank reacts with good humor to this reality and sings, "Now I know Annie understood. That's what happens when the getting gets good" (Ballard, 1954). An earlier song from 1951 also concerns male pleasure and mutuality. It is the Swalows' "It Ain't the Meat." The singer declares, "It ain't the meat, it's the motion. Makes your daddy want to rock. It's the movement that gives it the sock." He gives an example to illustrate the point. The girl "wraps all around me like a rubber band" (Swallows, 1951). Here sex is about how the partners fit together and it is the movement that gives the man further enjoyment.

Two other 1950s rhythm and blues songs of pleasure and mutuality are Shirley and Lee's 1956 hit, "Let the Good Times Roll," and Ray Charles' classic "What'd I Say" from 1959. Unlike the Hank Ballard songs, these two recordings crossed over to the Billboard top 40 charts. In these records, the sexual satisfaction of women as well as men are exhibited. They express joy and happiness during sex. Shirley and Lee alternately implore each other to let the good times roll. Lee's grunts, Shirley's request for Lee to close the door and rock some more, as well as her reference to being thrilled and feeling good all show that this song is about sexual congress (Shirlee & Lee, 1956). As is true of the second part of "What'd I Say," which was the B side of a hit record, and was too rawly sexual to be played on Top 40 radio in 1959. This track culminates in a simulation of sexual intercourse between Ray and his female backing group, the Raelettes, that is cathartic. This is a song of intimate togetherness and ecstasy. His howls indicate his sexual pleasure and are echoed by comparable responses form the female chorus (Charles, 1959). There is no more powerful recording about sexual intercourse than this Ray Charles performance. Of course, these selected rhythm and blues songs do not include other such genre records that are about the complications of romantic entanglements.

In contrast, in 1950s white male rock and roll records, references to sex are most often accompanied by ambivalence, a need to keep distance, possessiveness and/or fear of betrayal. For instance, Jerry Lee Lewis's first three Top 40 records from 1957 and 1958 are songs of sexual stimulation and lust. There is as much uneasiness as satisfaction in these songs. There are hints of pleasureful torture and sexual distance here that is not present in the aforementioned rhythm and blues records. In "Whole Lot of Shakin' Going On," Jerry Lee invites this female over to a barn. He requests her to "stand in one spot. Wiggle round just a little bit. That's what you gotta do, yea, oh baby." He wants to lustfully watch while she enacts a sexual tease. The thought of his watching from a distance sexually turns him on. Even though he asserts "Let's go one time," nothing materializes. At the end of the record, Jerry Lee is still imploring her to come on over (Lewis, 1957). The sexual enticement in this song is never consummated. He is both powerfully drawn to sex and reluctant to get too close.

In "Great Balls of Fire," sexual excitement makes Jerry Lee chew his nails, twittle his thumbs and become "real nervous." He adds that being so nervous is fun. Then adds "Too much love drives a man insane." If this is the ecstasy of sex, it is an unusual ecstasy. For Jerry Lee admits that his will has been broken, but this too is thrilling. In this song, he is a nervous, hyperactive lover more concerned with his physiological and psychological responses than what goes on between he and his partner. He is fidgety and self-involved, there is no sign of sexual satiation in this song, nor of a mutual pleasure filled union (Lewis, 1957). As with the earlier record, this is a song of the singer's sexual excitement.

Jerry Lee is so caught up with his own sexual responses in "Breathless," he confuses his own arousal with love. "Well, I shake all over, and you know why. I'm sure it's love. Cause when you call my name, you know I burn like wood in flame." Love and his own sexual shaking are equated. But as in the other records, a fulfilling sexual partnership does not come to fruition. He is aroused and uncertain, and worries that his love is a tease. He twice asks her to love him right, and tells her not to be shy (Lewis, 1958). In all three hit records we find a Jerry Lee Lewis persona that is

CHAPTER 12: DELIVER ME FROM THE SAYS OF OLD

aroused and uneasy, nervous and unconsummated. He is a sexual Sisyphus who does not get to the top of the sexual hill, and is excited but does not get too close to the females who arouse him.

In Gene Vincent's 1950's records, sex entails pleasure but also trails along with it possessiveness and exclusivity. For Vincent relationships arouses fear of violence, betrayal, and threats to masculinity. Both dancing and sex are where masculinity is proven. Masculine pride also entails exclusive possession. In his 1956 top 10 hit, "Be-Bop-A-Lula," his girl is seen as the queen of all the teens. He repeats over and over again that she is his baby doll, and "she loves me so." He then immediately follows this declaration with sexual gasps and a backing musician gives a wild triumphant yell. He acts as if he is victorious (Vincent, 1956). In his recordings, sex generally does not occur without a desire for an exclusive love relationship. In "Woman Love," sex can cure depression if he has the woman with him everywhere he goes. Vincent wants symbiosis. Still, he is fearful that relationship will not last. He fears infidelity, loss, and violence (Vincent, 1956). His girl is off with another man in "Cruisin." To retain her, he will need to get into a physical fight (Vincent, 1956). In "Who Slapped John," two men claim to possess the same woman, and one gets hit (Vincent, 1956). The loss of his girlfriend in "Teenage Partner," causes Gene to sob. His anticipation of romantic trouble makes him anxious and angry (Vincent, 1958). Relationships can be treasured when they enhance masculine pride, and dreaded for the uncertainties they often bring. There is more evidence of worry than fulfillment in many of his 1950s records.

With Elvis Presley, questions about him and sexuality are complicated. In his early stage act, Elvis simulated the hard thrusts of sexual intercourse, though the television audience of the time did not see these films. During his first television appearances he was sexy rather than sexual. He would gyrate his hips, shake his leg, and thrust his shoulders back and forth to the rhythms of the songs. He feels the music from head to toe in a way Chuck Berry would later celebrate. But if you compare his physical movements with the lyrics of his 1950s recordings, they are sometimes at variance with the performing Elvis.

A number of his hit records of that decade do have sexual overtones. In "Don't" and "I Want You, I Need You, I Love You," what starts out as sexual stimulation turns into conventional declarations of eternal devotion and the sex fades into the background (Presley, 1958 & 1956). Other hits like "All Shook Up," "I Need Your Love Tonight," and "A Big Hunk of Love" never get much beyond kissing, and sometimes leaves the singer aroused but feeling unfulfilled (Presley, 1957, 1958, 1958). "Love Me" and "Too Much" are romantic songs of masochism and martyrdom. In these two records, he actually asks to be treated mean and cruel, to have his faithful heart torn apart (Presley, 1956, 1957). In most of his 1950s top 40 singles, sex is either diluted by standard romantic imagery or Elvis is frustrated, unfulfilled or seeking to be mistreated.

The sexually direct Elvis of his early live shows is heard in two of his 1950s releases. They are his versions of "Good Rockin' Tonight," recorded for the Sun label, and Little Richard's "Tutti Frutti" for RCA Victor. In the first of these records, he says he will show his baby he is a mighty, mighty man; in the second how his girl's love making almost drives him crazy (Presley, 1954, 1956). These are songs of male prowess and pleasure, respectively. Another exception is his initially unreleased January 1957 take of Smiley Lewis's 1955 R & B hit, "One Night of Sin." Elvis later re-recorded this with cleaned up lyrics in February 1957 (Presley, 1957, 1983. In the earlier version the sin that was committed would make the earth stand still. In the later hit version, Elvis sings he never did no wrong (Presley, 1957). Still, this later version is one of Elvis's more powerful 1950s RCA recordings.

In the remainder of Elvis 1950s records, sex and romance are present. Sex is inseparable from love, and love contains devotion and possession. Disruption of domestic love is hell. The men in these songs suffer grievously over the loss of romance. Their masculinity cannot endure sorrow and dependence. To recover their pride, they must recover their superiority and independence. When women are virtuous and domestic, they can be objects of devotion. But should they deviate from these ideals, male agony results, and the suffering can only be relieved with the restoration of male dominance.

Elvis's 1956 RCA record of Arthur Crudup's "So Glad You're Mine" is a song of sexual pleasure and possession. Elvis can enjoy the sex because he is sure the woman is his (Presley, 1955). In his 1955 Sun studio recording of Ray Charles's "I Got A Woman," the sexual pleasure is enhanced because his partner knows her place is in his home. She never

CHAPTER 12: DELIVER ME FROM THE SAYS OF OLD

grumbles or fusses, and is there when he wants her (Presley, 1955). He sings of eternal love in "I Love You Because," "I'll Never Let You Go," "I'm Counting on You," "Anyway You Want Me," "Love Me Tender," "Loving You," and others (Presley, 1954, 1954, 1956, 1956, 1956, 1957).

Too often, high hopes for eternal romance do not work out. In the records of no other 1950s rock and roller stressed the pain of failed love as did Elvis. These include "That's When Your Heartache Begins," "Heartbreak Hotel," "My Baby Left Me," "A Fool Such As I" and more (Presley, 1957, 1956, 1956, 1958). In one of these forlorn songs, "How's the World Treating You," Elvis sings that since his breakup he has had "nothing but sorrow," All the sweet things that mattered "have been broken in two. All my dreams have been shattered" (Presley, 1956). He cannot remain in this defeated position for long and rallies his forces. Instead of just feeling bereft, he turns on the women. They will be to blame. Not him. His ex in "You're A Heartbreaker" is a "love faker" (Presley, 1954). In "Just Because" and "Lawdy Miss Clawdy" Elvis's ire is aroused by exploitative women (Presley, 1954, 1956). He asserts his independence, finds another love partner, and finds fault with the lovers who dumped him.

Leiber and Stoller's 1957 "Treat Me Nice" sums up much of the philosophy found in Elvis's 1950s recordings. "You know I'll be your slave if you asked me to. But if you don't behave, I'll walk right out on you" (Presley, 1957). Though he omits the suffering he will endure if she first leaves him. For the 1950s Elvis, sexual relationships are arenas for male dominance and assertions of masculinity. In these songs, there is more concern with pride and position, than pleasure and fulfillment.

In the songs of these 1950s male white rock and rock and rollers, sex is not only an area of enjoyment and happiness, it is regularly accompanied by anxiety, fear, and wounded pride. The struggle between tension, release, and enjoyment makes up much of the dialectic of 1950s rock and roll. In the white rockers of the 1950s the pull between pleasure and frustration is not resolved within heterosexual relationships, as it may be in selected rhythm and blues songs. The tension in 1950s rock and roll finds its release in dancing and music. These activities depend on more distance between the sexes.

For songs with rock and roll as the theme, Bill Haley's landmark "Rock Around the Clock" sets the tone. Rocking around the clock is not as it might be in other records a reference to sex, but here it is to dancing. The setting is not the bedroom, but a social dance. It is here on the dance floor that pleasure and rhythmic release occur; it can as Haley sings, place the partners in seventh heaven. In rock songs of this decade, dancing brings an uncontaminated delight that the complications of sexual intimacy may not provide.

Little Richard's songs with rock and roll as their theme emphasize fun. They too focus on heterosexual dancing in a social setting. The characters are "flat top cats" and "dungaree dolls" dancing at the "sock hop ball." Here rock and roll is a generational activity for hip teenagers eager to dance. Within these social boundaries, the kids let themselves go. "The joint's really jumpin,'" Little Richard sings, "the cats are going wild." At one dance, he joyfully declares, by ten o'clock "I'll be flying high, walk out into the sky… Cause tonight I'm gonna be one happy soul." For he is going rock it up, rip it up, and ball (Little Richard, 1956). Enjoyment and release are the themes of his rock and roll anthems.

These thrills might turn out to be temporary. His constituents are high schoolers and working-class young adults who just got paid. Good times may be for Saturday night and off hours. The grind of work and school can dominate the week. In Little Richard's "Rip It Up," he describes just getting paid on Saturday and what he intends to do is described just above. This Little Richard classic is akin to Fats Domino's "Blue Monday." Fats works like a slave all week and is too tired to play. But on Saturday he has his money, his honey and is ready to roar. Sunday morning, his head is bad, and he needs rest, because Monday is a mess (Domino, 1956). Among other things, rock and roll is an escape from the drudgery of work and school. It can be renewing, but remains a leisure time activity; one circumscribed by the school and work to which it is often contrasted. Deadening routine is the norm, rock and roll is the release.

And what a release it is. In songs like Carl Perkins "Boppin' The Blues," Fats Domino's "The Big Beat," and Johnny Cash's "Get Rhythm," the music is infectious and the lyrics have a message of healing. In Perkins's song, Carl complains to his physician of his ailments. The doctor responds, "Carl, you don't need no pills. Just a handful of nickels and a jukebox will

CHAPTER 12: DELIVER ME FROM THE SAYS OF OLD

cure your ills." He tries the remedy, and is transformed by the music (Perkins, 1956). Fats sings, "The Big Beat gets in your soul. Makes you jump. Makes you roll" (Domino, 1957). Johnny Cash advises "Get rhythm when you get the blues… A jumpy rhythm makes you feel so fine" (Cash,1956). 1950s rock and roll promises exciting pleasure through physical release to jumping music.

No one champions the redemptive power of rock and roll over the deadening impact of work and school than the maestro from St. Louis, Charles Edward Berry. Chuck in 1956 describes working at the mill, the gas station, serving in the Army, and the whole world of blue-collar employment as "too much monkey business for me to be involved in" (Berry, 1956). Similarly, in a 1957 top 10 hit, he describes being in school as harassing, challenging, annoying with a teacher who does not know how mean she looks. Students are subordinated and suppressed. But when three o'clock comes around, liberation tales place at the juke joint. "All day long you've been wanting to dance. Feelin' the music from head to toe." Rock and roll is enlivening; it is the antidote to a life denying world. Berry proclaims: "Hail hail rock 'n' roll, Deliver me from the days of old… The feeling is there body and soul" (Berry, 1957). In the name of liberty and the health of the soul, rock and roll is redeeming, it permeates one's whole being. Berry is a romantic of bodily movement, spurred on by danceable music in a public setting where couples join together in the delightful ritual of the dance. Rock and roll can satisfy desires for both liberty and belonging.

In his records, there is an implicit resentment and rebellion against adult social restraints on the spirits of the young. In 1958's "Around and Around," the joint was rocking; the music was reeling. Then the police arrived to dampen the feeling. But the partiers kept on dancing and never stopped dancing until the moon went down (Berry, 1958). In "Almost Grown," a well-behaved young man resents how interfering social authorities violate his privacy (Berry, 1959). By turning his auto into an airplane Chuck skillfully evades the arm of the law in "You Can't Catch Me" (Berry, 1955). Similar concerns have been discussed in "School Days" and "Too Much Monkey Business." Often leisure, pleasure and dancing are favored over conformity, respectability, and even responsibility.

Yet at times, he will affirm the American values he also sees as restrictive and life-denying. In "Back in the USA," he portrays America as a land of freedom, wealth, mobility, and adventure. "Anything you want, we got it right here in the U.S. A." (Berry, 1959). Suddenly the world of too much monkey business has become the land of opportunity and affluence. "Johnny B. Goode", which is a clear nominee for greatest 1950s rock and roll record, is about a little country boy who can really play guitar. His mother envisions success for her musician son. "Maybe someday your name will be in lights. Saying 'Johnny B. Goode Tonight'" (Berry, 1958). In the follow-up, "Bye, Bye, Johnny," success has come Johnny's way in the land of opportunity. His mother is giving her son a "goodbye kiss." Johnny is on his way to Hollywood to make motion pictures (Berry, 1960).

In the world of Chuck Berry songs, for some talent and drive can lead to glittering lights and well-earned fame. For others, freedom and fun are limited. "Sweet Little Sixteen" celebrates that all over the U.S., they are playing rock and roll, and "all the cats want to dance" with "sweet little sixteen." She shares in affluence by wearing high heel shoes, tight dresses, and lipstick. When everyone wants to dance with her, she is in her glory. But as Chuck sings, "She's got the grown-up blues." The reason being that "tomorrow morning. She'll have to change her trend. And be sweet sixteen, And back in class again" (Berry, 1958). She can only lay her burden down before and after school. On one hand, school and work demands are restrictive, and on the other, anything you want is readily available in the land of the free and the home of the brave.

1950s rock and roll songs are often about having fun in a world alternating between conformity and restriction, and liberty and opportunity. Still if the joy of the music is kept in the foreground and intimacy and necessity kept in the background the moments of pleasure can be sustained and difficulties be kept away. Some of Chuck Berry's songs hold out the promise of having your name in lights and getting anything you want. But while many songs reject pain for pleasure, nearby is that peak experiences are often followed by the restrictions of everyday reality. It is the dialectic of pleasure and denial, intimacy and distance, mutuality and romantic difficulties, rebellion and conformity, success and subordination that are central themes in the lyrics of 1950s rock and roll classics.

CHAPTER 12: DELIVER ME FROM THE SAYS OF OLD

REFERENCES

Anonymous (1956). *Elvis*. RCA Victor: LPM 1382.
Ballard, H. (2016). *The very best of Hank Ballard & The Midnighters*. One Day Music: DAY2CD315. (Original work released 1954)
Berry, C. (1984). *The great twenty-eight*. MCA Records: CHD-92500 (Original work released 1955-1959)
Cash, J. (2002). Get rhythm. On *The Essential Johnny Cash*. Columbia: C2K 86290. (Original work released 1956)
Charles, R. (1991). What'd I say. On *The Birth of Soul: The Complete Atlantic Rhythm & Blues Recordings, 1952-1959*. Atlantic 7 82310-2. (Original work released 1959)
Domino, F. (1971). *Fats domino*. Liberty Records: LWB509958. (Original work released 1956-1957)
Dominoes (1991). Sixty minute man. On *Risque Rhythm Nasty 50s R & B*. Rhino: R2 70570. (Original work released 1951)
Drifters (2003). Honey love. On *The Definitive Drifters*. Atlantic: WSMCD137. (Original work released 1954)
Ford, P. (n.d.). Rock around the clock and me. http://www.peterford.com/ratc.html.
Haley, B. (1985). *Bill Haley & his comets: From the original master takes*. MCA Records: MCAD-5539. (Original work released 1954)
Lewis, J. L. (1984). *Greatest hits*. Rhino: RNCD 5255. (Original work released 1957-1958)
Little Richard (1991). *The Georgia peach*. Specialty: SPCD-7012-2. (Original work released 1956)
Perkins, C. (1998). Boppin' the blues. On *The Very Best of: Blue Suede Shoes*. Collectables: COL-CD-6011. (Original work released 1956)
Presley, E. (1992). *Elvis: The king of rock 'n' roll: The Complete 50's Masters*. RCA: 66050-207863. (Original work released 1954-1958)
Shirley & Lee (1973). Let the good times roll. On *The Best of Shirley & Lee*. Ace: CH 47. (Original work released 1956)
Swallows. (1991). It ain't the meat. On *Risque Rhythm Nasty 50s r & B*. Rhino: R2 70570. (Original work released 1951)
Turner, J. (1986). TV Mama. On *Rhythm & Blues Years*. Atlantic: A1-81663. (Original work released 1953)

Vincent, G. (1974). *The bop that just won't stop*. Capitol: N-16209. (Original work released 1956)

Ward, E. (2016). *The history of rock & roll, Vol. One, 1920-1963*. Flatiron Books.

Whitburn, J. (2004). *The Billboard book of top 40 hits* (8th ed.). Billboard Books.

CHAPTER 13

WHERE HAVE ALL THE FLOWERS GONE?
A MEMORIAL TO PETER SEEGER

Pete Seeger, the eminent folksinger and political activist, died at the age of 94 on January 27, 2014. He was one of the few members of the 1930's Old Left who was influential with the youth generation of the 1960's. American left movements over the last century have often followed a developmental cycle that begins as youthful rebellion against unjust authority, followed by a period of ascendancy then diminishment and/or disillusionment. In these movements' early stages, immoral special interests are seen as preventing democracy, while the virtuous victims are seen as populist forces of redemption. As time goes on, many on the left become like those they once opposed, as many Communists became anticommunists, or New Leftists became yuppies. Pete Seeger followed a somewhat different path, yet his early rebellion was succeeded in middle age by a blander social rebellion.

His affiliation with radicalism began as a teenager in 1936 and lasted until he resigned from the Communist Party in 1949. Yet in 2004 he said, "I'm still a communist, in the sense that I don't believe the world will survive with the rich getting richer and the poor getting poorer" (Hajdu, 2004, para 28). Seeger's musical career combined his allegiance to politically progressive causes with his prominence within folk music circles.

His birth in 1919 meant he arrived on this planet too early to be called a red diaper baby (the child of members of the Communist party), but he picked up his radicalism from his family. His father and mother were both professional musicians. His dad, Charles, from an old-line New England family, established the University of California's music department. Charles' opposition to American involvement in World War I led to his resignation from "Cal" and a return to the east coast. The Seeger's had three sons. Peter was the youngest. His parents divorced when he was seven. During the Depression, Seeger's family was able to afford to send him to prominent boarding schools in Connecticut. After graduating from Avon Old Farms in 1936, Pete entered Harvard, but dropped out two years later, then went to work for Alan Lomax collecting folk music from throughout the U.S.

At the age of 17, Pete became another upper middle-class adolescent who found the ideas of Marx appealing, and joined the Young Communist League, then six years later became a member of the Communist Party. He was drawn to Communism during the party's Popular Front period, where they sought to collaborate with more mainstream reformers. After Hitler took power in Germany in 1933, Stalin became preoccupied with the Nazis. Parties under his control began to find common ground with anti-Nazi political parties. In the U.S. at this time the party slogan was "Communism is 20th Century Americanism." American Communists identified with the working class whether urban or rural.

For his entire career, Seeger remained somewhat true to the perspectives of the Popular Front period. He was interested in uncovering and recording folk songs from all regions of the United States and from countries throughout the world. Musically, Seeger was an internationalist and a champion of working people, wherever they might be. His own political songs also favored the lower classes over the economic bosses. Seeger believed that the people united can overcome the power of the elite. In this sense many of his political and non-political songs crossed the boundary between liberalism and radicalism and had a democratic flavor.

In the early 1940s, along with Woody Guthrie, Lee Hays, and Millard Lampell, Seeger founded the Almanac Singers, a politically radical folk group. Their first collection of songs was antiwar and anti-capitalist. President Roosevelt was seen as collaborating with Wall Street to promote war against the people's interest. Here youthful radicalism saw the powerful as destructive and championed the masses. Later these singers recorded pro-union songs. One of them, co-written by Seeger, is entitled "Talking Union." In this composition, it is the familiar opposition of workers and bosses, where the employees want to unionize and their employers want to destroy this effort by whatever means necessary. In the conflict between the people and the interests, Seeger and his collaborators proclaim, "But if you all stick together, boys... You'll win" (Seeger, 1941). The redeeming power of democratic unity can defeat entrenched economic power. This song contains rhetoric that has characterized American political insurgencies from the Stamp Act to the more recent Occupy Movement. Later, after Hitler invaded the USSR, the Almanac Singers reversed their anti-war stance and embraced American involvement in

CHAPTER 13: WHERE HAVE ALL THE FLOWERS GONE?

World War II with Seeger himself writing a song of pro-war support called "Dear Mr. President" (Almanac Singers, 1942).

Seeger's next important folk group was The Weavers, which he co-founded with Lee Hays, Ronnie Gilbert, and Fred Hellerman in 1948. The Weavers downplayed their political convictions and instead popularized folk songs from the U.S. and throughout the world. Their 1950 recording of "Goodnight Irene," composed by the African-American blues singer Leadbelly, was a number one record (The Weavers, 1950). Seeger was entering a new stage in his leftist career by accommodating with the power structure, recording for a major record company, and keeping his politics and music separate. He resigned from the Communist Party the year after The Weavers were formed.

The Weavers' popularity corresponded with the second Red Scare. Their record company succumbed to the pressure and dropped the group who disbanded in 1952. In 1955, the onetime Communist Party member, Peter Seeger, was interrogated by the House Committee on Un-American Activities (HUAC). While many individuals called before this group pleaded the Fifth Amendment, Seeger refused to answer questions on the grounds of the First Amendment. He was later convicted of contempt of Congress, though the conviction was subsequently overturned. Television and nightclubs would not allow Seeger to perform for many years, but he found other ways to get music to his audience. His fortunes began to alter as the U.S. slowly came out of the obsession with domestic subversion. Liberalism began to revive after the ascendancy of Martin Luther King Jr. in the mid-1950s and Kennedy's election in 1960. In 1957, Seeger introduced to Martin Luther King Jr. an old hymn that he had somewhat altered. The song was "We Shall Overcome," which, after King promoted it, soon became ubiquitous at civil rights rallies across the country.

In 1958 a folk group, the Kingston Trio, had a number one hit with "Tom Dooley." All of a sudden, a folk music revival spread throughout the country, eventually including television shows such as Hootenanny. One indication of Seeger's changing circumstances was his signing to Columbia Records in 1961 by another old 30s radical and legendary Columbia Records executive, John Hammond. Some of Seeger's less radical music was about to enter the mainstream. In 1955, he had composed an anti-war song, "Where Have All the Flowers Gone." As a member of The Almanac Singers, Seeger associated war mongering with capitalists. Here it was just war itself that was the enemy. Seven years later "Flowers" reached number 21 on the top 40 in a recording by the Kingston Trio. Also, in 1962, "If I Had a Hammer," a song co-written by Seeger and Lee Hays in 1949, reached number 10 in the Peter, Paul, and Mary version. This was a populist song about "love between my brothers and my sisters all over this land," the "hammer of justice," and the "bell of freedom" (Peter, Paul, and Mary, 1962). Here is a Seeger composition about social justice where the people unite but again there is no evil force standing in their way as was portrayed in the earlier "Talking Union." In 1954, when Seeger put music to and adapted lyrics from the book of Ecclesiastes for "Turn! Turn! Turn!" he added one phrase, after the line "a time for peace," he wrote "I swear it's not too late." The Byrds' rock version with this addition made it to the top of the charts for three weeks in 1965 (The Byrds, 1965).

The one occasion where a recording of Pete's actually made the top 100 was in 1964. The song was "Little Boxes," written by Malvina Reynolds, and is a satirical song about conformity and the loss of individuality in contemporary culture (Seeger, 1963). Another anti-war Pete Seeger song, "Waist Deep in the Big Muddy," was recorded in 1966 (Seeger, 1966). This song was about a fool army captain in the 1940s who, despite being repeatedly warned of the danger, died by wading too deep into the Missouri River (also known as Big Muddy). On the record, without quite saying so, Seeger made it clear he was also talking about Vietnam, but without any reference to a military industrial complex. While this recording never landed on the Billboard charts, it made its mark in other ways. Seeger taped the song for an airing of the Smothers Brothers Comedy Hour in November 1967, but the CBS censors removed it. The Smother Brothers objected, got their way, and early in 1968 Seeger sang this song on their program. Slightly earlier, in October 1967, prominent liberal journalist Richard Rovere wrote a lengthy anti-Vietnam war article for *The New Yorker* and titled his piece "Waist Deep in the Big Muddy" (Rovere, 1967).

With the revival of activism in the 1950s and 1960s, Pete Seeger's now watered-down political convictions reached a wide public audience through the mediums of popular music and television. However, the politically active folk singers of the mid-1960s added a dimension to some of their compositions that are not often found in Seeger's work: introspection and self-questioning. For instance, Bob Dylan's 1964 "My Back Pages" reflects on how he has felt younger when being less self-righteous, and "Changes" by Phil Ochs from 1966 concerns the impact of shifting events and feelings. In Ochs' 1966 satirical song "Love Me I'm A Liberal," he has his fictional narrator say, "I go to all the Pete Seeger concerts. He sure gets me singing those songs" (Ochs, 1966). There were ways then that Seeger made the transition from the old to the new left and other ways that, in keeping with the fate of his youth, he had somewhat different concerns than the generation of singer song-writers inheriting his mantle. His renewed popularity was related to making people feel connected without arousing anger at the power elite.

Pete Seeger kept continuity between the radicalism of his youth and the political activism of his middle and later years in his championing of world music and his anti-war stance. He persevered in these beliefs all his long adult life. Seeger was able to appeal to many by making his beliefs compatible with recurring American democratic concerns with freedom, justice, unity, equity, and peace. As have many other once youthful radicals, in middle age he found himself flirting with the mainstream he once vehemently opposed.

REFERNCES

Almanac Singers (2001). Dear Mr. President. On *Songs of Protest*. Prism Leisure: PLATCD 704. (Original work released 1942)

Hadju, D. (2004). Pete Seeger's Last War, *Mother Jones*, http://www.motherjones.com/ politics/2004/09/pete-seeger-*last-war*.

Ochs, P. (1966). Love me, I'm a liberal. On *In Concert*. Elektra: EKL 310.

Peter, Paul and Mary. (1962). If I had a hammer. On *Peter Paul and Mary*. Warner: 1449.

Rovere, R. (1967, October 28). Reflections: waist deep in the big muddy. *The New Yorker*. https://www.newyorker.com/magazine/1967/10/28/reflections-waist-deep-in-the-big-muddy

Seeger, P. & Almanac Singers (1955). Talking union. On *The Original Talking Union with the Almanac Singers & Other Union Songs with Pete Seeger & Chorus.* Folkways: FH 5285. (Original work released 1941)

Seeger, P. (1967). Little boxes. On *Greatest Hits.* Columbia: CS 9416. (Original work released 1963)

Seeger, P. (1967). Waist deep in the big muddy. On *Waist Deep in the Big Muddy.* Columbia: CS 9505.

The Byrds (1966). Turn, Turn, Turn. On *Turn! Turn! Turn!* Columbia.

Weavers. (1980). Goodnight Irene. On *Best of the Weavers.* MCA: MCA2-4052. (Original work released 1950)

CHAPTER 14

JAZZ, RACE, AND POLITICS: 1955-1975

The American civil rights movement of the 1950s and 1960s brought substantial change to the position of African-Americans in the U. S. It should not be surprising that many jazz musicians composed and wrote about issues surrounding these movement for freedom and equality. But the extent of these contributions has not been sufficiently focused on. This paper hopes to rectify this by discussing the history of jazz, race, and politics from 1955 to 1975. The outpouring of jazz songs about the condition of African Americans in this period far exceeded what proceeded and followed it. These recordings fall into various patterns that mirror the trends within the movement for civil rights. Starting with the 1954 Supreme Court decision nullifying segregation as a legal doctrine to the 1955 Montgomery bus boycott bringing Martin Luther King Jr. to prominence, the civil rights movement went through various stages and had a variety of components. The relative unity of the movement fragmented and led to liberal and radical wings. The relevant music reflected both the unity and the divisions. I try to cover both the history and how it is reflected in the themes prevalent in these songs and suites.

More attention has been paid to political protest music in folk and rock than jazz. Even before the post-World War II movement for racial equality, there were compositions showing racial pride, particularly in the works of Duke Ellington. Occasionally songs about oppression and injustice appeared in jazz music. This altered dramatically in the 1950s. There are well over 100 jazz songs and albums from 1955 to 1975 dealing with these issues.

Are there any groups in the United States who suffered more oppression than African-Americans? Most had been slaves in the U. S. until 1865, then a decade or so after reconstruction ended in 1877, the South made blacks second class citizens. States of the old Confederacy passed segregation statutes, blacks were kept from voting, lynching was tolerated. Tactics of fear and terror were the norm. Jump ahead half a century. In 1954, the Supreme Court declared segregation to be unconstitutional. The next year, Martin Luther King Jr. led the Montgomery bus boycott.

Racial Discrimination

There have been jazz songs that reflected the concern with discrimination, violence, and suffering among blacks. On April 26, 1955, famed trumpeter Louis Armstrong re-recorded the Fats Waller-Andy Razaf song, "(What Did I Do to Be So) Black and Blue," he had originally done in 1929. Jazz critic Dan Morgenstern says this is "the first non-religious protest song" (Morgenstern, 2004, para 9). Razaf's lyrics include:

> I'm white inside but that don't help my case
> 'Cause I can't hide what is in my face
>
> My only sin is in my skin
> What did I do to be so black and blue (Armstrong, 1955).

The next year for the Verve label, great jazz vocalist Billie Holiday made another version of her landmark 1939 "Strange Fruit":

> Southern trees bear a strange fruit
> Blood on the leaves and blood at the root
> Black bodies swingin' in the Southern breeze
> Strange fruit hangin' from the poplar trees
>
> Pastoral scene of the gallant South
> The bulging eyes and the twisted mouth
> Scent of magnolias sweet and fresh
> Then the sudden smell of burning flesh
>
> Here is a fruit for the crows to pluck
> For the rain to gather, for the wind to suck
> For the sun to rot, for the tree to drop
> Here is a strange and bitter crop (Holiday, 1956/2005).

These are two of the earliest jazz songs about the pain and terror of being black in the United States. Then in 1957, we have bassist Charles Mingus's powerful instrumental "Haitian Fight Song." The bassist told annotator Nat Hentoff that this "could just as well be called Afro-American Fight Song. ...I can't play it right unless I'm thinking about prejudice and hate

CHAPTER 14: JAZZ, RACE, AND POLITICS

and persecution, and how unfair it is. There's sadness and cries in it, but also determination" (Hentoff, 1957, para 12).

In 1961, for his album Africa/Brass, John Coltrane recorded a variation on a Negro spiritual, he entitled "Song of the Underground Railroad," a reference to the networks that helped slaves escape north to freedom, and he also performed for that album Cal Massey's "The Damned Don't Cry," an allusion to the plight of African-Americans (Coltrane, 1961). A variation on this theme was another Cal Massey composition, "The Cry of My People," a mournful ballad, recorded by trumpeter Lee Morgan in 1967 on The Sixth Sense. The trumpeter plays this ballad with a mute, that has a tone reminiscent of Miles Davis (Morgan, 1967).

The Real Ambassadors with music by Dave Brubeck and lyrics by Iola Brubeck was released by Columbia in 1962. It also had Louis Armstrong, Carmen McRae, and the singing group Lambert, Hendricks, and Ross on the date. Ostensibly it was about jazz artists touring other nations on a State Department good will tour, but civil rights were part of the undercurrent of this album and what preceded it. For on September 17, 1957, during the height of Governor Faubus forcibly keeping Little Rock's high school segregated, Louis Armstrong called President Eisenhower "two faced," and a leader with "no guts." The trumpeter also said, "It's getting almost so bad a colored man hasn't got any country." Louis's remarks made national headlines. A week later, the President sent troops to Little Rock to ensure the high school there was integrated (Margolick, 2017, para 6). On the Brubeck's record, Louis sang Iola's lyrics that the government does not represent some policies he is for, and ironically alluded that segregation is technically no longer legal. Later he sings that "They say I look like God. Could God be black?" He asks God "to set men free" (Brubeck, 1962).

Next, we come to the transformation of two songs from the 1920s recorded in the 1960s. In 1927, the Broadway musical version of Edna Ferber's Show Boat featured the song "Ol' Man River," written by Jerome Kern and Oscar Hammerstein. At the time, both the white Bing Crosby and the black Paul Robeson recorded it. Robeson also performed it in the 1936 film version. The song contrasts the Mississippi River, which keeps on rolling, with African Americans who plant potatoes and cotton, who sweat and strain, whose bodies are racked with pain, and are tired of living, but scared of dying. The original lyrics talk of niggers working while white folks play. In the movie, Robeson sang darkies where nigger had been in the original. In 1963, in one of his most moving recordings, Ray Charles, with backing by the Jack Halloran singers, re-framed the song. Now it is neither niggers nor darkies, but we who work while the white folks play. The record begins with just the backing vocalists performing the last choruses of the song, with singing about pulling the boats on the river from dawn to sunset, and working until you're dead. When Ray Charles enters, he croons of being racked with pain, toating the barge, and then adds "somebody said" before singing "lift that bale." The listener gets the sense of being ordered by a boss, with echoes of slaves and overseers. The burden of this back breaking work and subordination is clear in the pain in Charles's signing (Charles, 1963).

A different response to being an underling is evident in vocalist and pianist Nina Simone's alteration of "Pirate Jenny" from *The Threepenny Opera*. This is a 1928 musical, originally in German, with text by Bertrolt Brecht and music by Kurt Weill. "Pirate Jenny" originally was a song of working class resentment and revenge. When Lotte Lenya, Weill's wife, sang it in the 1955 New York production, the locale was a ratty waterfront, in a ratty old hotel. Simone changes it to a "crummy Southern town" and a "crummy old hotel." It remains a song about a maid taking orders, but Nina makes it a song about race. I do not know of a more harrowing vocal recording than this one. While the maid is bossed around, she is fantasizing about killing all of them. The song has her claiming that they are all murdered and their bodies loaded on a pirate ship in the harbor which sails out to sea with her on it, triumphantly making her escape and becoming liberated (Simone, 1964).

Songs about Civil Rights Events

A recurring stage in liberal/left movements has been organization and insurgency. This happened in the civil rights era, and in the jazz response to it. In 1957, courts ordered Little Rock high schools to be desegregated. Arkansas Governor Orville Faubus resisted the order, and President Eisenhower, as mentioned, eventually brought in federal troops to integrate the high school. Jazz bassist Charles Mingus was outraged. In 1959, for Columbia Records he recorded "Fables of Faubus," one of the earliest jazz compositions about the post 1954 civil rights movement

CHAPTER 14: JAZZ, RACE, AND POLITICS

Mingus, 1959). Mingus had written serious, yet tongue in cheek lyrics to his song, but the record label would not let him include the lyrics. The next year, for the Candid label, he did record the words, under the title "Original Faubus Fables." Here are some of them:

> Oh, Lord, don't let 'em shoot us!
> Oh, Lord, don't let 'em stab us!
> Oh, Lord, don't let 'em tar and feather us!
> Oh, Lord, no more swastikas!
> Oh, Lord, no more Ku Klux Klan!
> Name me someone who's ridiculous, Dannie.
> Governor Faubus!
> Why is he so sick and ridiculous?
> He won't permit integrated schools (Mingus, 1960).

Other jazz records followed in contemporary response to civil rights events. Drummer Max Roach's 1960 landmark album *We Insist! Freedom Now Suite* had on its cover a picture of the first sit-ins by African-American students at a lunch counter in North Carolina on February 1, 1960 (Roach, 1960). This occupation in Woolworth's sparked many other such events.

Also, in 1960, the Supreme Court declared that segregation in interstate transportation was illegal. On May 1, 1961, the Congress of Racial Equality (CORE) began freedom rides to integrate bus travel in the American south. Violence ensued. In response, on May 27, 1961, Art Blakey recorded a seven minute drum solo, "The Freedom Rider" (Blakey, 1964) in support of this civil rights campaign. Another Blakey recording three years later honored what CORE had accomplished in 1961 and what it continued to do. This was trumpeter Freddie Hubbard's "The Core," on the *Free For All* album. Hubbard said of the civil rights group, "They're getting at the core, at the center of the kinds of change that have to take place before this society is really open to everyone" (Blakey, 1964).

In the spring of 1963, things got even more heated in the deep south. Martin Luther King Jr. and allies started a desegregation campaign in Birmingham, Alabama in April, that led to King's arrest, the hosing of marching black children under the orders of Commissioner of Public Safety Bull Connor, and eventually the ending of whites only signs in the city in May. In June, the federal government made sure black students could enroll at the University of Alabama. The troubles in Alabama led President Kennedy to advocate for a national civil rights act in a speech on June 11, 1963. The next day, Mississippi civil rights leader, Medgar Evers was murdered, and in September a Birmingham black church was bombed killing four little girls.

Before the slaughter of the youngsters, Duke Ellington in early August 1963 performed the words and music to his composition "King Fit the Battle of Alabam." According to Bjarne Busk, this is "the most openly political song Ellington ever made" (Busk, 2012, para 6). Duke wrote:

> King fit the battle of Alabam,' Birmingham Alabam'
> King fit the battle of 'Bam
> And the Bull jumped nasty, ghastly, nasty
> Bull turned the hoses on the church people...
> Freedom rider, ride
> Freedom rider, go to town
> Y'all and us gonna git on the bus
> Y'all aboard, sit down, sit tight, sit down (Ellington, 1963).

Two months after the church bombing, to the cadences of King's funeral oration for the dead girls, John Coltrane recorded the somber, mournful song, "Alabama," As Ingrid Monson observes, this is "perhaps the most moving composition dedicated specifically to a civil rights event" (Monson, 2007, p. 211). In response to the Birmingham bombing and the assassination of Medgar Evers, in the spring of 1964, Nina Simone recorded: "Alabama has me so upset....and everybody knows about Mississippi Goddam." In another song from the same album, Simone declared:

> Old Jim Crow
> You've been around too long
> Gotta work the devil
> 'Til your dead and gone
> Old Jim Crow don't you know
> It's all over...

Back to "Mississippi Goddam," Simone (1964) sings:

CHAPTER 14: JAZZ, RACE, AND POLITICS

> Picket lines, school boycotts
> They try to say it's a communist plot
> All I want is equality
> For my sister, my brother and me....
> You don't have to live next to me
> Just give me my equality.

Following the historic events of the spring of 1963, in August of that year a massive march for civil rights occurred at the Lincoln Memorial in the nation's capital, where King delivered his "I Have A Dream Speech." On July 2nd, 1964, President Lyndon Johnson signed the civil rights act, marking the culmination of one phase of the movement for freedom for African Americans.

While segregation had now been legally abolished, getting Southern blacks to be able to vote was still a challenge. Civil rights leaders were now intent on getting to the ballot box. Along those lines, a march on Selma, Alabama was organized for a Sunday in March, 1965. More violence ensued, and that day has been labeled bloody Sunday ever since. Three contemporary jazz compositions marked the occasion. Guitarist Grant Green, on May 26, 1965 recorded "The Selma March," a funky, upbeat performance. Trumpeter Blue Mitchell wrote "March on Selma" in July, 1965. This song is in the hard bop tradition of 1960s Blue Note label. The ubiquitous Charles Mingus at a Minneapolis concert on May 13, 1965 played his "A Lonely Day in Selma, Alabama," though it was not released until 2012. This is a complex, ominous, prayerful composition. Mingus (2012) recited the following:

> It was a lonely day in Selma, Alabama
> People gathered there to walk and march for freedom
> Mother, child in arms
> I wonder about this freedom
> A freedom that is unjust.

About Freedom

Some of this injustice was to be diminished following President Johnson signing of the Voting Rights Act on August 6, 1965. The civil rights movement was accompanied by a number of jazz songs celebrating freedom, not only for American blacks, but in recognition of the new-found freedom of many nations in Africa.

Tenor saxophonist Sonny Rollins's 1958 "Freedom Suite" is a landmark. As with Mingus's "Haitian Fight Song," it is explicitly political. On the back of the album, Rollins (1958) wrote, "How ironic that the Negro, who more than any other people can claim America's culture as his own, is being persecuted and repressed, that the Negro, who has exemplified the humanities in his very existence, is being rewarded with inhumanity." The suite is a 19-minute composition, and is, according to A. B. Spellman, "a statement about the freedom of his people and about his own musical freedom... [It is also] ... one of the very first extended compositions for the tenor saxophone" (Spellman, 2001, para 6).

Other works by black American jazz artists about freedom would follow. In 1960, drummer Max Roach and singer-songwriter, Oscar Brown Jr. recorded We Insist! Freedom Now Suite. The first song, "Driva' Man," sung by Abbey Lincoln is about slavery and cruel overseers. "Freedom Day" is about the emancipation of the slaves, and their wonder that now they have liberty. "Triptych: Prayer, Protest, Peace" was conceived by Roach as a ballet, and contains powerful wordless vocals by Lincoln. "All Africa" celebrates the past, future, and music of that continent, while the last composition "Tears for Johannesburg" refers to the 1960 Sharpeville Massacre where 69 South Africans were gunned down by police (Roach, 1960).

Next year's Percussion Bittersweet album by Roach is a worthy successor to We Insist! The most important song about politics is "Mendacity," with music by Roach, lyrics by Chips Bayen and sung by Abbey Lincoln:

> Mendacity, mendacity, it makes the world go round...
> Now voting rights in this fair land we know are not denied.
> But if I tried in certain states, from tree tops I'd be tied.
> (Roach, 1961)

Other songs on the album include a tribute to the 1920s black leader, Marcus Garvey, a celebration of tender warriors who sit in at lunch counters, integrate the buses, and fight for civil rights. There are two songs in praise of what women do in this world, and another song about South

CHAPTER 14: JAZZ, RACE, AND POLITICS

Africa. The Jazz Crusaders entitled their first album, recorded in 1961, Freedom Sound. The title track features a marching drum, and funky, hard bop solos (Jazz Crusaders, 1961). Two years later, bassist Charles Mingus played a song entitled "Freedom" – for the *Mingus, Mingus, Mingus* album, for the Impulse label, though that song was not initially released. It first appeared on the CD version in 1995. The lyrics include the following lines:

> Freedom for your daddy
> Freedom for your momma
> Freedom for your brothers and sisters
> But no freedom for me. (Mingus, 1995)

Wayne Shorter's composition "Free For All" was the title of a 1964 Art Blakey album. The title track has a variety of meanings including all should be free, and that this performance is a musical free for all. This is a raucous, searing, thunderous performance (Blakey, 1964). "Freedom Jazz Dance" was composed and put on wax by Eddie Harris in 1965, and then revived the next year by Miles Davis (Harris, 1965, Davis, 1966). Billy Taylor in 1963 wrote the instrumental "I Wish I Knew How It Would Feel To Be Free" for his daughter. It took on a different meaning when in 1967, Nina Simone made a vocal version of the song with lyrics by Richard Lamb:

> I wish I knew how
> It would feel to be free
> I wish I could break
> All the chains holding me....
> And I wish you could know
> What it means to be me
> Then you'd see and agree
> Every man should be free... (Simone, 1967)

These lyrics fit into the civil rights sensibility and the need for freedom and being oneself that was part of a sixties sensibility.

Africa

One of the inspirations for many African-Americans in the fifties and sixties was that many African states were throwing off colonialism and becoming independent. The nationalism in Africa in time paralleled the fight for civil rights in these United States. Many songs with African nations or the continent in their titles were released. Wilbur Harden recording with John Coltrane and Curtis Fuller in 1958 with three songs about Africa: "Dial Africa," "Gold Coast", and "Tanganyika Strut" (Coltrane, 1958). In 1960, Randy Weston composed a theme album entitled Uhuru Afrika, or freedom Africa. It consists of a four-movement suite, and other songs about that continent (Weston, 1960). As Weston later says, "Africa, the cradle of civilization is my ancestral home, the home of my spirit and my soul" (Weston, 1972). He visited Africa in 1961 and moved there in 1968. In 1964, he recorded the powerful, "African Cookbook," with a remarkable Booker Ervin tenor solo (Weston, 1964/1972). Blues to Africa is his 1974 album, with the title tune being another version of a tune recorded in 1960 (Weston, 1974). Weston's being drawn to the continent from which most African-Americans ancestors came is echoed in others within the jazz world.

John Coltrane is generally considered to be non-political. His musical allegiances include his own compositions "Liberia" (Coltrane, 1960), "Africa" (Coltrane, 1961), and his recording Mongo Santamaria's "Afro-Blue" (Coltrane, 1961). Coltrane and Cannonball Adderley were in a classic Miles Davis quintet and sextet. Adderley in 1961 put "African Waltz" to wax, and in 1968 released an album entitled "Accent on Africa" (Adderley, 1962 & 1968). 1962 saw the release of Duke Ellington's beautiful "African Flower" and Art Blakey's album African Beat (Ellington, 1962; Blakey, 1962). "African Queen" by Horace Silver was a jazz hit in 1966, and in 1969 avant-garde drummer Sunny Murray released Homage to Africa (Silver, 1966, Murray, 1969). There was a link in the music from the fifties to the seventies between American blacks and their ancestral homeland.

Martin Luther King Jr.

The peak of the American civil rights movement in terms of practical achievements were these two pieces of landmark legislation on civil and

CHAPTER 14: JAZZ, RACE, AND POLITICS

voting rights. But the fight for black Americans was not over, as there was still a great deal of inequality in the land. The victories had occurred in the South, but many blacks had moved North starting at the time of World War I. From 1966 on, two things happened, the movement for black freedom moved north, and signs of splintering appeared. Insurgency continued, but was accompanied by emerging factions. The diminishment of vision and the fragmentation of liberal and left movements began to become clear, and impacted on what the goals were and the difficulties in sustaining a united front. A movement for black power emerged in 1966, later followed by black nationalism, and black separatism. Martin Luther King Jr. tried to hold the center together, but this became more difficult. His attempt to bring the civil rights movement to Chicago was a bust, and his opposition to the Vietnam War broke his alliance with President Johnson. Still, he was the most influential figure in the civil rights movement from 1955 to his assassination in 1968. He preached freedom, integration, equality, and non-violence. The passage of the two major civil rights laws in 1964 and 1965 owed a good deal to his prominence, campaigns, and influence.

There are a substantial number of jazz songs and suites about King, particularly after his April 4, 1968 murder. His death marked the end of an era, and the civil rights movement never fully recovered. Duke Ellington's 1963 homage to King has already been mentioned. John Coltrane recorded "Reverend King" in 1966, though it was not released until 1969 (Coltrane, 1969) when both he and King were gone. On April 7, 1968, just three days after King's murder, Nina Simone performed "Why (The King of Love Is Dead)," written by her bass player, Gene Taylor. A nearly six-minute version was part of her 1968 album 'Nuff Said. The full thirteen-minute performance was finally released in 2013 (Simone, 1968/2013).

Ella Fitzgerald was not known as a political activist, or as a writer of her own songs. King's murder inspired her to compose a song about him, "It's Up to You and Me," recorded on May 10, 1968. It was released as a 45 that year, and has not yet made it to an album. Ella sings of King's devotion to non-violence and peace, and that we have to continue his struggle. It is a powerful recording, from an unexpected source (Fitzgerald, 1968). Cecil Payne performed a mournful "Martin Luther King. Jr." on his Zodiac album, recorded in 1969 and 1970 (Payne, 1973).

Most extraordinarily, there are three extended recorded tributes to King by jazz artists. Herbie Hancock's *The Prisoner* was recorded for Blue Note in April, 1969 (Hancock, 1969); Oliver Nelson's *Black, Brown and Beautiful* is from 1970, and in 1973 Charles Earland played a live version of his "Suite for Martin Luther King." The first song on Hancock's album is "I Have A Dream," a reference to King's speech. The next song, "The Prisoner," refers the album's notes say to the struggles between oppressor and oppressed. The song "He Who Lives in Fear" is about the anxiety King had to live with over violence to his person. The last song, "Promise of the Sun," which the notes say is about the freedom the sun promises, while African-Americans have not been allowed to realize this freedom. I will return to Nelson's suite later. Earland's 16-minute performance is divided into two parts, "Offering" and "Mode for Martin" (Earland, 1973).

Other Slain Black Figures

There were also songs about other black activists who were murdered. Part of the inspiration for Nina Simone's "Mississippi Goddam," as mentioned was the killing of Medgar Evers. Songs about Malcolm X also abounded. Prior to his murder in 1965, many thought of Malcolm as a firebrand. The posthumous publication of his autobiography altered that somewhat, and to many he was a hero. Just a month after the murder, tenor player, Archie Shepp, recorded "Malcolm, Malcolm, Semper Malcolm" (Shepp, 1968). Leon Thomas in 1969 released his "Malcolm's Gone," singing Malcolm died to set me free (Thomas, 1969). Mongo Santamaria in 1972 composed his "Malcolm X" (Santamaria, 1972). In 1972, Archie Shepp had a song entitled "Blues for Brother George Jackson," the radical black prisoner who died staging a prison break (Shepp, 1972).

In 1974, avant-garde trombonist, Grachan Moncur III, released the album, Echoes of Prayer. It contained songs about murdered leaders Medgar Evers and Martin Luther King Jr., as well as a tribute to 1920s black leader, Marcus Garvey, and another to an alive black radical, Angela Davis (Moncur, 1974).

The Cities And Political Splintering

These songs about slain and other leaders reflect two other historical phenomena, in the second half of the 1960s and beyond attention was paid

CHAPTER 14: JAZZ, RACE, AND POLITICS

to blacks in the urban areas, especially as blacks had gathered in great numbers in cities throughout the country, and riots in many of them occurred.

Lou Rawls, on his 1966 live album, combined a verbal tour of life in black urban cities with the song, "Tobacco Road." Rawls talked about what the ghettos were like in a number of specifically identified American cities (Rawls, 1966).

In 1969, Leon Thomas turned his attention to life in a metropolis, with his "Welcome to New York," including the following lyrics:

> Welcome to New York, brother,
> It's a city full of fun....
> They've got plenty of rats and roaches
> Enough welfare for everyone
> They got a whole lot of police cars
> With their lights all flashing red
> But just try to find one
> When you're getting hit upside your head. (Thomas, 1969)

Another song about urban life is Stevie Wonder's "Living for the City." Ray Charles added his own dimension to this classic song in 1975. As Stevie wrote, "To find a job is like a haystack needle/ Cause where he lives they don't use colored people." Then reminiscent of his recording of "Busted," Ray interjects his own words in the middle of the song:

> Lord, what am I doing here
> With all this pain and suffering and misery
> With all the rape and the drugs
> And the murder in the streets
> And the rats and the roaches
> Crawling all over everything
> And I can't find a job nowhere
> My electricity has been turned off
> My gas don't burn no more
> And the water has stopped flowing
> And my poor family is cold and hungry
> Oh Lord, why has God forsaken m. (Charles, 1975)

Decades later, urban blight is still under addressed. There have been no easy solutions to the newer realities of life in the ghettos. While black middle and upper classes have emerged, there remains extensive deprivation for many African Americans. Since the mid-1970s, it has been rare in mainstream American political life for sustained focus to be placed on the socio-economic plight of urban blacks. Neither the center nor the left has workable solutions to these issues. Meanwhile, politically, the later 1960s and early 1970s saw various approaches, and this is reflected in the jazz of the era.

Jazz, Religion, and Activism

In the late 1960s and early 1970s, some recordings based on religious sensibilities and focused on political and racial concerns appeared. Mary Lou Williams had been a prominent jazz pianist, arranger and composer since the 1920s. In 1968, she had composed "Music for Peace." Soon after she also recorded what became known as Mary Lou's Mass, which was initially released in 1975 and came out in more complete fashion on CD in 2005. This extended composition focuses on both religious and civil concerns and incorporates some of the earlier composition. The last two songs, "Tell Him Not To Talk Too Long," and "I Have A Dream," are about Martin Luther King Jr., and were initially recorded the year after his killing (Williams, 1975/2005).

Also, combining religious perspectives and political concerns was popular pianist Dave Brubeck. In 1969, he released an album on Decca that combined religious and social concerns, and was a classical composition with jazz elements. It was called The Gates of Justice, and was re-recorded in 2001. Brubeck writes in the original program notes that he focused "on the historic and spiritual parallels of Jews and American blacks," and hoped "to construct a bridge" between these two groups. But as he continued to write this composition, he recognized he had been led to "the more basic problem of man…and ultimately to God" (Brubeck, 2001).

In 1972, Brubeck released an album that combined classical, jazz, and rock elements. It was inspired by the Old Testament prophet, Isaiah, and was, Brubeck writes, "dedicated to the slain students of Kent University and Mississippi State, and all other innocent victims caught in the cross-fire between repression and rebellion" (Brubeck, 1972). Brubeck was extending his commitment to social justice that included his cancelling shows in the 1950s segregated south when they would not permit him to include his black bass player in the performances and his early 1960s recording of The Real Ambassadors with its civil rights overtones.

Jazz Activists: Centrist and Radical

In the divided 1960s, alto saxophonist, composer and arranger, Oliver Nelson was in the center of the political mainstream. He was one of the few who remained there. In the fall of 1961, he wrote and recorded *Afro-American Sketches*. In the liner notes, he says "Jungleaire" "is an account of a contest for freedom between the African warriors and the slave traders." It is an "attempt to depict what freedom must have meant to the American Negro when he was told 'You Are Free!'" is given in "Emancipation Blues." Nelson's "Going Up North" concerns the journey above the Mason-Dixon line to have a better life away from the South. "Disillusioned" shows that despite the trip north, "the Negro position in society, politics, culture has not really changed," though here "the right to become somebody is... within the realm of possibility." The album concludes with "Freedom Dance," which Nelson dedicates "to the thousands of militant youths, Freedom Riders (of all races) and all people with the desire and maturity to be free" (Nelson, 1961).

Six years later, Oliver Nelson wrote The Kennedy Dream: A Musical Tribute to John Fitzgerald Kennedy. This album intersperses John Kennedy's speeches with songs about the President's accomplishments. "Let the Word Go Forth" is from Kennedy's inaugural address that the torch has been passed to a new generation. "A Genuine Peace" quotes from Kennedy's 1963 American University address that that led to the above ground nuclear test ban treaty. "The Rights of All" cites Kennedy's address on civil rights from June 11, 1963. There are also songs about religious tolerance, and promotion of the arts. The last song on the album composed by Nelson is a somber "Day in Dallas," the end of the Kennedy dream. Not many African American jazz artists have written about recent American presidents, yet alone with reverence (Nelson, 1967).

The notion of a dream recurs in Nelson's aforementioned Black, Brown, and Beautiful, from October 1969. This extended suite is about the death of Martin Luther King Jr. It begins with "Aftermath," and the disarray and sadness following King's murder, followed by a requiem, then a tribute entitled "Martin Was A Real Man, A Real Man." Another song is called "I Hope in Time A Change Will Come." This remarkable album has been given little attention, and was finally issued on compact disc in 2017 (Nelson, 1969/2017).

In his albums about Kennedy and King, Oliver Nelson recognizes how centrist leaders have been inspiring heroes. In July 1969 in an interview in Jazz & Pop magazine after Nelson had been to Africa, he said that whatever problems are present in the U.S., in Africa "poverty is a way of life." He says, "The African is very busy trying to become as Western as possible." Recognizing Nelson's mainstream views, he was asked what he would say to militants such as LeRoi Jones, Eldridge Cleaver, Stokely Carmichael and others. Nelson said he would not give them advice, except they should go to Africa themselves. Nelson said, "We have to develop what we have here" (Rivelli & Levin, 1970, pp. 69 & 75). Separate from his political and social views, Oliver Nelson's three extended suites have not been given sufficient recognition in the jazz literature.

Still in the political center is a jazz song with an anti-Vietnam War lyric that made the Billboard Top 100 single chart in early 1970 and the LP from which it was taken was on the Top 40 album chart for 5 weeks the same year (Billboard, 2020; Whitburn, 1995 & 200). The song was "Compared to What." The lyric was: "The President has got his war. Folks don't know just what it's for... Have one doubt they call it treason" (Harris, 1969). The recording was by pianist-vocalist Les McCann and Saxophonist Eddie Harris. Written by former pop singer Gene McDaniels, McCann first recorded it in 1966 when Lyndon Johnson was President, but the live version with Harris added became popular after Nixon took office.

A more recognized jazz artist is the remarkable Charles Mingus, who was politically concerned. He falls more within the radical perspective. Mingus wrote songs with political titles throughout his career, a number have already been discussed. In 1960 at Antibes, he performed his "Prayer for Passive Resistance," an allusion to the lunch-counter sit-ins from that year. Mingus composed a piece originally entitled "Meditation," but which he gave various titles, including 1964s "Meditation on a Pair of Wire Scissors," but he most often called it "Mediation on Integration," which when played at the 1965 Monterrey Jazz Festival led to an enthusiastic standing ovation. Less than a week later at UCLA, he recorded his "Once There Was A Holding Company Called Old America," reflecting his belief that big business controlled the country (Mingus, 2012). The last political composition he recorded was 1974s, "Remember Rockefeller at Attica," which refers to the 1971 rebellion of prisoners and their killing after Governor Rockefeller ordered force to be used to put down the insurrection (Mingus, 1974).

Even more overtly radical in the 1960s and 1970s than Mingus was tenor saxophonist, Archie Shepp. In addition to his songs about Malcolm and George Jackson, Shepp recorded "Attica Blues," as a song and the title of a 1972 album (Shepp, 1972). Shepp collaborated with trumpeter and composer Cal Massey, whose songs had been recorded by Coltrane and Lee Morgan, among others. In 1969, the radical Black Panthers commissioned Massey to write "The Black Liberation Suite." Shepp recorded three parts of Massey's piece. The full suite was not recorded until 2011 by Fred Ho and Quincy Saul. Six of the nine movements are for black leaders including Eldridge Cleaver, Malcolm X, Martin Luther King Jr., Huey Newton, John Coltrane, and Marcus Garvey. Newton and Cleaver were Black Panthers. Massey was including a full spectrum of black leaders all working in their own way for liberation (Ho, 2011).

Nina Simone remained in the forefront of black consciousness in this period. Along with Mingus and Max Roach, she is the jazz artist who throughout the sixties most frequently addressed issues of race and politics. In 1967, Simone sang Langston Hughes's poem "Backlash Blues," which contains the following lines:

> You give me second class houses,
> Second class schools.
> Do you think that colored folks
> Are just second class fools? (Simone, 1967)

In 1969, she wrote that to be young, gifted, and black is where it's at (Simone, 1969). Her moving version of "Why? The King of Love is Dead" by Gene Taylor was first sung just a few days after King was assassinated. It expressed King's non-violent philosophy. But Nina sang we are now on the brink, and my people are rising. She said, "we cannot afford any more losses....they are shooting us down one by one... Dr. King's murder has left me so numb" (Simone, 1968). The loss of King was a major turning point, the center was no longer holding. In 1969, Nina sang about revolution, saying the constitution has to bend. She sings revolution is about change, and that you have to get your foot off my back. What the revolution was going to be was not actually specified (Simone, 1969).

As in the politics of the period, some of the rhetoric in jazz songs became more militant, and reflected that there were divisions in the movements for black freedom. Leon Thomas, who had expressed admiration for Malcolm X, in 1969 declared he is not going to Vietnam. He contrasts the cost of sending a man to the moon while hungry children are not being taken care of. This disparity is a reason he declares being in Vietnam is off limits for him (Thomas, 1969). In 1970, Gary Bartz, in his "Vietcong," wrote favorably about this group fighting for their homeland. Bartz wrote about not fighting your filthy battles, as he has battles of his own. He won't raise your children, instead he will raise his own. He sings, "hell no." Bartz is renouncing serving the whites to take care of his own. The interests of blacks and whites can diverge (Bartz, 1970).

Another album about Vietnam is the 1971 Freddie Hubbard's record "Sing Me a Song of Songmy." This was about the 1968 My Lai massacre. Songmy is another name for this South Vietnamese village. The album also refers to the 1969 murder by Charles Manson and crew of the movie actress Sharon Tate, and the 1970 shootings by the National of protesters at Kent State (Hubbard, 1971).

With a similar sense of the need for refusal and change, in 1971, Gil-Scott Heron recorded the witty socio-political satire, "The Revolution Will Not Be Televised." Here are a sample of the lyrics:

> There will be no pictures of you and Willie May
> Pushing that shopping cart down the block on the dead run
> Or trying to slide that color TV into a stolen ambulance
> NBC will not be able predict the winner at 8:32
> Or report from 29 districts
> The revolution will not be televised
> There will be no pictures of pigs shooting down
> Brothers on the instant replay

CHAPTER 14: JAZZ, RACE, AND POLITICS

> There will be no pictures of pigs shooting down
> Brothers on the instant replay
> There will be no pictures of Whitney Young
> Being run out of Harlem on a rail with a brand new process
> There will be no slow motion or still life of Roy Wilkens
> Strolling through Watts in a red, black and green
> Liberation jumpsuit that he had been saving
> For just the proper occasion
> The revolution will not be right back after a message
> About a white tornado, white lightning, or white people
> You will not have to worry about a dove in your bedroom
> The tiger in your tank or the giant in your toilet bowl
> The revolution will not go better with Coke
> The revolution will not fight the germs that may cause bad breath
> The revolution will put you in the driver's seat
> The Revolution will not be a rerun, brother
> The Revolution will be live. (Scott-Heron, 1971)

Scott-Heron also advised his brothers to get out of the ghetto, it could keep one psychologically as well as economically trapped, and even worse addicted to drugs. He is also worried about police brutality and murder, particularly the killing of black militants. Yet he remains skeptical of opportunistic, hypocritical black revolutionaries, who do not help out those for whom they claim to be advocating. Scott-Heron then presents a picture of political and socio-economic life for blacks in the early seventies. He shows both the aspirations for revolution and political and economic divisions.

After the Mid-1970s

Given this splintering reflected in politics and song, after the mid-seventies, there was less heard on jazz records or on the national scene of racial remedies. In 1978, a black sociologist, Wilson (1978), wrote The Declining Significance of Race. Though by this time, the civil rights movement and black radicalism had more or less dissipated. Black power champion Stokely Carmichael had permanently moved to Africa in 1969. A number of Black Panthers had been murdered in the late sixties and early seventies. By the late seventies, the Black Panther elite leadership were living in fashionable penthouse apartments on expensive Lake Merritt in Oakland. Black Panther hero, Huey Newton, drove a Mercedes-Benz. Other civil rights leaders began to run for political office as Democrats. Martin Luther King disciple, Andrew Young became Mayor of Atlanta, John Lewis of SNCC was elected to Congress, as was former Black Panther Bobby Rush. The civil rights movement was not only fragmented, by the end of the seventies it had no unified direction. Those who had worked outside the system began to work within the system, move away from their prior views, become those whom they warned against, or left politics altogether.

The jazz performers of this most recent era also had their ups and downs. Radicals Max Roach and Archie Shepp were less politically active as they aged, both becoming faculty at the University of Massachusetts. Herbie Hancock has also been less political in the last four decades. Oliver Nelson made a successful career in the Hollywood studies, but died at age 43 of a heart attack. Mingus kept alive his political consciousness, unfortunately he developed Lou Gehrig's disease and died in 1980. Nina Simone left the United States in 1970. In the 1980s she was diagnosed with bipolar disorder, and her recordings were intermittent after becoming an expatriate. In 1985, she shot a gun at a record company executive. Nina died in 2003. Her reputation has been growing in recent years, including a profile of her in the last few years in the New Yorker. Gil Scott-Heron had a successful recording career and kept alive his political consciousness in the 1970s. Later he was arrested and imprisoned for drug abuse, developed HIV and died at the age of 62 in 2011. Among the most influential jazz artists of the sixties was John Coltrane. It could be said Coltrane was to jazz as Martin Luther King Jr. was to civil rights. Coltrane died from liver cancer in 1967 at age 40.

The legacy of the civil rights era and the political jazz of the fifties through seventies lives on. It has been revived by a number of jazz artists, most particularly by Leo Smith, especially in his 2012 multi-album recording "Ten Freedom Summers." He recorded his first album in the early 1970s. In the height of the civil rights era, jazz artists got more activated by political events than at any other time since jazz began at the end of the nineteenth century. It was a vibrant music at its inception, and remains so. Hail, hail jazz, the feeling is there body and soul.

CHAPTER 14: JAZZ, RACE, AND POLITICS

REFERENCES

Adderley, C. (1961). *African waltz*. Riverside: RLP 377. .
Adderley, C. (1968). *Accent on Africa*. Capitol: ST-2987.
Armstrong, L. (1997). (What Did I Do To Be So) Black and Blue. On *Louis Armstrong's Greatest Hits*. Columbia: CK 65420. (Original work released 1955)
Bartz, G. (1971). Vietcong. On *Harlem Bush Music*. Milestone: MCD-47101-2.
Billboard. (2020). Les McCann. https://www.billboard.com/music/les-mccann.
Blakey, A. (1962). *African beat*. Blue Note: BST 84097.
Blakey, A. (196). Free for all. On *Free For All*. Blue Note: ST 84170.
Blakey, A. (1964). Freedom rider. On *Freedom Rider*. Blue Note: BST 84156.
Blakey, A. (1964). The core. On *Free For All*. Blue Note: ST 84170.
Brubeck, D. (1962). *The real ambassadors*. Columbia: OL 5850.
Brubeck, D. (1969). *The gates of justice*. Naxos: 8.559414.
Brubeck, D. (1972). *Truth is fallen*. Atlantic: 1606.
Busk, B. (2012). My people. On *My People: The Complete Show* Storyville: 1018430.
Charles, R. (1963). Ol' man river. On *Ray Charles: A Man and His Soul*. ABC Records: ABC-590X.
Charles, R. (1975), Living for the city. On *Renaissance*. Crossover: CR 9005.
Coltrane, J. (1985). Dial Africa, Gold Coast, Tanganyika Strut. On *Africa* Savoy Jazz: ZD70818. (Original work released 1958)
Coltrane, J. (1964). Liberia. On *Coltrane's Sound*. Atlantic: SD-1419.
Coltrane, J. (1961). Africa. On *Africa Brass*. Impulse: A-6-S.
Coltrane, J. (1964). Afro-Blue. On *Live at Birdland*. Impulse: AS-50.
Coltrane, J. (1964). Alabama. On *Live at Birdland* . Impulse: AS-50.
Coltrane, J. (1969). Reverend king. On *Cosmic Music*. Impulse: AS-9148.
Davis, M. (1966). Freedom jazz dance. On *Miles Smiles*. Columbia: CS 9401.
Earland, C. (1974). Suite for Martin Luther King. On *In Concert*. Prestige: PRCD 24267-2.
Ellington, D. (1987). Fleurette Africaine (African Flower). On *Money Jungle*. Blue Note: CDP: 546398.

Ellington, D. (2012). King fit the battle of Alabam. On *My People: The Complete Show*. Storyville: 1018430.

Fitzgerald, E. (1968). It's up to me and you. Capitol: 2212.

Green, G. (1965). The Selma march. On *His Majesty King Funk*. Verve: VS-8627.

Hancock, H. (1969). *The Prisoner*. Blue Note: BST 84321.

Harris, E., (1965). Freedom jazz dance. On *The In Sound*. Atlantic: 1448.

Hentoff, N. (2009). Charles Mingus: The clown. *Pithecanthropus Erectus The Clown*. On Essential Jazz Classics: EJC55437. (Original work released 1957)

Ho, F & Sau, Q. (2011). *The Music Of Cal Massey: A Tribute*. Mutable Music: 004.

Holiday, B. (2005). Strange fruit. On *Billie Holiday: The Complete Verve Master Takes*. Verve: 0249880302. (Original work released 1956).

Hubbard, F. (1971). *Sing Me A Song Of Songmy*. Atlantic: SD 1576.

Jazz Crusaders. (1961). *Freedom Sound*. Pacific Jazz: ST-27.

Margolick, D. (2007). The day Louis Armstrong made noise. *New York Times*. https://www.nytimes.com/2007/09/23/opinion/23margolick.html.

McCann, L. and Harris, E. (1969). Compared to what , On *Swiss Movement* . Atlantic: SD 1537.

Mingus, C. (2009). Haitian fight song. On *Pithecanthropous Erectus + The Clown*. Essential Jazz Classics EJC55437 (Original work released 1957).

Mingus, C. (1959). Fables of Faubus. On *Mingus Ah Um*. Columbia: CK 40648.

Mingus, C. (1960). Original fables of Faubus. On *Presents Charles Mingus*. Candid: CJS 9005.

Mingus, C. (1965). Meditations. On *Live At The Jazz Workshop*. Fantasy 86017.

Mingus, C. (1975). Remembering Rockefeller at Attica. On *Changes One*. Atlantic SD 1677.

Mingus, C. (1976). Prayer for passive resistance. On *Mingus at Antibes*. Atlantic: SD 2-3001. (Original work released 1960)

Mingus, C. (1995). Freedom. On *Mingus, Mingus, Mingus*. Impulse: IMPD-170.

Mingus, C. (2012). Meditations On a pair of wire cutters. On *The Jazz Workshop Concerts, 1964-65*. Mosaic: MD7-253.

CHAPTER 14: JAZZ, RACE, AND POLITICS

Mingus, C. (2012). Meditations on integration. On *The Jazz Workshop Concerts, 1964-65.* Mosaic: MD7-253.
Mingus, C. (2012). A lonely day in Selma. Alabama/Freedom. On *The Jazz Workshop Concerts, 1964-65.* Mosaic: MD7-253.
Mitchell, B. (1965). March on Selma. On *Down With It.* Blue Note: BST 84214.
Moncur III, G. (1974). *Echoes of prayer.* JCOA Records: JCOA LP 1009.
Monson, I. (2007), Freedom sounds: Civil rights call out to jazz and Africa . Oxford University Press.
Morgan, L. (2004), The Cry of my people. On *The Sixth Sense.* Blue Note: 724359242323. (Original work released 1967)
Morgenstern, D. (2004). Louis Armstrong, On *The Essential Louis Armstrong.* Columbia: C2K 89280.
Murray, S. (1969). *Homage to Africa.* Actuel: 3.
Nelson. O. (1961). *Afro-American Sketches.* Prestige: PRST 7225.
Nelson, O. (1967). *The Kennedy Dream.* Impulse: A-9144
Nelson, O. (1970). *Black, Brown and Beautiful.* Flying Dutchman: FDS-116.
Payne, C. (1973). Martin Luther King Jr. On *Zodiac.* Strata-East: SES-19734.
Rawls, L. (1966). Southside monologue /Tobacco Road. On *Live!* Capitol: ST 2459.
Rivelli, P. (1970). Oliver Nelson's African Tour. In P. Rivelli & R. Levin (Eds.), *Black Giants* (pp. 68-77). World Publishing Company.
Roach, M. (1960). *We Insist: Freedom Now Suite.* Candid: CJS 9002.
Roach, M. (1963). Mendacity. On *Percussion Bittersweet.* Impulse: A-8.
Rollins, S. (1958). *Freedom Suite.* Riverside: RLP 12-258.
Santamaria, M. (1973). Malcolm X. On *Fuego.* Vaya: VS-18.
Scott-Heron, G. (1971). The revolution will not be televised. On *Pieces Of A Man.* Flying Dutchman: FD 10143.
Shepp, A. (1965). Malcolm, Malcolm – Semper Malcolm. On *Fire Music.* Fire Music. Impulse: AS-86.
Shepp, A. (1972). Blues for Brother George Jackson. On *Attica Blues.* Impulse: AS-9222
Silver, H. (1966). African queen. On *Cape Verdean Blues.* Blue Note: BST 84220.
Simone, N. (1990). Mississippi goddam. On *In Concert/I Put A Spell On You.* Mercury:846543-2. (Original work released 1964)

Simone, N. (1990). Old Jim Crow. On *In Concert/I Put A Spell on You*. Mercury: 846543-2. (Original work originally released 1964)

Simone, N. (1990). Pirate Jenny. On *In Concert/ I Put A Spell on You*. Mercury:846543-2. (Original work released 1964)

Simone, N. (1967). Backlash blues. On *Sings the Blues*. RCA Victor: LSP 3789.

Simone, N. (1968). Why (The King of love is dead). On *'Nuff Said*. RCA Victor: LSP-4065.

Simone, N. (1969). Revolution. On *To Love Somebody*. RCA Victor: LSP-4152.

Simone, N. (1970). To be young, gifted, and black. On *Black Gold*. RCA Victor: LSP 4248

Simone, N. (2013). Why (The king of love is dead). On *Forever Young, Gifted and Black: Songs of Freedom and Spirit*. Sony Music: 2876744132.

Spellman, A. B. (2001). Sonny Rollins: Freedom Suite. *NPR*. https://www.npr.org/2011/06/20/4182012/sonny-rollins-freedom-suite.

Thomas, L. (1969). Damn nam. On *Spirits Known and Unknown*. Flying Dutchman: FD-10115.

Thomas, L. (1969). Malcolm's gone. On *Spirits Known and Unknown*. Flying Dutchman: FD-10115.

Thomas, L. (1973). Welcome to New York. On *Facets: The Legend of Leon Thomas*. Flying Dutchman: FD 10164. (Original work released 1970)

Weston. R. (1961). *Uhuru Africa*. Roulette: SR 65001.

Weston, R. (1972). *African cookbook*. Atlantic: SD 1609.

Weston, R. (1975). *Blues to Africa*. Arista Freedom: AL 1014.

Williams, M. L. (2005). *Mary Lou's mass*. Smithsonian Folkways. (Original work released 1975)

Wilson, W. (1978). *The declining significance of race*. University of Chicago Press.

ABOUT THE AUTHOR

Ken Fuchsman taught history, interdisciplinary studies, and administered an undergraduate degree program of 1200 students at the University of Connecticut. His articles connecting Freud's theories with his life have appeared in academic journals in Great Britain and the United States. He has reviewed film in peer reviewed publications, and hosted radio shows on the history of rock-and-roll and jazz for six years.

Dr. Fuchsman was President of the International Psychohistorical Association from 2016 to 2020. His co-edited book, *Psychoanalytic and Historical Perspectives on the Leadership of Donald Trump* was published by Routledge in 2020. The same publisher in 2021 released *Healing, Rebirth, and the Work of Michael Eigen,* a collection of articles he co-edited. At University of Connecticut, he designed and taught a course on the "Nature of Being Human" and is working on turning his course, lectures, and further research on the topic into a book.

www.ingramcontent.com/pod-product-compliance
Lightning Source LLC
Chambersburg PA
CBHW060953230426
43665CB00015B/2176